Facebook®

FOR

DUMMIES®

A Wiley Brand

5th Edition

Facebook®

FOR DUMMIES®

A Wiley Brand

5th Edition

by Carolyn Abram

FOR DUMMIES®
A Wiley Brand

Facebook® For Dummies®, 5th Edition

Published by
John Wiley & Sons, Inc.
111 River Street
Hoboken, NJ 07030-5774

www.wiley.com

Copyright © 2013 by John Wiley & Sons, Inc., Hoboken, New Jersey

Published by John Wiley & Sons, Inc., Hoboken, New Jersey

Published simultaneously in Canada

For general information on our other products and services, please contact our Customer Care Department within the U.S. at 877-762-2974, outside the U.S. at 317-572-3993, or fax 317-572-4002.

For technical support, please visit www.wiley.com/techsupport.

Wiley publishes in a variety of print and electronic formats and by print-on-demand. Some material included with standard print versions of this book may not be included in e-books or in print-on-demand. If this book refers to media such as a CD or DVD that is not included in the version you purchased, you may download this material at http://booksupport.wiley.com. For more information about Wiley products, visit www.wiley.com.

Library of Congress Control Number: 2013939160

ISBN 978-1-118-63312-0 (pbk); ISBN 978-1-118-63304-5 (ebk); ISBN 978-1-118-63303-8 (ebk); ISBN 978-1-118-63305-2 (ebk)

Manufactured in the United States of America

10 9 8 7 6 5

Contents at a Glance

Table of Contents

Introduction

· ·

Facebook connects you with the people you know and care about. It enables you to communicate, stay up-to-date, and keep in touch with friends and family anywhere. It facilitates your relationships online to help enhance them in person. Specifically, Facebook connects you with the *people* you know around *content* that is important to you. Whether you're the type to take photos or look at them, or write about your life, or read about your friends' lives, Facebook is designed to enable you to succeed. Maybe you like to share websites and news, play games, plan events, organize groups of people, or promote your business. Whatever you prefer, Facebook has you covered.

Facebook offers you control. Communication and information sharing are powerful only when you can do what you want within your comfort zone. Nearly every piece of information and means of connecting on Facebook come with full privacy controls, allowing you to share and communicate exactly how — and with whom — you desire.

Facebook welcomes everyone: students and professionals; grandchildren (as long as they're at least age 13), parents, and grandparents; busy people; socialites; celebrities; distant friends; and roommates. No matter who you are, using Facebook can add value to your life.

About Facebook For Dummies

Part I of this book teaches you all the basics to get you up and running on Facebook. This information is more than enough for you to discover Facebook's value. Part II teaches you about friends and how you can communicate and interact with them on Facebook. Part III explores all the fun and interesting things you can do on Facebook. Finally, Part IV explores the creative, diverse, touching, and even frustrating ways people have welcomed Facebook into their lives.

Here are some of the things you can do with this book:

- **Find out how to represent yourself online.** Facebook lets you create a profile (called a Timeline) that you can share with friends, co-workers, and people-you-have-yet-to-meet.

- **Connect and share with people you know.** Whether you're seeking close friends or long-lost ones, family members, business contacts, teammates, businesses, or celebrities, Facebook keeps you connected. Never say, "Goodbye" again . . . unless you want to.

- **Discover how the online tools of Facebook can help enhance your relationships offline.** Photo sharing, group organization, event planning, and messaging tools all enable you to maintain an active social life in the real world.

- **Bring your connections off Facebook and on to the rest of the web.** Many websites, games, apps, and services on the Internet can work with your Facebook information to deliver you a better experience.

- **Promote a business, cause, or yourself to the people who can bring you success.** Engaging with people on Facebook can help ensure that your message is heard.

Foolish Assumptions

In this book, I make the following assumptions:

- You're at least 13 years of age.

- You have some access to the Internet, an e-mail address, and a web browser that is not Internet Explorer 6 (Internet Explorer 7, Safari, Chrome, Firefox, and so on are all good).

- There are people in your life with whom you communicate.

- You can read the language in which this sentence is printed.

Facebook pages and features — such as the Facebook Groups or the Settings page — are called out with capital letters. Brackets like *<this>* denote generic text that will be different on your screen, such as looking at *<Your Name>*.

I often state my opinions throughout this book. Though I have worked for Facebook in the past, the opinions expressed here represent only my perspective, not that of Facebook. I am an avid Facebook user and became one long before I worked for Facebook.

Icons Used in This Book

What's a *For Dummies* book without icons pointing you in the direction of great information that's sure to help you along your way? In this section, I briefly describe each icon I use in this book.

The Tip icon points out helpful information that is likely to improve your experience.

The Remember icon marks an interesting and useful fact — something that you may want to use later.

The Warning icon highlights lurking danger. With this icon, I'm telling you to pay attention and proceed with caution.

Where to Go from Here

Whether you've been using Facebook for years or this is your first time, I recommend you start by reading Chapter 1, which sets the stage for most of what I describe in detail in the rest of this book. After reading the first chapter, you may have a better sense of which topics will be more relevant to you, and you can, therefore, flip right to them. However, I recommend that *everyone* spend some quality time in Chapter 5, which covers privacy on Facebook. Facebook is an online representation of a community, so it's important that each person understands how to operate in that community to ensure a safe, fun, and functional environment for everyone.

If you're new to Facebook and looking to use it to enhance your own personal connections, I recommend reading this book from Part I straight through Part IV.

You may already be quite familiar with Facebook when you pick up this book. But because the site is constantly growing and changing, there is always more to know. The detailed information in Parts II and III should keep you ahead of the curve.

No matter which category you fall into, it's time to get started: Let one hand flip the pages of this book, the other drive your computer mouse, and let your mind open up to one of the most popular, fun, and useful websites out there.

Part I
Getting Started with Facebook

getting started
with
Facebook

In this part . . .

- ✔ What you can and can't do on Facebook
- ✔ Getting confirmed and verified
- ✔ Looking around
- ✔ Filling out and your information
- ✔ Sharing with your friends
- ✔ Visit www.dummies.com for great Dummies content online.

Chapter 1

The Many Faces of Facebook

Think about the people you interacted with throughout the past day. In the morning, you may have gone to get the paper and chatted with the neighbor. You may have asked your kids what time they'd be home and negotiated with your partner about whose turn it is to cook dinner. Perhaps you spent the day at the office, chatting, joking, and (heaven forbid) getting things done with your co-workers. In the midst of it all, you may have sent an e-mail to all the people in your book club, asking them what book should be next, and what date works for the most people. Maybe while you sat on the bus you read the newspaper, or called your mom to wish her a happy birthday, or searched on your phone for a good restaurant to go to for drinks with friends. This is your world, as it revolves around you.

Each of us has our own version of the world, and as we interact with each other, those worlds intertwine, interplay, and interlock. Maybe your best friend from college was the one to introduce you to the book club, and then someone from the book club recommended a good restaurant. This network of people you interact with — your friends, acquaintances, and loved ones — exists online. Facebook is the online representation of the web of connections between people in the real world. Facebook (and other Internet companies) like to call this network the *social graph*.

Now, you may be asking, if this graph or network exists in the real world, why do I need it online, too? Good question (gold stars all around). The answer is that having it online facilitates and improves all your social relationships. In other words, Facebook makes your life easier and your friendships better. It can help with very practical things like remembering a friend's birthday or coordinating a party. It can also help with the more abstract aspects of relationships, things like staying close with family you aren't physically near or talking about your day with friends.

Getting set up and familiar with Facebook does take a little work (which you know, or else you wouldn't be starting out on this book-length journey). It may feel a little overwhelming at times, but the reward is worth it — I promise you.

So . . . What Is Facebook, Exactly?

"Yes, Carolyn," you're saying. "I know it's going to help me stay in touch with my friends and communicate with the people in my life, but what *is* it?"

Well, at its most basic, Facebook is a website. You'll find it through a web browser like Safari, Google Chrome, Firefox, or Internet Explorer, the same way you might navigate to a search engine like Google or to an airline's website to book tickets. Figure 1-1 shows what you will probably see when you navigate to www.facebook.com.

Facebook is a website where you go to accomplish certain tasks. These tasks usually fall under the umbrella category of *social maintenance*. For example, you may go to Facebook to

- Check out what your friends are up to today.
- Tell your friends and family about your recent successes, show them your photos, or let them know you're thinking of them.
- Show off the pictures from your latest vacation.

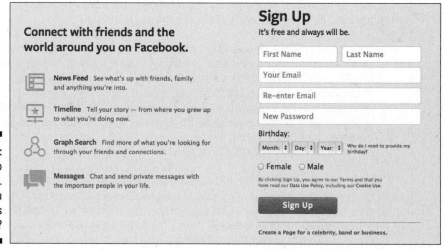

Figure 1-1: Welcome to Facebook. Would you like fries with that?

- ✔ Make a contact in a city you're moving to or at a company where you're applying for a job.

- ✔ Plan an event.

- ✔ Get in touch with an old friend.

- ✔ Garner support for a cause.

- ✔ Get recommendations from friends for movies, books, music, and restaurants.

- ✔ Remember everyone's birthday.

So what Facebook *is,* exactly, is a website built to help you represent yourself online and share with your real-world friends online. The rest of it — how that's accomplished, what people typically share on Facebook, and how it all works — is what this book is all about.

Discovering What You Can Do on Facebook

Now that you know Facebook is a means by which you can connect with people who matter to you, your next question may be, "How?" More gold stars for you! In the next few sections, I give you an overview.

Establish a Timeline

When you sign up for Facebook, one of the first things you do is establish your *Timeline,* originally referred to as Profile. The reason Facebook calls this a Timeline and not a profile (other than to be a bit confusing) is because Timelines are much more than just an at-a-glance bio. Timelines become an ongoing history of your life on Facebook. When you (or your friends) are feeling nostalgic, you can explore your history the same way you might flip through an old photo album.

At first, the thought of putting a photo album of your entire life online may feel sort of scary or daunting. After all, that stuff is personal. But one of the things you'll discover about Facebook is that it's a place to be personal. The people who will see your Timeline are, for the most part, the people you'd show a photo album to in real life. They are your friends and family members.

That "for the most part" is an important part of Facebook, too. You will encounter other people on Facebook, including potential employers or professional contacts, more distant friends, and casual acquaintances. This distinction — between your close friends and everyone else — is an important one to be aware of.

Fundamentally, you create a Timeline on Facebook because it's required. But Timelines have this funny habit of starting out as a bare-bones regulation and then becoming something more. They become your home on the Internet, with the same comfort of walking into your own bedroom. As you start to collect posts, photos, and interactions with friends there, your Timeline becomes an indispensable record of what's going on with you, both now and in the past. You can even use your Facebook info to log in to other websites on the Internet — meaning your profile picture and name are transferred with the click of a button, no need to create a new profile. In other words, the Timeline is the only website profile you'll need.

The Timeline, shown in Figure 1-2, is set up with all kinds of privacy controls to specify *who* you want to see *which* information. Many people find great value in adding to their Timeline just about every piece of information and then unveiling each particular piece cautiously. The safest rule here is to share on your Timeline any piece of information you'd share with someone in real life. The corollary applies, too: Don't share on your Timeline any information that you wouldn't share with someone in real life.

Chapter 2 provides lots of detail about the Timeline and what you might choose to share there. For now, think of it as a personal web page that Facebook helps you create to facilitate sharing with friends and represent yourself online.

Figure 1-2:
An example
of a
Facebook
Timeline.

Connect with friends

Now that you know about Timelines, you should also know about ways to connect your Timeline to the Timelines of your acquaintances. These connections are called *friendships*. On Facebook, it's pretty common to refer to *friending* people you know. This just means establishing the virtual connection. Friending people enables you to communicate and share with them more easily. Friends are basically the reason Facebook can be so powerful and useful to people. After all, you can sit and stare at your own Timeline for only so long. Facebook offers the following tools to help you find your friends:

- ✔ **Facebook Friend Finder:** Enables you to scan the e-mail addresses in your e-mail address book to find whether those people are already on Facebook. Selectively choose among those with whom you'd like to connect.

- ✔ **People You May Know:** Shows you the names and pictures of people you likely know. These people are selected for you based on commonalities like where you live or work or how many friends you have in common.

- ✔ **Search:** Helps you find the people who are most likely already using Facebook.

After you establish a few connections, use those connections to find other people you know by searching through their connections for familiar names. I explain how to find people you know on Facebook in Chapter 6.

Communicate with Facebook friends

As Facebook grows, it becomes more likely that anyone with whom you're trying to communicate can be reached. These days it's a fairly safe assumption that you'll be able to find that person you just met at a dinner party, an old professor from college, or the childhood friend you've been meaning to catch up with. Digging up a person's contact information could require calls to mutual friends, a trip to the white pages (provided you know enough about that person to identify the right contact information), or an e-mail sent to a potentially outdated e-mail address. Facebook streamlines finding and contacting people in one place. If the friend you're reaching out to is active on Facebook, no matter where she lives or how many times she's changed her e-mail address, you can reach one another.

And Facebook isn't just about looking up old friends to say hi. Its messaging system is designed to make it easy to dash a quick note off to friends and get their reply just as fast. The comments people leave on each other's photos, status updates, and posts are real conversations that you will find yourself taking part in.

Share your thoughts

You have something to say. I can just tell by the look on your face. Maybe you're proud of the home team, maybe you're excited for Friday, or maybe you can't believe what you saw on the way to work this morning. All day long, things are happening to all of us that make us just want to turn to our friends and say, "You know what? . . . That's what." Facebook gives you the stage and an eager audience. In Chapter 7, I explain how you can make short or long posts about the things happening around you and how they're distributed to your friends in an easy way.

Share your pictures

Since the invention of the modern-day camera, people have been all too eager to yell, "Cheese!" Photographs can make great tour guides on trips down memory lane, but only if you actually remember to develop, upload, or scrapbook them. Many memories fade away when the smiling faces are stuffed into an old shoe box, remain on undeveloped rolls of film, or are forgotten in some folder on a hard drive.

Facebook offers three great incentives for uploading, organizing, and editing your photos:

- ✔ **Facebook provides one easy-to-access location for all your photos.** Directing any interested person to your Facebook Timeline is easier than e-mailing pictures individually, sending a complicated link to a photo site, or waiting until the family reunion to show off the my-how-the-kids-have-grown pics.

- ✔ **Every photo you upload can be linked to the Timelines of the people in the photo.** For example, you upload pictures of you and your sister and link them to her Timeline. Whenever someone visits her Timeline, he sees those pictures; he doesn't even have to know you. This is great because it introduces longevity to photos. As long as people are visiting your sister's Timeline, they can see those pictures. Photo albums no longer have to be something people look at right after the event and maybe then again years later.

- ✔ **Facebook gives you the power to control exactly who has access to your photos.** Every time you upload a photo or create a new photo album on Facebook, you can decide whether you want everyone on Facebook to see it, just your friends, or even just a subset of your friends based on your comfort level. You may choose to show your wedding photos to all your friends, but perhaps only some friends see the honeymoon. This control enables you to tailor your audience to those friends who might be most interested. All your friends might enjoy your baby photos, but maybe only your co-workers will care about photos from the recent company party.

Plan Events, join Groups

Facebook isn't meant to be a replacement for face-to-face interaction; it's meant to facilitate interactions when face time isn't possible or to facilitate the planning of face time. Two of the greatest tools for this are Events and Groups.

Events are just what they sound like: a system for creating events, inviting people to them, sending out messages about them, and so on. Your friends and other guests RSVP to events, which allows the event organizers to plan accordingly and allows attendees to receive event reminders. Facebook Events can be used for something as small as a lunch date or something as big as a march on Washington, D.C. Sometimes events are abstract rather than physical. For example, someone could create an event for Ride Your Bike to Work Day and hope the invitation spreads far and wide (through friends and friends of friends) to promote awareness. I use Events to plan barbecues for my friends as well as to put together a larger reading series. I cover Events in detail in Chapter 11.

Groups are also what they sound like: groups of people organized around a common topic or real-world organization. One group may be intimate, such as five best friends who plan several activities together. Another group could be practical — for example, PTA Members of Denver Schools. Within a group, all members can share relevant information, photos, or discussions. My groups include one for my family where we might post photos we don't want to share with the world at large, one for my *For Dummies* editorial team so we can update each other on how the writing is going, and one for a group of friends who are all planning to take a trip together next year. Groups are covered in detail in Chapter 9.

Facebook and the web

Facebook Photos, Groups, and Events are only a small sampling of how you can use Facebook to connect with the people you know. Throughout this book, you find information about how Facebook interacts with the greater Internet. You might see articles recommended by friends when you go to *The New York Times* website, or information about what music your friends like when you use Spotify, an Internet radio website. Additionally, in Chapter 14, I explain in detail the games, apps, and websites that you can use with your Facebook information.

Many of these websites and applications have been built by outside developers who don't work for Facebook. They include tools to help you edit your photos; create slideshows; play games with friends across the globe; divvy up bills among people who live or hang out together; and exchange information about good movies, music, books, and restaurants. After you become a little more comfortable with the Facebook basics, you can try some of the thousands of applications and websites whose services allow you to interact with your Facebook friends.

Promote a cause or business

In addition to your friends and family, you interact with tons of other things or entities every day. These may be a newspaper or magazine, a celebrity whose marriage travails you can't help but be fascinated by, a television show that has you on the edge of your seat, or a cause that's near and dear to your heart. All these entities can be represented on Facebook through Pages (with a capital P). These Pages look almost exactly like Timelines, just for the not-quite-people among us. Instead of becoming friends with Pages, you can like them. So when you like a television show (say, *The Daily Show with Jon Stewart*), you'll start to see updates from that Page *(The Daily Show)* on your Home page. Liking Pages for businesses or causes helps you stay up-to-date with news from them.

If you're the one managing something like a small business, a cause, or a newsletter, you can also create a page. After you've created that page, your users/customers/fans can like it, and then you can update them with news about whatever's going on in the world of your store/cause/thing. I talk about all the ins and outs of Pages in Chapter 13.

Keeping in Mind What You Can't Do on Facebook

Facebook is meant to represent real people and real associations; it's also meant to be safe. Many of the rules of participation on Facebook exist to uphold those two goals.

There are things you can't do on Facebook other than what's listed here. For example, you can't send multiple unsolicited messages to people you're not friends with; you can't look at the photos of someone who has really tight privacy settings; you can't spin straw into gold. These rules may change how you use Facebook, but probably won't change *whether* you use it. The following four rules are highlighted in this section because, if any are a problem for you, you probably won't get to the rest of the book.

You can't lie

Okay, you can, but you shouldn't, especially not about your basic information. Lying about your identity is a violation of the Statement of Rights and Responsibilities and grounds for your Timeline being disabled. Although many people try, Facebook doesn't let anyone sign up with an obviously fake name like Marilyn Manson or Fakey McFakerson. Those who do make it past the name checks will likely find their account flagged and disabled.

You can't be twelve

Or younger. Seriously. Facebook takes very seriously the U.S. law that prohibits minors under the age of 13 from creating an online Timeline for themselves. This rule is in place for the safety of minors, and it's a particular safety rule that Facebook does enforce. If you or someone you know on Facebook is under 13, deactivate (or make him deactivate) the account now. If you're reported to the Facebook User Operations team and they confirm that you're underage, your account will be disabled.

You can't troll or spam

On the Internet, *trolling* refers to posting deliberately offensive material to websites in order to get people upset. *Spamming* refers to sending out bulk promotional messages. If you do either of these things on Facebook, there's a good chance your account will be shut down.

The logic for this is that Facebook is about real people and real connections. It's one thing to message a mutual friend or the occasional stranger whose Timeline implies being open to meeting new people if the two of you have matching interests. However, between Facebook's automatic detection systems and user-generated reports, sending too many unsolicited messages is likely to get your account flagged and disabled.

Similarly, Facebook aims to be a "trusted" environment for people to exchange ideas and information. If people deliberately disturb the peace with pornographic, hateful, or bullying content, that trust is pretty much broken.

Chances are that you have no intention of spamming or trolling, so keep in mind that if you see either of these things happening, you can report the content or person to Facebook (you can find out how to report a photo, for example, in Chapter 10), and its User Operations team investigates the report. If you're getting warnings about things like spamming, chances are you just need to tweak *how* you're using Facebook. For example, you may need to create a Page instead of using your personal account for mass messaging. You can find out how to promote your business (or yourself) in Chapter 13.

You can't upload illegal content

Facebook users live in virtually every country in the world, so Facebook is often obligated to respect the local laws for its users. Respecting these laws is something Facebook has to do regardless of its own position on pornography (where minors can see it), copyrighted material, hate speech, depictions of crimes, and other offensive content. However, doing so is also in line with Facebook's value of being a safe, happy place for people 13 and older. Don't confuse this with censorship; Facebook is all about freedom of speech and self-expression, but the moment that compromises anyone's safety or breaks any law, disciplinary action is taken.

Realizing How Facebook Is Different from Other Social Sites

Lots of social sites besides Facebook try to help people connect. Some popular sites are Twitter, LinkedIn, Google+, Instagram, Tumblr, and many others.

I'll start with the biggest reason Facebook is different. Literally, the biggest: Facebook has over one *billion* users across the world (yes, billion with a *b*). Other social sites might be popular in one country or another, but Facebook is popular pretty much everywhere.

If you're going to use only one social networking site, choose Facebook — everyone you want to interact with is already there.

You'll see a lot of similar functionality across different sites: establishing connections, creating Timelines, liking content, and so on. However, each site brings a slightly different emphasis in terms of what is important. LinkedIn, for example, helps people with career networking, so it puts emphasis on professional information and connections. Match.com, on the other hand, is about matchmaking, so it's not exactly meant for those of us who aren't looking to get a date. Twitter encourages its members to share short *tweets*, 140-character posts with their connections; and Instagram (which is actually owned by Facebook) encourages its members to share cool photos taken with mobile phones.

You might find some or all of these sites useful at different points in time, but Facebook wants to be the one that is always useful in one way or another — so it tries to offer all the functionality I just mentioned . . . *and more.*

How You Can Use Facebook

Now that you know what you can do, generally, on Facebook, it's time to consider some of the specific ways you may find yourself using Facebook in the future. The following list is by no means comprehensive, and I've left out some of the things already mentioned in this chapter (things like sharing photos and events and groups). These are more specific-use cases than an advertisement for Facebook's features.

One billion people use Facebook, but not all of them can see your whole Timeline. You can share as much or as little with as many or as few people as you so desire. Put under lock and key the posts or parts of your Timeline you *don't* want to share with everyone. Chapter 5 goes into much greater detail on how to protect yourself and your information.

Getting information

At any age, you may need to find someone's phone number or connect with a friend of a friend to organize something. Facebook can make these very practical tasks a little bit easier. As long as you can search for someone's name, you should be able to find her on Facebook and find the information you're looking for.

Keeping up with long-distance friends

These days, families and friends are often spread far and wide across state or country lines. Children go to college; grandparents move to Florida; people move for their job or because they want a change of scenery. These distances make it hard for people to interact in any more significant way than gathering together once per year to share some turkey and pie (pecan, preferably). Facebook offers a place where you can virtually meet and interact. Upload photos of the kids for everyone to see; write posts about what everyone is up to. Even the more mundane information about your life ("I'm at jury duty") can make someone across the world feel like, just for a second, she's sitting next to you and commiserating with you about your jury summons.

Am I signing up for a dating site?

Throughout this book, you read about ways to communicate: messages, chatting, poking, liking, and commenting. These fairly neutral activities can take on a whole new meaning and spark when they happen between two people interested in each other.

Although Facebook is not technically a dating site, plenty of people do take advantage of its social nature to boost their dating lives in different ways:

✔ You can inform people through your Timeline whom you're looking to meet (women, men, or both).

✔ You can certainly use Facebook's systems to flirt, get to know, and yes, do a little background research on dating prospects.

✔ If you're happily ensconced in couple-dom, listing your relationship status and linking to your partner's Timeline is an easy way to broadcast, "Move along; I'm taken."

Moving to a new city

Landing in a new city with all your worldly belongings and an upside-down map can be hugely intimidating. Having some open arms or at least numbers to call when you arrive can greatly ease the transition. Although you may already know some people who live in your new city, Facebook can help connect with all the old friends and acquaintances you either forgot live there or have moved there since you last heard from them. These people can help you find doctors, apartments, hair stylists, Frisbee leagues, and restaurants.

As you meet more and more new friends, you can connect with them on Facebook. Sooner than you thought possible, when someone posts about construction slowing down his commute, you know exactly the street he means, and you may realize, *I'm home.*

Getting a job

Plenty of people use Facebook as a tool for managing their careers as well as their social lives. If you're looking at a particular company, find people who already work there to get the inside scoop or to land an interview. If you're thinking about moving into a particular industry, browse your friends by past jobs and interests to find someone to connect with. If you go to a conference for professional development, you can keep track of the other people you meet there as your Facebook friends.

Reunions

Thanks to life's curveballs, your friends at any given time may not be the people in your life at another. The memories of people you consider to be most important in your life fade over the years so that even trying to recall a last name may give you pause. The primary reason for this lapse is a legitimate one: There are only so many hours in a day. While we make new, close friends, others drift away because it's impossible to maintain many intense relationships. Facebook is an extremely powerful tool; however, it hasn't yet found a way to extend the number of hours in a day, so it can't exactly fix the problem of growing apart. Facebook can, however, lessen the finality and inevitability of the distance.

Because Facebook is less than ten years old (and because you're reading this book), you probably don't have your entire social history mapped out. Some may find it a daunting task to create connections with everyone they've ever known, which I don't recommend. Instead, build your graph as you need to or as opportunity presents. Perhaps you want to upload a photo taken from your high school graduation. Search for the people in the photo on Facebook; form the friend connection; and then *tag*, or mark, them as being in the photo. Maybe you're thinking about opening a restaurant, and you'd like to contact a friend from college who was headed into the restaurant business after graduation. Perhaps you never told your true feelings to the one who got away. For all these reasons, you may find yourself using the Facebook Search box.

Frequently, I receive reports from adopted children who connect with their biological parents or estranged siblings who find each other on Facebook. I once heard from my sixth-grade bully, who found me on Facebook and apologized for his behavior as a kid. I, in turn, used it to apologize to someone I treated terribly around the same time.

Organizing movements

If you kept up on the news of the "Arab Spring" uprisings in the early part of 2011, you couldn't avoid hearing about the role Facebook played. Young people used Facebook as an organizing tool, letting each other know about protest locations and times. People in geographically distant regions could share ideas about their countries and what they wanted to see outside of the watchful eye of oppressive regimes.

And as the drama unfolded, plenty of people with family in the affected areas turned to Facebook to make sure their loved ones were okay. People unrelated but concerned offered their support through their own status updates and more.

The birth of the 'Book

In the old days, say, ten years ago, most college freshmen would receive a thinly bound book containing the names and faces of everyone in their matriculating class. These *face books* were useful for matching names to the students seen around campus or for pointing out particular people to friends. There were several problems with these face books. If someone didn't send his picture in, the books were incomplete. They were outdated by junior year because many people looked drastically different, and the books didn't reflect the students who had transferred in or who were from any other class. Finally, they had little information about each person.

In February 2004, Mark Zuckerberg, a sophomore at Harvard, launched an online "book" to which people could upload their photos and personal information, a service that solved many of these problems. Within a month, more than one-half the Harvard undergraduates had signed up.

Zuckerberg was then joined by others to help expand the site into other schools. I was the first Stanford student to receive an account. During the summer of the same year, Facebook moved to Palo Alto, California, where the site and the company kept growing. By December 2004, the site had grown to one million college students. Every time Facebook opened to a new demographic — high school, then work users, then everyone — the rate at which people joined the site continued to increase.

At the end of 2006, the site had more than 10 million users; 2007 closed out with more than 50 million active users. At the time of this book's publication in 2013, that final count has grown to in excess of one billion people across the globe using Facebook to stay in touch.

The term *movement*, here, can apply to anything. Whether it's a campaign to raise awareness about gay teen suicides or a campaign to raise money for victims of a natural disaster, Facebook can be used to bring support and spread the word.

Chapter 2

Adding Your Own Face to Facebook

In This Chapter

▶ Signing up and getting started

▶ Creating your Timeline

▶ Getting confirmed and verified

In Chapter 1, I cover why you might want to join Facebook. In this chapter, I actually get you signed up and ready to go on Facebook. Keep a couple of things in mind when you sign up. First, Facebook becomes exponentially more useful and more fun when you start adding friends. Without friends, it can feel kind of dull. Second, your friends may take a few days to respond to your Friend Requests, so be patient. Even if your first time on Facebook isn't as exciting as you hope, be sure to come back and try again over the following weeks. Third, you can have only one account on Facebook. Facebook links accounts to e-mail addresses, and your e-mail address can be linked to only one account. This system enforces a world where people are who they say they are on Facebook.

Signing Up for Facebook

Officially, all you need in order to join Facebook is a valid e-mail address. When I say *valid,* I just mean that you need to be able to easily access the messages in that account because Facebook e-mails you a registration confirmation. Figure 2-1 shows the crucial part of the sign-up page, which you can find by navigating to `http://www.facebook.com`.

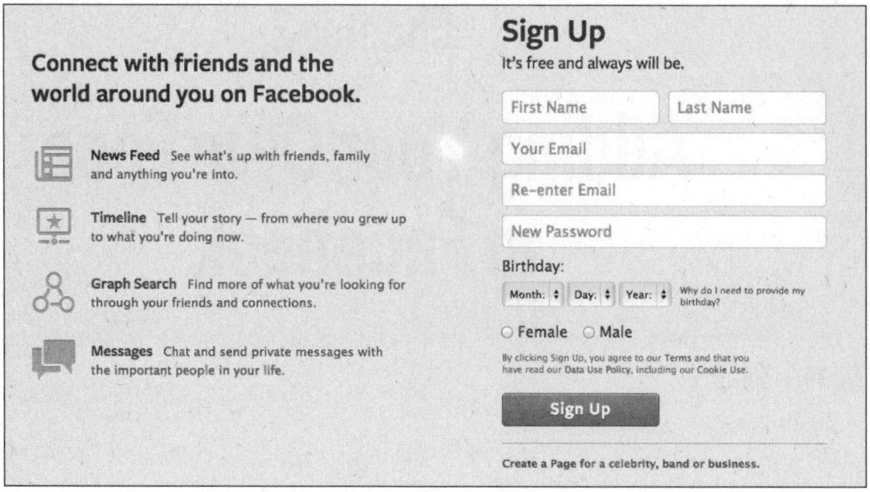

Figure 2-1:
Enter infor-
mation here
to create a
Facebook
account.

As you can see, you need to fill out a few things:

- **First and Last Name:** Facebook is a place based on real identity. Sign up with the name people know you by. I don't recommend signing up with a fake name or alias because that will make it hard for you to be found by friends. After you've signed up, you can add nicknames or maiden names to your Timeline to make it even easier for friends to find you. But for now, just use your real first and last names.

- **Email:** You need to enter your valid e-mail address here. Facebook asks you to enter your e-mail twice to make sure that there are no typos and your e-mails will actually get to you.

- **Password:** Like with all passwords, using a combination of letters and numbers is a good idea for your Facebook password. It's probably not a good idea to use the same password for every site you join, so I recommend using something unique for Facebook.

- **Birthday:** Enter your date of birth. If you're shy about sharing your birthday, don't worry: You'll be able to hide this information on your Timeline later.

- **Gender (Female or Male):** Facebook uses your gender information to construct sentences about you on the site. Especially in other languages, it's weird to see sentences like "Jennifer added a photo of themself." If you want to hide your gender on your Timeline, you can do so after you sign up.

After you fill out this information, click Sign Up (that's the big green button). Congratulations: You officially joined Facebook!

When you click Sign Up, you're agreeing to Facebook's Statement of Rights and Responsibilities and Privacy Policy. Most websites have fairly similar terms and policies, but if you're curious about just what Facebook's are, you can always follow the Terms and Privacy links at the bottom of every Facebook page.

Getting Started

Although you have this book to help guide you through the ins and outs of Facebook, lots of Facebook users do not. (How sad for them!) That's why Facebook puts all its users through a three-step Getting Started Wizard to help start them out on the right foot. This is one of those places where what I think you should do and what Facebook thinks you should do line up exactly, so I'll go through all three of these steps together, covering what to enter as well as why these steps are important to using Facebook.

In certain cases, depending on whether you were invited to join Facebook by a friend or you joined with an e-mail address from your workplace or school, you may get slightly different steps than those detailed as follows. Don't worry; the same principles apply.

Step 1: Find Your Friends

The Find Your Friends step, shown in Figure 2-2, is first because it's that important to enjoying Facebook. Without friends, Facebook can feel a little bit like going to an amusement park alone. Sure, the rides were fun, and the food was greasy, but no one was there to appreciate it with you.

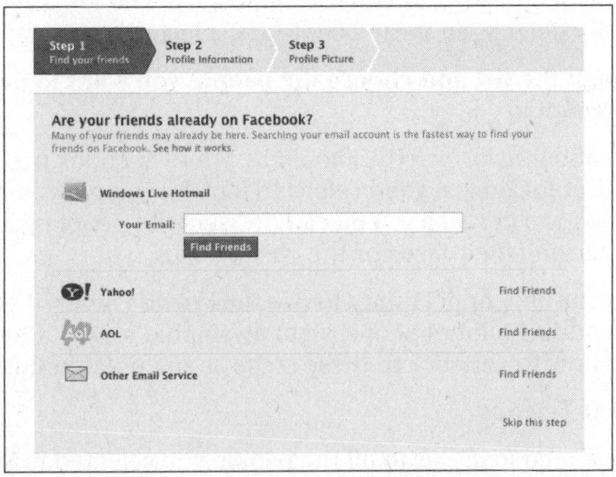

Step 1 Find your friends	**Step 2** Profile Information **Step 3** Profile Picture

Are your friends already on Facebook?
Many of your friends may already be here. Searching your email account is the fastest way to find your friends on Facebook. See how it works.

 Windows Live Hotmail

Your Email: [   ]

Find Friends

 Yahoo!   Find Friends

 AOL   Find Friends

 Other Email Service   Find Friends

                                                               Skip this step

Figure 2-2:
Find your
friends early
and often.

You have many ways to find friends on Facebook. I go over all of them in Chapter 6, as well as talking more about what friendship really means on Facebook. The method Facebook is highlighting in this step is the *Friend Finder.*

The Friend Finder works by allowing Facebook access to your e-mail account. Facebook then combs through your e-mail contacts and matches the e-mails it finds with e-mails attached to the Facebook accounts of the people you e-mail. So if Joe Smith, your friend, e-mailed you from `jsmith@email.com` and also had a Facebook account he created with that e-mail address, the Friend Finder presents you with Joe's name and profile picture and asks if you want to be friends on Facebook.

To use the Friend Finder, follow these steps:

1. **Select the e-mail provider you're using.**

   This may be Windows Live Hotmail, Gmail, Yahoo!, or another e-mail client. Facebook automatically selects a provider based on the e-mail you used to register.

   I used a nonstandard domain, so Figure 2-2 shows nothing prefilled.

   Depending on what e-mail service you use, importing your contacts and looking for friends may entail a few extra steps. Facebook provides instructions for these steps. If you follow those steps, come back here and skip to Step 4 on this list.

2. **Enter your e-mail address and e-mail password.**

   Remember to enter your e-mail password, not the password you just created for Facebook.

3. **Click Find Friends.**

   Behind the scenes, Facebook searches your contact list and presents you with the people in your e-mail Contacts list who are already on Facebook. By default, all these people are selected to be your friends.

4. **Look through the list and choose the people you want to be friends with on Facebook.**

   I talk more about *who,* exactly, should be your Facebook friends in Chapter 6, but for now, a good rule is to look for people you're friends with or related to in real life. You can deselect the people you don't want to add by clicking their faces or the check boxes.

   This isn't your only opportunity to use the Friend Finder. If you aren't sure about adding a lot of people right away, that's okay. Chapter 6 shows you how to get back to these steps at any point in time.

5. **Click Add as Friends.**

   This sends *Friend Requests* to all the people you selected in Step 4. On Facebook, all friendships have to be agreed to by both people. A request to your friend needs to be approved by her before you are officially Facebook friends.

After you add friends, Facebook looks at the e-mail addresses it didn't find matches for and asks you whether you want to invite those people to join Facebook.

6. **Select people you want to invite to join Facebook.**

   Much like selecting friends to add, you can select and deselect friends' e-mail addresses by selecting the check box next to their e-mails.

   If you don't want to invite anyone to join Facebook just yet, look on the bottom right of the screen for a Skip link. It's right next to the Send Invites button.

7. **Click Send Invites to send out invitations to your friends via e-mail.**

   They'll receive e-mails from Facebook letting them know you invited them to join.

The Friend Finder is very useful when you're just getting started on Facebook because it allows you to find a whole bunch of friends all at once. If you had to look for each of your friends by name, it could take a while. Friend Finder allows you to speed up that process.

Step 2: Profile Information

Your *Facebook Profile,* or *Timeline,* is the online representation of who you are. Most likely, you have online profiles for various websites. Facebook Timelines tend to be a little more comprehensive and dynamic, for reasons that I detail in Chapter 4.

While you're getting started, Facebook asks for only a little bit of Profile Information, the part that I like to call the *bio.* Facebook asks for this bio because this is the information that will help your friends find you. The Profile Information step is shown in Figure 2-3.

There are five fields that Facebook asks for. You can fill out all or none of them, but I definitely recommend filling them all out:

✓ **High School:** Enter the high school you attended. If you attended more than one high school, pick just one to enter now; you'll be able to add the rest of them later.

✓ **College/University:** If you attended college, enter your school. If you attended more than one school, either because you transferred or because you also attended a graduate program, just pick one school for now. You'll be able to add the rest later.

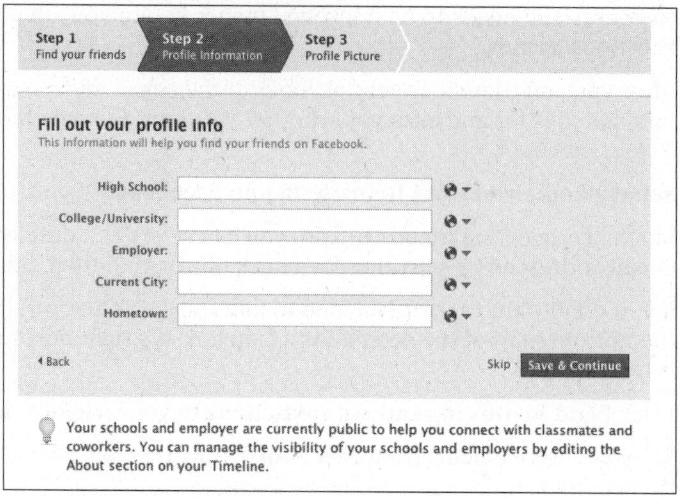

Figure 2-3:
Profile
Information
helps your
friends
find you.

Step 1
Find your friends

Step 2
Profile Information

Step 3
Profile Picture

Fill out your profile info
This information will help you find your friends on Facebook.

High School:

College/University:

Employer:

Current City:

Hometown:

◂ Back   Skip   Save & Continue

Your schools and employer are currently public to help you connect with classmates and
coworkers. You can manage the visibility of your schools and employers by editing the
About section on your Timeline.

- **Employer:** Enter the name of the company you work for. For now, enter wherever you're currently working or where you worked most recently. You'll be able to enter a full work history later on.

- **Current City:** Enter the city where you currently reside.

- **Hometown:** Enter the place you identify as your hometown. That may be the place you were born or the place you moved to when you were 10 years old. It's up to you.

You may notice that as you type the name of your high school or college, a list of names appears below the field where you're typing. Get used to seeing these *autocomplete* menus around Facebook. As you type, Facebook tries to guess the rest of the word you're typing. When you see what you're looking for, use the arrow keys to highlight the correct match and press Enter. You'll find similar menus later when you start using search, tagging photos, and sending messages.

Next to each field is a globe icon with an upside-down triangle next to it, shown next to this paragraph. This is one version of the Privacy Menu that appears throughout Facebook. Also known as the Audience Selector, you can click this icon to change who can see the information you just entered.

Privacy on Facebook is important. And complex. That's why all of Chapter 5 is dedicated to understanding it. But for now, decide who can see each of these items. So, for example, if you're choosing privacy for your High School, you would click the globe icon to open the privacy menu and select from the following options:

- **Public or Everyone:** Anyone who visits your Timeline can see where you went to high school. Additionally, anyone who searches for People Who Went to *<High School Name>* will see you in the search results.

✔ **Friends:** Only people you add as friends will be able to see where you went to high school.

✔ **Only Me:** Only you will be able to see where you went to high school. A friend visiting your Timeline won't see this information.

✔ **Custom:** A specific set of people you choose will or will not be able to see where you went to high school. This option doesn't usually become very useful until people have responded to your Friend Requests.

✔ **Lists (Close Friends and Family):** Facebook tries to help you sort your friends into categories such as Close Friends or Family (or other types of categories, detailed in Chapter 6). You can choose to allow only people in those lists to see where you went to high school. Much like Custom, this option may not be very useful at this time.

If you don't want to share this information publicly, simply click the globe icon and select with whom you do want to share it. Each privacy setting has its own icon to represent it, so if you choose Friends, the globe icon will be replaced by the icon of two silhouettes.

Because these are the fields that help friends find you, I recommend leaving them set to Public. Especially if you have a common name, having some biographical details makes it easier for friends to find and identify you. (Yes, you are the right Jane Smith because you're from Kalamazoo, Michigan.) But if you aren't comfortable with that, you of course can change the privacy setting. Privacy settings aren't set in stone; you can always adjust them (either to make information more or less private) later.

When you're done filling out these fields, click the blue Save & Continue button to move on to the next step.

Sometimes Facebook will use the information you just entered to show you some people it thinks you may know. In that case, after you finish Step 2, but before you get to Step 3, you may see an Add People You Know screen. This screen displays the name and photos of people you may want to add as friends. Click the Add Friend button next to the images of people you know and want to add as friends. You can also choose to skip that part of the step using the Skip link (next to the Save & Continue button).

Step 3: Profile Picture

Much like Step 2, Step 3 is about helping your friends find you, whereas Step 1 was about helping you find them.

Like your biographical information, your profile picture helps set you apart from other people with similar names. Step 3 is shown in Figure 2-4.

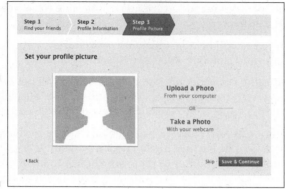

Figure 2-4:
Add a profile picture to get your own face on Facebook.

To add your profile picture, make sure you have a photo you want to use saved somewhere on your computer's hard drive, and follow these steps:

1. **Click Upload a Photo.**

    This brings up a dialog box similar to the one shown in Figure 2-5.

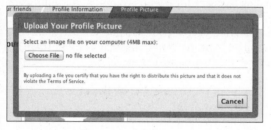

Figure 2-5:
Start here to navigate your computer's hard drive.

2. **Click Choose File.**

    Depending on what kind of computer you have, this may say something slightly different, but the gist is the same: Choose a file from your hard drive. This opens a navigation interface.

3. **Select your desired photo and click Select or OK.**

    This brings you back to the Getting Started Wizard, except now there's a preview of your new profile picture.

4. **Click Save & Continue.**

I talk a lot about your profile picture and the many ways it's used on Facebook in Chapter 4, but here are a few quick tips on selecting a profile picture:

✔ **Make a good first impression.** Your profile picture is one of the first ways people interact with your Timeline and how you choose to represent yourself. Most people pick pictures that are flattering or that represent what's important to them. Sometimes, profile pictures include other people — friends or significant others. Other times, the location matters. If the first photo you see of someone is at the beach versus at a party or sitting at his desk, you may draw different conclusions about that person. What picture represents you?

✔ **Consider who will see your profile picture.** By default, your profile picture appears in search results that are visible to all of Facebook and can even be made available to the larger Internet population. So, generally, people who search for your name can see that picture. Make sure it's something you're comfortable with everyone seeing.

✔ **Pick a photo *you* like.** As you use Facebook, you actually wind up seeing your own photo quite often. Small versions appear wherever you make a comment, post something, or are part of a group. So pick a photo you like looking at.

✔ **You're not stuck with it.** After I put all this pressure on you to pick the perfect photo, keep in mind that you can easily change your profile picture at any time. Is it the dead of winter, and that photo of you on the beach last summer is just too depressing to look at? No problem; simply edit your profile picture, which you can find out how to do in Chapter 4.

Well, those are pretty much the basics of getting started on Facebook. Hopefully, by now you've added a few friends, some information about yourself, and a profile picture.

Your New Home Page

After you complete your Getting Started Wizard, you arrive at your Home page. This is where Facebook starts to look like the Facebook you would see if you'd been using the site for a while already. The Home page is what you see when you log in to Facebook.

What's interesting about the Facebook Home page is that while some parts remain the same (such as the big blue bar on top, and the menu on the left-hand side), the bulk of what you see is constantly changing. This is because the Home page (also known as the News Feed) updates to show you what your friends are posting, sharing, and talking about on Facebook.

At the beginning of this chapter, I pointed out that Facebook gets exponentially better once you have friends. This is absolutely true on the Home page. Until your friends respond to your requests, you may not see much here except prompts to learn more about Facebook, find more friends, or fill out information you didn't fill out in Steps 1–3. After you add the people you know as friends, take a break. Stretch. Take a walk. Drink some water. Come back over the next few days to see the interesting photos, status updates, and links your friends are sharing.

Trust Me: Getting Confirmed and Verified

As I say over and over, Facebook is a website for real identity and real people. To protect this fact, Facebook has systems in place to detect any fake accounts. Fake accounts may be jokes (for example, someone creating an account for her dog), or they may be *spammers* (robots creating accounts to send thousands of fake Friend Requests). Regardless, they're not allowed on the site.

You, however, aren't fake or a spammer; how does Facebook know that? Facebook figures that out by confirming and verifying you.

Confirmation

Confirmation is Facebook's way of trying to make sure that you are really you and that the e-mail address you used to sign up is really yours. After you finish the earlier three Getting Started steps, you may see a yellow banner across the top of your Home page, asking you to check your e-mail to finish signing up for Facebook.

When you click the Sign Up button (as I describe earlier), Facebook sends you an e-mail asking you to confirm your account. In other words, Facebook is double-checking that you are the person who owns your e-mail address.

To confirm that you are, in fact, you, and that the e-mail address is, in fact, yours, go to your e-mail, look for that message, and open it. (It will usually have a subject like *Just One More Step to Get Started on Facebook* or *Facebook Confirmation*.) That e-mail contains a link. Click the link in that e-mail, and you will be confirmed.

You may have already confirmed your e-mail address by using the Friend Finder or other normal activities. If Facebook isn't bugging you about it with banners or follow-up e-mails, you can pretty much assume you're good to go.

Am I too old for Facebook?

No. Most emphatically, no. This is a common misconception, mainly because Facebook was originally exclusive to college students. Facebook's origins, even its name, are rooted in college campuses, but its utility and nature aren't limited to being useful to only college students.

Everyone has networks of friends and people with whom they interact on a day-to-day basis. Young or old, in college or working, this is true. Facebook tries to map these real-world connections to make it easier for people to share information with their friends.

If you're reading this section and thinking maybe you're just too old for Facebook, you're wrong. More and more people in older age demographics are signing up for Facebook every day to keep in touch with old friends, share photos, create events, and connect with local organizations. Almost everything I discuss in the book is non-age-specific.

Obviously, how people use the site can be very different at different ages, but you will discover these nuances when you use Facebook more and more. Generally, you should feel confident that you and your friends can connect and use Facebook in a meaningful way.

More than one billion people are using Facebook, and that number isn't made up of "a bunch of kids." Rather, it's a bunch of people from every age group, every country, and every walk of life.

Verification

Verification is a way to make sure that beyond just owning an e-mail account (which, unfortunately, any evil robot can do), you are a real human being who won't abuse Facebook or post inappropriate content. Unfortunately, Facebook has a bit of a "guilty until proven innocent" attitude about all of this. And Facebook puts you through a series of tests to prove your innocence.

Most of these tests aren't ones you have to actively take. Instead, just use the site as your lovely, non-spamming self, and eventually you'll be verified. If you're concerned about being verified right away, however, you can do so by adding a mobile number to your account. Follow these steps:

1. **Click the link on your Home page to add a mobile number.**

   If this link doesn't appear on your Home page, click the gear icon in the top-right corner, select Account Settings, choose Mobile from the left menu, and click the Add a Phone button. A pop-up window appears, as shown in Figure 2-6.

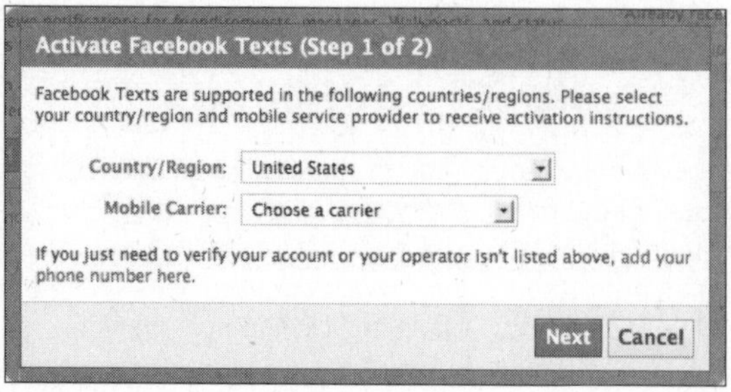

Activate Facebook Texts (Step 1 of 2)

Facebook Texts are supported in the following countries/regions. Please select your country/region and mobile service provider to receive activation instructions.

Country/Region: United States

Mobile Carrier: Choose a carrier

If you just need to verify your account or your operator isn't listed above, add your phone number here.

Next   Cancel

Figure 2-6:
Activate
Facebook
Texts to
verify
yourself.

When you add a mobile number, you're signing up for Facebook Texts, a service that will send text messages to your phone to notify you of certain events on Facebook, like receiving a message or getting a Friend Request. If you're not ready to be part of that service (using Facebook on a mobile phone is covered in detail in Chapter 12), you can still verify your account by clicking the blue line of text at the bottom of the window that reads Add Your Phone Number Here.

2. **Click the Add Your Phone Number Here link.**

   This opens the Confirm Your Number window, shown in Figure 2-7.

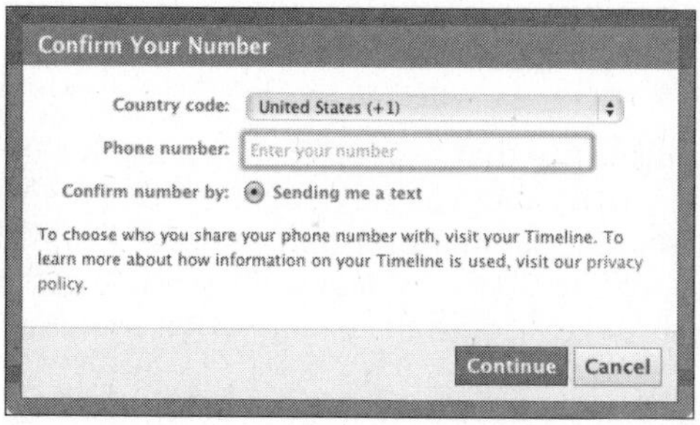

Confirm Your Number

Country code: United States (+1)

Phone number: Enter your number

Confirm number by: ● Sending me a text

To choose who you share your phone number with, visit your Timeline. To learn more about how information on your Timeline is used, visit our privacy policy.

Continue   Cancel

Figure 2-7:
Confirm
your phone
number to
prove you're
real.

3. **Select your Country Code.**

4. **Enter your phone number into the Phone Number box.**

5. **Click Continue.**

   This sends a text message containing a code to your phone.

6. **Back at your computer, enter that code into the designated box on the screen and click Confirm.**

   After you confirm this code, your account will be verified.

Chapter 3

Finding Your Way Around Facebook

*H*ere's the thing about using Facebook: It has a lot of options. Now, this is actually one of the best things about Facebook. You can upload photos, look at photos, chat with a friend, message a friend, read updates from friends . . . the list goes on and on. What does get a little confusing is that there's no one way to do anything on Facebook. Depending on what page you're on, you'll see slightly different things. Depending on who your friends are, you'll see slightly different things. Using Facebook can't exactly be broken down into ten easy steps.

However, you can learn to recognize a few more constant places. Starting from when you log in, you will always start on your *Home page.* The Home page, though continually evolving, has a few constants that I detail in this chapter. If you ever find yourself lost on Facebook (it happens; trust me), click the Home link or the Facebook logo to go to the Home page, where you'll be able to reorient yourself.

Figure 3-1 shows a sample Home page. This chapter details the elements of the Home page that you're likely to see, too: menus and links to other parts of the site. Some of these links can be found no matter where you are on Facebook, some appear only when you're on your Home page, and some will be there, well, sometimes. Learning about these links helps you understand how to find your way around Facebook and enables you to work with some of Facebook's features and options.

Figure 3-1:
Your Home
page may
look a little
like this.

Checking Out the Blue Bar on Top

I happen to spend a lot of time in coffee shops working alongside writers, students, businesspeople, and hobbyists — all drinking steamy beverages and manning laptops. I can always tell at a glance when someone is browsing Facebook by the big blue bar across the top of the page. The blue bar is home to many of the important navigational links on Facebook. And anytime you're looking at a Facebook page, you'll have the blue bar accompanying you, like a really loyal puppy. Figure 3-2 shows the blue bar.

Figure 3-2:
The blue bar
at the top.

Here's what you need to know about the different parts of the blue bar:

✓ **Facebook logo:** The "f" Facebook logo on the left of the blue bar serves two purposes. First, it reminds you what website you're using. Second, no matter where you are on Facebook, if you click this icon, you're back at the Facebook Home page.

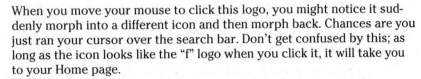

When you move your mouse to click this logo, you might notice it suddenly morph into a different icon and then morph back. Chances are you just ran your cursor over the search bar. Don't get confused by this; as long as the icon looks like the "f" logo when you click it, it will take you to your Home page.

✔ **Search:** The white text next to the logo reads `Type to Search for People, Places and Things`. This text area is where you can type any sort of search query. Simply click that text and start typing what you're looking for. After you click, Facebook opens up a menu with suggested searches. I cover the ways Facebook Search is special later in the "Graph Search" section of this chapter.

The area of the blue bar that lets you know about Search on your Home page will actually change depending on where you are on Facebook. For example, when you're on a friend's Timeline, it will show your friend's name. When you're exploring a group, it will show the group's name. This is one way to keep from getting lost.

✔ **Home:** This link is always there to bring you back to the Home page. When in doubt, just go Home and start over.

✔ **Friend Requests:** Next to the Home link is an icon of two people, intended to depict friends. Clicking this icon reveals a menu that shows you any pending Friend Requests you may have. Whenever you receive brand-new Friend Requests, a little red number totaling the number of new requests shows up on top of this icon. When you view the new requests, regardless of whether you respond to them, the red flag goes away. I cover sending and receiving Friend Requests in more detail in Chapter 6.

✔ **Messages:** An icon depicting two speech bubbles lets you access a preview of your Messages Inbox. Clicking it shows you snippets from your most recent messages, as well as links to use if you want to send a new message or go to your Inbox. As with the Friend Requests, a little red flag appears to show you how many new messages you have. When you click that flag and view the preview of the new messages, the flag disappears. I cover Facebook Messages in Chapter 8.

✔ **Notifications:** When someone on Facebook has taken an action that involves you, you're notified by a red flag on top of the next icon — the globe. Maybe the person has tagged you in a photo, posted to your Timeline, liked a comment you made, or posted something to a group you belong to. Click the globe to scroll through your most recent notifications, as well as a link to change your notification settings or see all your notifications on another page.

✔ **Account menu (down arrow):** In this book, I reference the *Account menu*. That's the menu that appears when you click this arrow. Here's a rundown of some of the options you can find on the Account menu:

   • *Settings:* Choosing this brings you to the Settings page, where you can change your name, your e-mail address or password, your mobile information (which allows you to access the site from a mobile phone), or the language you want to use on the site. This is also where you go to find privacy settings (detailed in Chapter 5), notification settings, and to deactivate your account.

- *Log Out:* Clicking this ends your Facebook session. If you share your computer with others, always be sure to log out to ensure that another person can't access your Facebook account.

If you have the Remember Me option selected when you log in, you won't ever be logged out until you click Log Out. Remember Me keeps you logged in despite closing the browser; therefore, I recommend using the Remember Me option only on a computer you don't share with others.

- *Help:* Clicking Help switches over to a Help menu with links to frequently asked questions and a search box. If you ever have a problem and you can't find the answer in this book, the Help menu and the Help Center are good places to start.

- *Your Pages:* In Chapter 13, I go over creating a *Page,* or special profile for businesses or organizations. If you create or manage Pages, you'll be able to find links to use Facebook on behalf of your Pages from the Account menu.

- **Your Ads:** I also briefly cover ads in Chapter 13. If you create an ad to be shown on Facebook, you'll find links to manage and create more ads in this menu.

The Left Sidebar

The left side of any screen on Facebook — regardless of whether you're on the Home page — is taken up by what Facebook calls the *sidebar.* The sidebar is the menu on the left side of the page that provides links to frequently used areas of the site, as well as access to your online friends for easy chatting. This menu is black, with various colorful icons representing the section of the site they will take you to.

Depending on the width of your browser window, you may see the sidebar in either its minimized or its expanded state. If your browser window isn't wide, the minimized state shows just a few icons. You can hover over the menu to expand it and select the link you need. You can see the comparison between the minimized and expanded versions of the sidebar in Figure 3-3.

The sidebar is divided into two sections. The top section provides links to the parts of Facebook you use the most. For that reason, I refer to this as the *favorites* section. The bottom part of the sidebar is the *friends* section. It functions a lot like a buddy list to allow you to chat easily with your friends.

Figure 3-3:
Expand the sidebar by hovering your mouse over it.

The favorites section

Some of the items in the top part of your sidebar may vary depending on which parts of the site you use more. For example, certain apps may appear here if you use them a lot. If you've never joined a group, you won't see any here. However, in general, starting at the top and working your way down, you should see most, if not all, of these items:

✔ **Timeline (<*Your Name*>):** If you squint really hard you may recognize that this small photo is the same photo you see on your Timeline, the profile picture. Clicking this photo brings you to your Timeline (you'll know you're there because the text next to the little "f" logo now shows your name). See Chapter 4 for more on Timelines.

✔ **Privacy Shortcuts (lock icon):** Chances are that you, like many other people reading this book, care a lot about your privacy and exactly who can see your content on Facebook. Although there are lots of privacy configurations, all of which are covered in Chapter 5, opening this menu lets you check on your current settings, edit settings, and access links to other privacy tools you may find useful.

Here are three basic questions Facebook thinks you might have about privacy that need to be answered from these shortcuts:

  • Who can see my stuff?

- Who can contact me?

- How do I stop someone from bothering me?

✔ **News Feed:** News Feed is actually the main focus of your Home page. It's a constantly updating list of stories by and about your friends. News Feed is a way to keep up with what your friends are doing, as well as see their most recent photos, videos, and activities. Because it's so important to using Facebook, I cover it in the section "Viewing News Feed," later in this chapter, and then again in Chapter 7. You can always go back to your Home page and News Feed by clicking this link, the Home link in the blue bar, or the "f" logo in the blue bar.

✔ **Messages:** This link opens your Messages Inbox. Facebook's messaging system is actually fairly different than what you may be used to in your e-mail, but it's very useful. See Chapter 8 for the details on this topic.

✔ **Events:** This link brings you the Events page, where you can see upcoming birthdays and events you've been invited to. Events can range from intimate birthday parties to big talks or lectures. I cover this topic in detail in Chapter 11.

✔ **Apps:** In Figure 3-3, the item below Events is Candy Crush Saga. This is an app I use. *Apps* are games or features that aren't built by Facebook employees, but that use (with your permission) Facebook data to function. I cover apps in detail in Chapter 14. As you start to use apps, they may appear here. Clicking a link to one will bring you to that app's Home page.

✔ **Groups:** My sidebar shows a few groups that I use frequently. Groups are ways to communicate with (you guessed it) groups of related people. That might be a group of people all going on vacation together or a group of people who are in a book club together. Chapter 9 covers Facebook Groups in detail, but for now, just keep in mind that when you click a link to a group, you're taken to its Home page on Facebook where you can see recent posts and discussions. If you often participate in discussions with a particular group, it may appear here in the sidebar.

✔ **See More:** As I mention, the apps and groups I use most frequently appear in my sidebar, but these aren't all the apps I use or groups I belong to. To get to my less frequently used groups or apps, I simply click the See More link to view a complete list.

Next to the icons in the sidebar are small numbers letting you know how many "new" items are in that area of the site. In Figure 3-3, for example, the *2* next to the Messages icon indicates that I have two unread messages. The *4* next to the group icon indicates that two new posts are in that group. These numbers also appear when the menu is expanded.

The Friends section

The bottom part of the sidebar is basically a buddy list. It shows you all your friends who are online (signified by green dots next to their names) or using Facebook mobile (signified by a mobile phone icon next to their names). Facebook puts the friends you interact with most often at the top of this section; you can scroll down to see all your friends who are currently online. Clicking a friend's name opens a chat window at the bottom of the screen, where you can type a message directly to that person. Chatting (and other forms of messaging) is covered in Chapter 8.

Viewing News Feed

This chapter is about navigating Facebook, which is why the blue bar and the sidebar are so important. At the same time, these menus aren't really the focus of the Home page. Instead, these menus serve as a bit of a background to the main event: News Feed. As I mention earlier, News Feed is what you see as the main focus of your Home page.

So what is News Feed? Imagine that your morning paper, news show, or radio program included an additional section that featured articles solely about the specific people you know. That's what News Feed is. As long as the people you know are active on Facebook, you can stay up-to-date with their lives via your News Feed. A friend may post photos from his recent birthday party, another may write a post about her new job, and another may publish a public event for her upcoming art show. These may all show up as stories in your Facebook News Feed. A News Feed bonus: You can often use it to stay up-to-date on current events just by seeing what your friends are talking about or by liking the Pages of real-world news organizations and getting their updates in your News Feed. When there's unusual weather, I find out about it on Facebook first because I see a flurry of posts asking if that was really hail.

News Feed is possibly one of the best and most interesting things about Facebook, but also one of the hardest to explain. This is because no matter how I describe seeing a photo of my friend and her new baby pop up in my News Feed, it won't be as exciting as when *your* friend posts those photos. I do my best to capture at least a bit of this excitement in Chapter 7.

On the right side of the Home page, next to News Feed, are two boxes. The top box is what I call the *News Feed menu*. It can be used to change your *view* of News Feed. By view, I mean who or what you see in the News Feed portion of the Home page. By default, News Feed doesn't show you absolutely everything that is happening on Facebook; it tries to show you stories about people you care about, and it tries to show you interesting stories about those people. If you don't like the mix that Facebook creates for you, though, you can choose a different view from this News Feed menu.

You can see some of the options in the News Feed menu if you click the down arrow beneath it. This expands the menu to some of the most common views. For example, you may just want to see stories from and about close friends (the people you interact with most on Facebook). Or you may want to see the most recent posts. Or you may want to see all the content related to music, such as what people are listening to or the artists people like. You can see posts from certain groups or from all the people who went to high school or college with you. You get the idea.

The second box on the right side of the page is what I think of as the *reminders box*. Reminders include things like friends' birthdays, upcoming events, Friend Requests, and requests from apps. You may also see notifications here about life events people add on Facebook — for example, a couple getting engaged or having a baby.

The bottom part of the reminders box is a reminder of something else: that although Facebook is free for you to use, the way it makes its money is through showing you (and everyone else) ads. The sponsored section of this box shows a variety of ads.

Graph Search

Search has become an integral part of using the Internet. It's the way we find the info we need — whether that's a businesses address, a person's contact info, or the year of the great San Francisco earthquake. Facebook's search is also important, though it works a bit differently from the way a search engine like Google or Bing does. Instead of just looking for the best match for what you searched for, Facebook tries to give you a way to explore the best your friends have to offer through what Facebook calls *Graph Search*.

Graph Search is named for the web of connections between you and your friends that is sometimes referred to as the *social graph*. Graph Search allows these connections to be surfaced to you in interesting ways. On the most practical level, this is why when you search for a friend with a common name on Facebook, the top results will be people with the same common friends as you, or people in your city, or from your hometown. Search doesn't just look for people with a specific name; it looks for all the connections that might matter in a search.

What's cool about Graph Search is that it allows you to discover new and interesting things through search. For example, you can search for "Restaurants my friends like in Seattle" and see all the restaurants in the city that your friends have taken the time to like on Facebook. You can search for "Photos of my friends" or "Music my friends like" to discover content you might not know about. You could even search for something like "Friends of my friends who like my photos" and see who likes your photos whom you might not know about.

To use Graph Search, start typing something in the search box in the big blue bar on top (refer to Figure 3-2). It can be anything, but you might try something like **TV shows my friends like**. As you type, Facebook actually recommends several different searches. For example, as I typed "TV shows my friends," I realized I could search for my friends' favorite TV shows, the favorite TV shows of people who live near me, the favorite TV shows of people who like the same science fiction blog I like, and so on. When I finally pick an actual search, Facebook shows me the results in a list. (It's no surprise that *Arrested Development* tops out the list.) I can then refine the search using the options on the right side of the search results page.

Depending on the type of search, you may have different options for both refining and expanding the search. Figure 3-4 shows the *search refinement box,* which gives possibilities for changing the search when I look for restaurants that people in Seattle like. In addition to the map of locations, I can narrow the search down to a certain type of cuisine by clicking the Category drop-down menu. I can also add a Liked By category so that I see only restaurants that people in Seattle like *and* that my friend Phil likes. Additionally, I can actually expand the search to look at photos from these restaurants.

If you want to search for something cool but don't even know what to search for, click the Discover Something New link found at the bottom of the search refinement box. Facebook will generate a random search, and you might just learn something cool about your friends or about yourself.

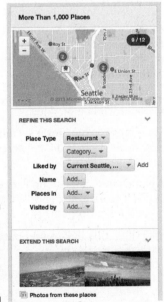

Figure 3-4: Graph Search can be a bit of a rabbit hole.

Although Graph Search is interesting to play with, you may find that more often than not, you're using the search bar to get quickly to someplace on Facebook. You might want to hop over to a friend's Timeline to leave a post, or you might be trying to remember what time that particular event is. In both these cases, simply typing the name of the person or event into the search bar will bring up the correct results. Facebook autocompletes as you type, and before it recommends complicated searches, it usually recommends a person, Page, group, or event that you are likely to be looking for.

Exploring the Lowest Links: The Footer

In blue type at the very bottom of every Facebook page, you see a set of links collectively called the *footer*. The footer is the catch-all for important information about Facebook the social network, Facebook for business, Facebook the company, and the Facebook policies.

As you scroll down your Home page to find these links, it may seem like you've been scrolling forever and that the links keep on jumping down the page. This isn't your imagination. When you scroll down the Home page, Facebook assumes you want to read more News Feed posts, so it shows you more. And more. And more. If you're trying to get to these bottom links, I recommend logging out of Facebook and clicking them from Facebook's log-in page.

Here is a description of each link:

- **About:** This link takes you to the official Facebook Page, where you can read about key features of Facebook, see the latest headlines and announcements from the company, discover the newest Facebook features, and see links to recent articles written about Facebook.

- **Create Ad:** If you're running ads on Facebook, or want to, this is where you go to get started and keep track of any ad campaigns.

- **Create Page:** *Pages* are basically Timelines for businesses, causes, and other non-people. This link takes you to the Create a Page screen. I cover Pages in detail in Chapter 13.

- **Developers:** Many of the apps and games you can use on Facebook are written by outside developers who don't work at Facebook. If you're interested in creating a new Facebook application, this is your link.

- **Careers:** Want to work for Facebook? Click this link to find out what jobs are available and all about the working environment.

- **Privacy:** Details the Facebook Data Use Policy, if you're looking for a little light bedtime reading.

✔ **Cookies:** Sadly, clicking this link doesn't make chocolate chip cookies suddenly appear in your hand. Instead, it brings you to a page that
explains how Facebook uses *web cookies,* or stored data on your web
browser. Cookies are used on many websites to keep your experience
more convenient (for example, automatically displaying Facebook in the
language of whatever country your computer is in) and also to deliver
ads to you.

✔ **Terms:** This link takes you to a page where you can view all of
Facebook's Terms and Policies, including the Statement of Rights and
Responsibilities (which you agreed to when you signed up) and the Data
Use Policy.

✔ **Help:** The Help Center gives you all sorts of tools for finding out how
to use the site and how to stay safe on Facebook. If you can't find an
answer in this book, I suggest searching for an answer in the Facebook
Help Center.

Chapter 4

Timeline: The Story of You

. . . .

In This Chapter

▶ Navigating the Timeline

▶ Filling out and editing your Timeline information

▶ Sharing with your friends through your Timeline

. . . .

O ne of the fun things about writing *Facebook For Dummies* has been noting what's important in my life based on the examples I use to explain certain concepts. When I wrote the first edition, I was just out of college and every example usually related to Ultimate Frisbee, whether it was posting photos (of a Frisbee game) or planning an event (like a Frisbee match). By the second edition, I'd been working a little bit longer and used examples related to some really fun travels I'd taken. The third edition was all about my wedding, the fourth about my time in grad school, and for this edition, my new baby makes more than a few cameos. As it turns out, your life can change a lot over the course of several years.

That moment of looking backward and seeing how far you've come is the idea behind the Facebook Timeline. Like many websites, Facebook wants you to establish a profile with the basic biographical information — where you're from, what you do, where you went to school. But in addition to that, Facebook also wants you to keep updating and posting and sharing and marking events that define you. Then it turns all that information into a virtual scrapbook that you and your friends can explore. That virtual scrapbook is your Timeline.

Although Facebook does a lot of the work, this is *your* Timeline, so all aspects of it can be edited, modified, and changed based on how you want to represent yourself and your history. This chapter covers all the ways you edit the information and appearance of your Timeline, as well as who can see what on your Timeline.

Scrolling Through Time

Figure 4-1 shows the top of a Timeline. The Timeline has a few different portions: the big cover photo and the smaller profile picture, the navigation tabs beneath the cover photo, the About box, the Share box, and the Timeline itself, extending from the present back and back and back to the day you were born.

Figure 4-1:
The top of a
Timeline.

In terms of navigating the Timeline, the most important thing to know is that *you scroll down the page to go back in time.* As you scroll down, posts you and your friends have made and life events you have added keep on showing up. When you start scrolling down, a new menu appears at the top of the page (below the blue bar at the top). I call this the *Timeline navigator* (see Figure 4-2).

Figure 4-2:
Use the
navigator to
activate your
nostalgia.

The Timeline navigator uses a series of drop-down menus to help you jump around in time. Click any of the buttons to view a drop-down menu of options:

- ✔ **Timeline:** This drop-down menu lets you switch from the Timeline itself to the About section of your Timeline. I cover the About section in the "All About Me" section later in this chapter.

- ✔ **Year:** This drop-down menu lets you hop from year to year on your Timeline.

- ✔ **Highlights/Month:** By default, when you scroll back in time, Facebook shows you *Highlights* — what it thinks are the most important posts or events. You can use the Timeline navigator to change from Highlights to All Stories. When you switch to all stories, you can use this menu to view specific months within a certain year.

First Impressions

If you're brand new to Facebook, your Timeline may seem a little empty compared to those of your friends. That's okay; your Timeline will fill up as you start to update your status, post links, and so on (see the upcoming "Telling Your Story" section). But before you do all that, you want to get the basics filled out so that people can find you, recognize you, and learn a little bit about you. This section covers the very first thing people see when they arrive on your Timeline: your cover photo and your profile picture.

These two photos at the top of your Timeline present the first impression to all visitors to your Timeline. The cover photo is the larger photo that serves as a background to your Timeline. People often choose visually striking photos or images that speak to who they are and what they love. To change your cover photo, follow these steps:

1. **Hover over your existing cover photo.**

   A Change Cover button appears on the right side of the photo.

2. **Click the Change Cover button.**

   The Change Cover menu appears with four options: Choose from Photos, Upload Photo, Reposition, and Remove.

   If you're using a Facebook Mobile app that syncs with your phone, you may also see an option to Add Synced Photo.

3. **Click Choose from Photos to select a cover photo from photos you've already added to Facebook.**

   The Choose from Your Photos window appears, as shown in Figure 4-3. By default, it shows Recent Uploads. You can get to a full list of your photos by clicking View Albums in the upper-right corner.

Figure 4-3:
Use the
Choose
from Photos
window to
choose a
cover photo.

4. **Choose Upload Photo to select a cover photo from your computer.**

   A window for navigating your computer's files appears.

5. **Select your cover photo by clicking your desired album and then the desired photo.**

   This brings you back to your Timeline, where you should see the new cover photo in place with the overlaid message, Drag to Reposition Cover.

6. **Select the photo file you want as your cover and click Open.**

   This brings you back to your Timeline, where you should see the new cover photo in place with the overlaid message, Drag to Reposition Cover.

   Because the cover photo spans the width of your Timeline, you may occasionally find that when you try to add some photos as your cover, you get an error telling you that it isn't wide enough. Make sure your cover photo is at least 720 pixels wide to ensure that it will fit.

7. **Click and drag your cover photo to position it correctly within the frame of the screen.**

8. **Click Save Changes.**

   Your new cover photo is now in place.

If you don't like the way your cover photo is positioned, you can use the same Change Cover menu to either reposition or remove your cover photo. You can change your cover as often as you want.

Your profile picture is the smaller photo. This photo is what sticks with you all around Facebook, appearing wherever you comment or post something. For example, your friends may see your status post in their News Feeds, accompanied by your name and profile picture. Most people use some variation on a headshot for their profile picture. There are several ways to add a profile picture.

Add a profile picture that's already on Facebook

If you skip to Chapter 10, you'll see that Facebook is the number-one photo-sharing site on the web, which means there's a good chance someone has already added a photo of you to Facebook that you might like to use as a profile picture.

Use these steps to change your profile picture to one that is already on Facebook:

1. **Hover your mouse over your existing profile picture.**

   The Edit Profile Picture button appears.

2. **Click the Edit Profile Picture button.**

   The Profile Picture menu appears with five options: Choose from Photos, Take Photo (only for people with a webcam), Upload Photo, Edit Thumbnail, and Remove.

3. **To choose from the photos of you on Facebook, click Choose from Photos.**

   The Choose from Photos window appears, which by default shows you all the photos that you're tagged in on Facebook. Page through these photos by clicking the arrows in the bottom-right corner. You can also get to the photos you've added to Facebook by clicking View Albums in the upper-right corner.

4. **Select the photo you want as your profile picture by clicking it.**

   This brings you to the photo with a cropping interface, as shown in Figure 4-4.

5. **Using the cropping functions, choose the portion of the photo you want as your profile picture.**

   Move the transparent box around the photo by clicking and dragging it. Click and drag the corners of the transparent box to include more or less of the original photo.

Drag the corners of the transparent box above to crop this photo into your profile picture. Done Cropping | Cancel

Figure 4-4:
Crop profile
pictures to
focus on
just you.

6. **Click Done Cropping when you've finished.**

   It's a small link right beneath the photo. This step takes you back to your Timeline. The new profile picture should be visible.

Add a profile picture from your hard drive

If there aren't any photos of you on Facebook that would make suitable profile pictures, you can choose a photo from your computer's hard drive:

1. **Hover the mouse over your existing profile picture.**

   The Edit Profile Picture button appears.

2. **Click the Edit Profile Picture button.**

   The Profile Picture menu appears with five options: Choose from Photos, Take Photo (only for people with a webcam), Upload Photo, Edit Thumbnail, and Remove.

3. **Select Upload Photo.**

   An interface for navigating your computer's hard drive appears.

4. **Locate and click the desired photo.**

5. **Click Open or Choose.**

   The photo is added and appears in place of your old profile picture.

Take a photo of yourself using your webcam

If you have a camera built into your computer or an external webcam, you can also take a photo to be your profile picture by following these steps:

1. **Hover the mouse over your existing profile picture.**

   The Edit Profile Picture button appears.

2. **Click the Edit Profile Picture button.**

   The Profile Picture menu appears with five options: Choose from Photos, Take Photo (only for people with a webcam), Upload Photo, Edit Thumbnail, and Remove.

3. **Select Take Photo.**

   An interface for shooting a photo using your computer's webcam appears.

4. **Click the button at the bottom of the screen to take your photo.**

   Remember to smile!

5. **If you're happy with the photo, click Save as Profile Picture.**

   The photo is added and appears in place of your old profile picture.

Much like your cover photo, you can change your profile picture as often as you choose. Every photo you select as your profile picture is automatically added to the Profile Pictures album.

Your cover photo and profile picture are visible to anyone who searches for you and clicks on your name. Make sure you're comfortable with everyone seeing these images.

Telling Your Story

Getting back to the main focus of your Timeline, take a look at the stuff below the cover photo. Two columns run down the page:

✔ The skinny column on the left side is full of interests, recent activity, and application activity (I cover these parts of your Timeline in the upcoming "Sections" section).

✔ The wider right column is where posts and life events live. These posts might be something you've added to Facebook, like a status or a photo or something someone has added to Facebook about you, like a photo tag. These posts constitute your Timeline. As you scroll down your past, you can see what you were posting last week, last month, last year.

Whether you joined Facebook yesterday or five years ago, you can use Facebook to highlight important events in your life that are happening now or in years past. This section goes over the basics of sharing your story, from the ongoing process of status updates and photo posts to the posting of life events to the capability to curate your Timeline to highlight your favorite posts and events.

Posts

Posts are the type of sharing you'll be doing most often on Facebook. These are the bread and butter of sharing. People post multiple times a day about an array of topics. And they post things from the Share box, also known as the Publisher. The Share box is the text field at the top of your Timeline's right column, as shown in Figure 4-5.

Figure 4-5:
The Share
box on the
Timeline.

The Share box is what you use to post content — statuses, photos, places, links, and so on — to your Timeline. When you post content, you can also choose who can see it. Friends and subscribers then may see these posts in their News Feeds when they log in. (For more information on News Feed, check out Chapter 7.)

Status

The most common type of post that you see people make from the Share box is a basic text update that answers the question, "What's on your mind?" On Facebook, people refer to this type of post as a *status update* or just as their *status*. Status updates are quick, short, and completely open to interpretation. People may update them with what they may be doing at that moment ("Eating a snack"), offer a random observation ("A cat in my backyard just caught a snake!"), or request info ("Planning a trip to India this summer. Anyone know where I should stay?"). It's very easy for friends to comment on statuses, so a provocative update can really get the conversation going. I comment on commenting in Chapter 7.

Status updates sound small and inconsequential, but when they're added together, they can tell a really big story for one person or for many people.

For close friends, these statuses let you keep up-to-date on their daily lives and share a casual laugh over something that you might never hear about otherwise. As a collective, statuses are how news spreads quickly through Facebook. Because your posts go into your friends' News Feeds, a single update can have a big impact and is somewhat likely to be repeated in some way or another. For example, news of a minor earthquake in my area spread faster on Facebook than it did on news sites.

To update your status, follow these steps:

1. **Click in the What's on Your Mind field of the Share box.**

   This step expands the Share box.

2. **Type your comment/thought/status.**

3. **(Optional) Click the person icon in the bottom gray bar of the Share box to add tags to your post.**

   Tags are ways of marking people you're with when you're writing a status update. The tags link back to your friends' Timelines and notify them of your update. When you tag someone, an additional bit of text is added to the status, so it looks like this:

   Off to play board games — with *<Eric>*.

   Eric then receives a notification that you tagged him.

   If you want to tag someone as part of a sentence as opposed to just noting that he's with you, add an @ symbol and begin typing the person's name. Facebook autocompletes as you type, and the tag appears as part of your status update: for example,

   <Eric> kicked my butt at Settlers of Catan.

4. **(Optional) Click the location pin icon to add a location.**

   Facebook Places is a feature I cover in Chapter 12 You can click this pin and begin typing a city or place name, and Facebook tries to autocomplete the place where you are. Letting friends know where you are (also called *checking in*) is a great way to increase the chances of serendipitous encounters. I've often had a friend text me when she sees a status to ask if I'm still at the coffee shop, wanting to know if she can swing by to say hi.

5. **(Optional) Click the smiley face icon to add info about what you're doing, interacting with, or feeling.**

   Much like tagging a person, or checking in to a location, you can add details to your status about what you're reading, watching, listening to, feeling, doing, and so on. Facebook looks to autocomplete things as you type, so if you add that you're at the movies, you can start typing in a movie's title, and Facebook will automatically add it to the list of movies that you've watched.

6. **(Optional) Click the audience menu in the bottom-right corner to change who can see this particular post.**

   Just like the information in your About section, you can choose from the basic privacy options: Public, Friends, Friends Except Acquaintances, Only Me, and Custom. Whatever you select will be saved for your next status post. In other words, if I post a link to Friends, the next time I go to update my status, Facebook assumes I also want to share that with Friends.

7. **Click Post.**

If that made you feel like updating your status requires wayyyy too much work, I want to remind you how many of those steps are optional. You can follow the abridged version of the preceding if you prefer:

1. **Click in the Share box.**
2. **Type your status.**
3. **Click Post.**

Posts with links

Frequently, people use their status updates to bring attention to something else on the Internet. It may be an article they found interesting, or an event, a photo album, or anything else they want to publicize. Usually, people add a comment to explain the link; other times, they use the link itself as their status, almost as though they're saying, "What I'm thinking about right now is this link."

Posts with links mean you can share something you like with a lot of friends without having to create an e-mail list, call up someone to talk about it, or stand behind someone and say, "Read this." At the same time, you're almost more likely to get someone to strike up a conversation about your content because it's going out to more people, and you're reaching a greater number of people who may be interested in it.

To post a link, simply follow the instructions for updating a status and copy and paste the link you want into the field where you normally type a status. This automatically expands a preview of what your post will look like, including a preview of the content (as shown in Figure 4-6).

A preview usually contains a headline, a thumbnail photo, and teaser text. Hover over either the headline or teaser text and click to edit what appears in the preview. Use the arrows at the bottom of the preview to change the thumbnail that appears alongside the preview. You can also edit your own comment.

If you delete the URL text from the Share box, it doesn't actually remove the link from your post. In fact, deleting the link can make your post look cleaner and leave more room for your own thoughts about the link.

Figure 4-6:
A preview of
your post.

Photo

Facebook is actually the Internet's number-one photo-sharing website. In other words, people love to share photos, and they post a lot of them on Facebook. Consider this fact a teaser trailer for Chapter 10, where I go over the entire Photo application, including adding photos from the Share box. Photo also gives you the capability to add videos, which I also cover in Chapter 10.

Place

The third type of post that Facebook gives you a special tab for within the Share box is a location check-in. Typically, check-ins are part of another post, like a status, but if all you want to do is note where you are, click Place and start typing the name of your location. You can also add tags or a comment to your check-in. Click Post when you're done.

Life events

Part of what's nice about Facebook is the way it lets you connect with friends over the small stuff: a nice sunset on your walk home, a funny observation in the park (cats in strollers! Hilarious!). But Facebook is also awesome for letting you connect over the big stuff. Babies being born, houses being purchased, pets being adopted. The milestones, if you will. The Life Events section lets you make a note of that event on your Timeline.

Although it's not required, you may also feel an urge to fill out your history on your Timeline. If you're new to Facebook, you may want to expand your Timeline back past the day you joined. Life Events is a good way to think about what you want to add in your history.

To add a life event, follow these steps:

1. **Click the Life Event section in the Share box.**

   A menu of various types of life events appears. The categories are listed here although when you click each one, you'll find many subcategories as well:

   - *Work & Education*
   - *Family & Relationships*
   - *Home & Living*
   - *Health & Wellness*
   - *Travel & Experiences*

   Milestones can be big or small; if you check out the subcategories, you'll see things that range from getting your braces removed to learning a new hobby to having a baby. And you should feel free to make up your own. Lots of people use Life Events to represent small accomplishments in a humorous way. For example, one of my friends posted a life event to commemorate the day he successfully canceled his cable service.

2. **Select the event you want to create from the menu.**

   This opens a pop-up window with specific text fields to fill out and space for photos to go along with the event. You can see an example in Figure 4-7.

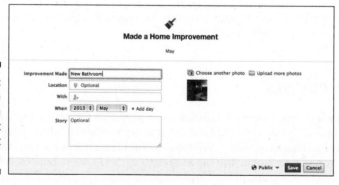

Figure 4-7:
Add a life event from the recent or distant past.

3. **Fill out the details you want to share.**

   You don't have to fill out all the fields, but it's pretty important to fill in the date of the event so that it goes to the right place on your Timeline.

4. **Add a photo to illustrate the event.**

   Click Choose from Photos if there is already a photo on Facebook you want to use, or choose Upload Photos to add photos from your computer.

5. **Use the Privacy menu to choose who can see this event in your Timeline.**

   You have the same five options you have all over Facebook: Public, Friends, Friends Except Acquaintances, Only Me, or Custom.

6. **Click Save.**

   The event is then added to your Timeline, with any photos you've added featured prominently.

As you scroll down through your history, you may realize that you want to add an event or milestone. Don't worry about scrolling back up to the top of the page. The Timeline navigator should be following you as you scroll down, showing your name and the year you're looking at. Click the Life Event icon on the right side of this bar to add a milestone to your past.

Editing posts

If you've been on Facebook for a while and start scrolling backward through time, you may notice that you're not actually seeing everything. You see everything that you've done in the last week, sure. And most things from the last month. If you scroll back a year, you might not see every photo you added, but maybe one photo from a big event that a lot of people commented on.

Facebook knows that not all posts are created equal, so it attempts to create a selection of the best posts to represent your history, and it calls these posts *Highlights.* When you look at your Timeline highlights, you see what Facebook thinks are the most important posts and bits of information. Facebook does this based on algorithms that look at things like how many likes or comments a certain post got. It favors things like photos. But Facebook doesn't always get it right, so you can always go back and choose your own highlights.

Hover over any post in your Timeline to reveal two buttons in the upper-right corner of that post (see Figure 4-8). The star button allows you to highlight a post. Highlighting it puts a little blue flag over the corner of the post. Click that flag again to remove the highlight.

Clicking the pencil icon allows you to edit the post. Editing it includes four options: Change Date, Change Location, Hide from Timeline, or Delete. Keep in mind that these options are available for only your own posts. Posts that your friends have left on your Timeline have two editing options: change date and hide from Timeline. You can also delete or report posts your friends have left on your wall.

Figure 4-8:
Highlight,
edit, or
remove a
post.

Photo posts contain an additional option: Reposition Photo. Because the post boxes are uniform sizes, sometimes your photos get cropped on your Timeline. Click this option to reposition which section of a photo is seen in the post on your Timeline.

Hiding a post is different from deleting it. When you hide a post, you keep that post from appearing on your Timeline, but the post still exists. So if, for example, you hide a particularly bad photo from your Timeline, the photo album still exists. Anyone with permission to see it could navigate to your Photos section and check it out. But it's not going to get called out on your Timeline. If you delete a post, it's gone forever; even you won't be able to find it on Facebook.

If you're looking to remove things like photos or videos that exist only on Facebook, keep in mind that once they're gone from Facebook they're gone forever. It might be more practical to change the audience that can see the photo album than to delete it entirely. Trust me; one hard-drive crash, and your photos are Facebook-only.

Sections

Whereas the right column of your Timeline is dedicated to posts and life events, the left column is for everything else. This includes some biographical information about you, your interests, your friends, previews of your photos, and recent activity on Facebook. Represented as a series of boxes, Facebook refers to these as *sections.* I like to think of sections as compilations of information. You might become friends with one new person per month and be tagged in three photos. Rather than take up space on the right side of your Timeline and overshadow the very interesting posts, this information is instead compiled in a Recent Activity box on the left side. Here are a few of the sections you may see on your Timeline:

- **About:** The About box actually shows only a portion of the information you may have added to your About section (which I cover soon in the "All About Me" section). The part it does show includes the things that help identify you as you.

  I think of it as "dinner party introduction." These pieces of info — where you work, where you live, where you went to school, who your spouse is — are the sorts of things you might talk about the first time you meet someone.

- **Friends:** The Friends box shows thumbnail photos of, you guessed it, your friends. Usually, friends you recently added will appear here, and as you scroll back in time, this box highlights whom you added when. For example, when I scroll back a month, I see the ten friends I added from my parenting support group. When I scroll back a few years, I see all the friends I added from my graduate program.

- **Photos:** The Photos box shows thumbnails of photos you've been tagged in, starting with the most recent one. When you scroll back in time, it will show other details about the photos from that time. For example, when I scroll back, the Photos box shows the last year I was tagged in 13 photos with my husband and 4 photos with one of my other friends.

- **Places:** The Places box displays locations where you've checked in recently. As you scroll back in time, it shows a map of all the places you checked in at that time period, and usually highlights one in particular on the map. For example, when I scroll to 2011, the Places box lets me know I checked into 20 places, and the map highlights that, at one point, I was in the New York City Public Library's reading room.

- **Activity:** The Activity box (shown in Figure 4-9) highlights actions you've taken on Facebook that aren't posts. These include things like people you've become friends with or an event you attended.

  These aren't meaty stories like your posts, but more of a garnish helping to round out the story of what's going on with you.

  As you scroll back in time, you'll see this box reappear to give summaries of, for example, how many friends you added last year, or how many people posted on your Timeline for your birthday.

- **Likes:** The Likes box shows pages that you have liked, starting with the most recent one. As you scroll back in time, this box shows pages you liked at particular times.

- **Interests:** There are actually multiple interest boxes for things like Music, Movies, Books, and so on. In theory, these are filled out naturally as you add information to your posts. For example, if you post that you're reading *The Great Gatsby,* and tag that book using the @ symbol, *The Great Gatsby* is added to the Books box.

Figure 4-9:
Recent
activity
shows what
you've been
up to.

✔ **Application Activity:** Applications are websites, games, and other programs that allow you to integrate some aspect of Facebook into using them. For example, Spotify is a music-streaming program that you can add to your computer. You can also integrate Facebook into Spotify so your friends can see what you are listening to.

Many applications may have some aspect of automatic sharing, so after you sign up, every time you take a certain action — reading articles on *The Washington Post,* watching a TV show on Hulu — that activity will be added to your Timeline. This sort of activity gets its own box with info about the application you used.

If you don't want activity published to your Timeline from a particular application, you can always hide that app's section. Hover the mouse over the recent activity box from that app and then click the pencil icon that appears in the upper-right corner. You can then select Hide Section. You can learn more about controlling your apps in Chapter 14.

Adding to your interest sections

Interest sections are a part of the Timeline that can be really fun way to let your friends know the music, movies, television shows, books, and other things that really define you. Most of you have at least one book that's your favorite, and maybe another that you're reading right now and would really like to talk about with someone.

You can share both books you have read and your favorite books with your Facebook Friends following these steps:

1. **Navigate to the expanded Books section of your Timeline by clicking the More link beneath your cover photo and selecting Books from the drop-down menu.**

TIP

Although I'm using Books as an example, the same applies to the other Interest sections.

This takes you to the expanded Books section of your Timeline, shown in Figure 4-10. There are three subcategories of books that you can add to: Read, Want to Read, and Likes.

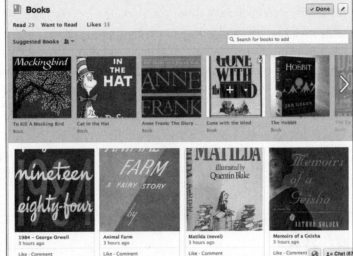

Figure 4-10: An expanded Books section on your Timeline.

2. **Click into the section you want to be adding books to.**

   By default, you will be in the Read section.

3. **Type the name of the book you want to add into the Search box.**

   Facebook will attempt to autocomplete as you type. When you see the book you want to add, click it or press Enter. You may also be able to click from a selection of suggested books that Facebook displays.

4. **Repeat Step 3 until you add every book you've read ever.**

5. **Click the Want to Read or Likes section to add books that are on your list or that you want to actively recommend to people.**

TIP

   Adding books in those sections is exactly the same: Search for the ones you want to add and then click them to select them.

Editing sections

You can decide which compilation boxes appear on your Timeline as well as the order they appear as you scroll down. To edit which sections appear and how they show up, hover your mouse over any of the Interest boxes in the left column; then click the blue pencil icon that appears in the upper-right corner of that box. Say that you do this with the Movies box. In that case, you'll see this menu of options:

- **Edit Sections:** Select this to view a list of all the possible sections you could have on your Timeline. Deselect the ones you don't want appearing, and click and drag the various sections to change the order of how they appear.

  Make sure you click Save when you're done.

- **Hide Section:** Select this if you want to hide the Movies section from appearing on your Timeline.

- **Activity Log:** Click this to be taken to Activity Log and see all activity related to movies that could appear in the Movies box. Activity Log gets a little more attention later on in this chapter in the "Timeline Privacy" section.

- **Edit Privacy:** Click this to edit who can see all the movies you have liked on Facebook. The privacy options are the same as for your posts: Public, Friends, Friends Except Acquaintances, Only Me, or a Custom set of people.

All About Me

The About box gives you (and your friends) the dinner party basics: where you live, what you do, where you're from, whom you're with. But there's a lot more information about you that Facebook gives you the opportunity to share. Clicking the About link beneath your cover photo opens the expanded About section of your Timeline (see Figure 4-11).

This page houses lots of information about you: Work and Education, Basic Information, Living, Relationships and Family, Contact Information. Much of this information won't change very much over time, so it needs to be edited only once or when something big happens, like you move to a new city.

You can visit the About section to edit this information as well as edit who can see it. Unlike the cover photo and profile picture, you choose who gets to see this information. By default, your information is public, meaning everyone can see it. When you go to adjust it, there are five basic privacy options to remember:

- **Public or Everyone:** This means that anyone who finds your Timeline, potentially anywhere on the Internet, can see this piece of information.

This is a good setting for the things that are not very personal or are already public knowledge.

By default, almost all your information is public. If you want only Friends to see your information, you need to change each privacy setting individually.

✔ **Friends:** This means that only your Friends can see that piece of information. This setting is useful for more personal things like your contact information.

✔ **Friends Except Acquaintances:** This option refers to the "acquaintances" smart list that Facebook creates for many users. People who have been added to this list will be unable to see this information.

✔ **Only Me:** This option allows you to keep information on your Timeline for your own reference, but not show it to anyone else on Facebook.

✔ **Custom:** You can use custom settings to show items to specific groups of people. You can choose a setting like Friends of Friends if you want something to be visible to more than just friends, but not to the public; or you can even choose to show something only to specific friends, or to hide it from specific friends. For more on these privacy options and how to use them, check out Chapter 5.

All information fields in the About section are optional. If something doesn't apply to you, or you don't want to share that information, just leave it blank.

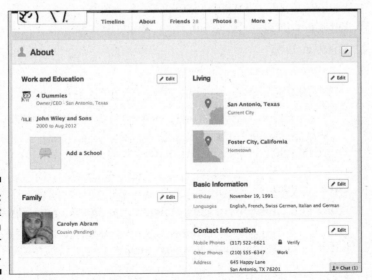

Figure 4-11: The About section of your Timeline.

Work and Education

If you've been through Chapter 2 (getting started on Facebook), you were asked to enter your education and work history. If you didn't do that or want to add a more complete online resume, you can add more schools and employers on this page. Remember that this sort of information can really help old friends find you for reunions, recommendations, or reminiscing. From the About section of the Timeline, first click the Edit button in the upper-right corner of the Work and Education section. You can then add and edit professional and educational information. When you're done editing, click the Done Editing button in the upper-right corner.

See the little privacy icon to the right of the Where Have You Worked field? That icon represents who can see this information, and clicking it allows you to change who can see it. This is true of virtually every field in the About section. Look for the privacy icons and adjust according to your comfort levels.

To add an employer, follow these steps:

1. **After you click the Edit button, click in the Where Have You Worked field.**

2. **Start typing the name of the company where you worked or currently work.**

   Facebook tries to find a match while you type. When that match is highlighted, or when you finish typing, press Enter.

3. **Enter details about your job in the fields that appear.**

   These include

   - *Position:* Enter your job title.

   - *City/Town:* Enter where you physically went (or go) to work.

   - *Description:* Provide a more detailed description of what it is you do.

   - *Time Period:* Enter the amount of time you worked at this job. If you select I Currently Work Here, it appears at the top of your Timeline.

4. **Click Add Job.**

5. **Either add more jobs or click Done Editing in the upper-right corner.**

   You can change any of the information about this job (or others) in the future by clicking the Edit link next to it.

If you're interested in using Facebook for professional networking, you can also add specific projects to your work history. For example, underneath my job at *Facebook For Dummies,* I could click Add a Project and fill out information about the most recent edition: who my editors are, how long the project took, and a description of what I'm doing.

To add a college, follow these steps:

1. **Click in the field Where Did You Go to College?**

2. **Start typing the name of the college you attended (or attend).**

   Facebook tries to find a match while you type. When that match is high-lighted, or when you finish typing, press Enter.

3. **Enter details of your school in the fields that appear.**

   These include

   - *Time Period:* Click the blue text Add Year to show when you started and finished your degree.

   - *Description:* Add details about your time at school that you think may be relevant.

   - *Concentrations:* List any majors or minors you had.

   - *Attended For:* Choose whether you attended as an undergraduate or a graduate student. If you select Graduate Student, you will have additional space to enter the type of degree you received.

4. **Click Add School.**

To add a high school, follow these steps:

1. **Click in the High School field, where it says Where Did You Go to High School?**

2. **Start typing the name of the high school you attended (or attend).**

   Facebook tries to find a match while you type. When that match is high-lighted, or when you finish typing, press Enter.

3. **Enter details of your school in the fields that appear.**

   These include

   - *Time Period:* Click the blue text Add Year to show when you started and finished your degree.

   - *Graduated:* Check this box if you graduated from this school.

   - *Description:* Add details about your time at school that you think may be relevant.

4. **Click Add School.**

You can edit any of this information (for example, if you leave your current job or remember that you were actually in the class of '45, not '46) by clicking the Edit link next to the employer or school you want to edit. The same fields reappear, and you can change any and all information.

When you're done adding and editing your professional and educational history, click Done Editing to save your changes.

Living

This section contains two pins on two maps: one to show where you're from, and one to show your current city. Click Edit to change either of these and to control who can see this information. Remember to click Save when you're done.

Basic Information

Your Basic Information is just what it sounds like: the very basics about you that you might use to identify who you are and where you're from. Click Edit to open a pop-up window to edit any of these fields and who can see them.

By default, your basic information (with the exception of your birthday) is public. Change your privacy settings using the drop-down menu to the right of each item in the list.

- **Sex (I Am):** You entered your sex when you signed up for Facebook, and Facebook mirrors your selection here. If you don't want people to see your sex on your Timeline, you can deselect the check box below this field.

- **Birthday:** You also entered your birthday when you registered for Facebook. Here, you can tweak the date (in case you messed up) as well as decide what people can see about your birthday. Some people don't like sharing their age, their birthday, or both. If you're one of these people, use this drop-down menu to select what you want to share.

Although you can change your birthday and year at will most of the time, Facebook's systems prevent you from shifting to under 18 after you've been listed as over 18. If, through a legitimate mistake, this happened to you, contact Facebook's User Operations team from the Help Center.

- **Interested In:** This field is primarily used by people to signal their sexual orientation. Some people feel that this section makes Facebook seem like a dating site, so if that doesn't sound like you, you don't have to fill it out.

- **Relationship Status:** You can edit who, if anyone, you're seeing, and what type of relationship you're in both here and in the Relationship section.

- **Languages:** Languages might seem a little less basic than, say, your city, but you can enter any languages you speak here.

- **Religion:** You can choose to list your religion and describe it.

- **Political Views:** You can also choose to list your political views and further explain them with a description.

Whenever you edit a section of your information, click Save (a button at the bottom of the box) so you don't lose your work.

Relationship and Family

The Relationship section and the Family section provide space for you to list your romantic and family relationships. These relationships provide a way of linking your Timeline to someone else's Timeline, and therefore require confirmation. In other words, if you list yourself as married, your spouse needs to confirm that fact before it appears on both Timelines.

You can add a relationship by following these steps:

1. **Click the Edit button in the upper-right corner of the Relationship section.**

   A pop-up window for editing this information appears.

2. **Click the Relationship Status menu to reveal the different types of romantic relationships you can add.**

   These include Single, In a Relationship, Engaged, Married, It's Complicated (a Facebook classic), Widowed, Separated, Divorced, In a Civil Union, and In a Domestic Partnership.

3. **You can either stop here or choose to link to the person you're in this relationship with. Type the person's name into the box that appears.**

   Facebook autocompletes as you type. Press Enter when you see your beloved's name highlighted. This sends a notification to that person.

4. **(Optional) Add your anniversary using the drop-down menus that appear.**

   If you add your anniversary, your friends will see a small reminder on their Home pages on that date.

5. **Click Save.**

For many couples, the act of changing from Single to In a Relationship on Facebook is a major relationship milestone. There's even a term for it: Facebook official. You may overhear someone saying, "It's official, but is it Facebook official?" Feel free to impress your friends with this knowledge of Facebook customs.

You can add a family relationship by following these steps:

1. **Click the Edit button in the upper-right corner of the Family section.**

   A pop-up window for editing this information appears. It is the same menu that is used to edit Relationship information.

2. **Click in the text box for Family Member and start typing your family member's name into that box.**

   Facebook tries to autocomplete as you type. When you see your sister's or mother's or whomever's name appear, click to select it.

3. **Select the type of relationship from the drop-down menu.**

   Facebook offers a variety of family relationships ranging from the nuclear to the extended.

4. **Click Save at the bottom of the pop-up window.**

Contact Information

I know, it may seem a little scary to add your contact information to the Internet, and if you're not comfortable with it, that's okay. Facebook itself is a great way for people to reach you, so you shouldn't feel that it's required that you add other ways for people to contact you as well.

That being said, it can be very useful for your friends to be able to get ahold of your number or address if needed, and there are privacy options that can help you feel more comfortable sharing some of this information. There's more information on Timeline Privacy at the end of this chapter, so if you want to edit your contact information, follow these steps:

1. **Click the Edit button in the upper-right corner of the Contact Information section.**

   A pop-up window for editing this information appears.

2. **Click in the respective text fields for adding e-mail addresses, phone numbers, IM handles, addresses, and websites.**

   If you've already added any of these, and want to add more, look for the links to Add Another <phone>.

3. **Enter the appropriate information.**

4. **Click Save.**

Your Friends and Your Timeline

Your Timeline is what your friends look at to get a sense of your life, and it's also where they leave public messages for you. In this way, your friends' posts become part of your history (just like in real life). Think about all the things you learn about a friend the first time you meet his parents, or all the funny stories you hear when your friend's significant other recounts the story of how they met. These are the types of insights that your friends may casually leave on your Timeline, making all your friends know you a little better.

When friends visit your Timeline, they'll also see a version of the Share box that you see. They can't add life events, but they can post text and photos to your Timeline. Check out the posts on your friends' Timelines. Chances are that you'll see a few "Hey, how are you, let's catch up" messages; a few "That was an awesome trip/dinner/drink" messages; and maybe a few statements that make so little sense, you're sure they must be inside jokes.

If you're on a friend's Timeline around his birthday, you're sure to see many "Happy Birthday" posts. There aren't many rules for using Facebook, but one tradition that has arisen over time is the "Happy Birthday" post. Because most people see notifications of their friends' birthdays on their Home pages, the quickest way to say "I'm thinking of you" on their special day is to write on their Timeline.

Although I think that the back and forth between friends is one of the delights of the Timeline, some people find it a little hard to let go. If you're someone who doesn't like the idea of a friend being able to write something personal on your Timeline, you can prevent friends from being able to post on it within your Settings page. You can also limit who can see the posts your friends leave. From the Settings page, go to the Timeline and Tagging section and look for the settings related to who can post on your Timeline and who can see what others post on your Timeline.

The best way to get used to the Timeline is to start using it. Write on your friends' Timelines, post a status update or a link on your own, and see what sort of response you get from your friends. After all, that's what the Timeline is all about — sharing with your friends.

Timeline Privacy

As I go through the different parts of the Timeline in this chapter, I try to point out where you can change privacy or control who can see what. I cover privacy in great detail in Chapter 5, so most of the information in this section may be a bit redundant. However, I hope it can help clarify the age old question of "Who can see what?"

Posts privacy

Privacy on your posts and life events is something you usually adjust as you're creating them. Next to the Post button in the Share box, Facebook displays the audience for that post. Click the audience to open a drop-down menu for changing who can see it. Remember, there are usually five options for privacy: Public, Friends, Friends Except Acquaintances, Only Me, or Custom.

You can edit the privacy on a post after the fact as well. To do so, follow these steps:

1. **When you're looking at the post you want to edit, click the privacy icon.**

   The privacy icon mirrors the current privacy setting for that post. For example, a public post displays a globe icon next to the information about when it was posted. When you click it, the Privacy menu appears. If you're having trouble locating the icon, check out Figure 4-12.

Figure 4-12:
Change the
privacy on
individual
posts.

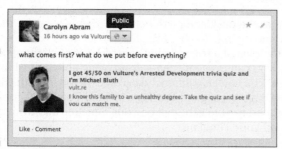

2. **Select your desired privacy setting from the drop-down menu.**

   Your new privacy setting is automatically saved.

Editing the privacy for a post edits the privacy *only* for that post. If you normally post publicly and you change the privacy for one post to Friends, the rest of your posts will still be visible to everyone.

About privacy

The About information, such as where you went to school or your relationship status, changes infrequently, if ever. You can edit the privacy for this content in the same place you edit the information itself. To get there, go to your Timeline and then click the About link beneath your cover photo.

The About page has several sections, each representing a different information category. Click the Edit button in the upper-right corner of a section to access the editing options for that category. Next to each piece of information, a privacy icon appears signifying who can see that piece of information. By default, most of this information is set to Public and Visible to Everyone, although contact information is only visible to Friends by default.

About information is one of the places where the Only Me setting might come in handy. For example, lots of people don't like sharing their birthdays on Facebook, but Facebook requires you to enter a birthday when you sign up. Making it visible only to you effectively hides your birthday from everyone.

Click Save Changes when you're done editing privacy settings. Otherwise, the new settings won't stick.

Interest sections privacy

Interests are sorted into categories like Movies, Music, Books, and so on. For your TV Shows section, for example, you can add TV shows that you've watched, TV shows that you want to watch, and TV shows that you like. Each time you add a TV show to the list of shows you've watched or want to watch, you can also control who sees that you've added that particular show to that list.

Figure 4-13 shows me editing who can see that I've watched the BBC show *Sherlock*. I opened this incarnation of the Privacy menu by hovering over the show's image and then clicking the privacy icon that appeared beneath it.

Figure 4-13:
Selecting
who
can see
what I've
watched.

Additionally, I can control who can see what TV shows I like. Unlike the Watched and Want to Watch sections, where I can edit this individually, I decide who can see *all* the shows I've liked. To edit who can see what you've liked, follow these steps:

1. **Make sure you're looking at the correct section on your screen.**

   In this case, I'm looking at the TV Shows box.

2. **Click the pencil icon button in the upper-right corner of the box.**

   A menu of options related to this section appears.

3. **Click Edit Privacy.**

   A pop-up window appears.

4. **In the section of the window labeled Likes, click the Privacy menu.**

   The familiar Privacy menu appears with these options: Everyone, Friends, Friends Except Acquaintances, Only Me, Custom, or Lists.

5. **Choose who can see the TV shows you have liked.**

6. **Click Close.**

   The changes are saved when you click Close.

Privacy tools

With so many posts and so much information living on your Timeline, it's understandable that you may be a little confused about who is seeing what. To that end, Facebook offers two tools for keeping track. I cover these in more detail in Chapter 5, when I talk about all things privacy, but here's an overview for now.

View As

You can get to the View As tool by clicking the gear button on your cover photo and selecting View As from the menu that appears. Clicking that option brings you to your Timeline as though you were someone who was not your friend. In other words, you can see what strangers can see, click on, and know about you if they come to your Timeline.

In the black bar on top of this view of your Timeline, there's a white, bold link named View as Specific Person. If you want to check on, for example, what acquaintances or people you've added to a particular Friend List can see, click this link and enter a Friend's name in the text box that appears. If you're surprised by what that Friend can see, you can go change the privacy on any content you want hidden from him.

Activity Log

For your own reference, Facebook provides an Activity Log of your Timeline that only you can see. To get to it, click the Activity Log button that's found in the right corner of your cover photo. This takes you to your Activity Log. This is a condensed version of your Timeline and all your activity on Facebook. Scan through the items in this log. Click the privacy icon to the right of any item to change who can see it. You can also click on the pencil icon to decide whether something should be hidden from or highlighted on your Timeline.

Chapter 5

Privacy and Safety on Facebook

In This Chapter

▶ Navigating the many privacy options on Facebook

▶ Protecting yourself online and on Facebook

▶ Deciding what to share and when

*W*hen people talk about privacy online — and on Facebook in particular — I like to remind them that there's a spectrum of privacy concerns. On one end of the spectrum are true horror stories of predators approaching minors, identity thefts, and the like. Hopefully (and most likely), you will never deal with these issues although I do touch on them at the end of this chapter. On the other end of the spectrum are issues I usually categorize as "awkward social situations" — for example, posting a photo of your perfect beach day that your co-workers can see on a day when you called in "sick" (not that you would ever do something like that). Somewhere in between are questions about strangers seeing your stuff and security issues like spamming and phishing. All these privacy-related topics are legitimate, though you'll probably deal with the awkward end of the spectrum more often than anything else.

Regardless of where on the spectrum your particular question or problem falls, however, you should be able to use your privacy settings to make things better. I can't promise that you'll be able to prevent 100 percent of the situations that make you annoyed or uncomfortable or leave you with that sort of icky feeling, but I can tell you that you should be able to reduce how often you feel that way. The goal is to get as close to 100 percent as possible so you can feel as comfortable as possible sharing on Facebook.

Of course, there's also a spectrum of what "being comfortable" means to different people. That's why talking about privacy can get kind of confusing: There are a lot of options, and what makes me comfortable might not make you comfortable. This chapter is meant to be a guide to all the privacy options Facebook offers so that you can figure out the right combinations that make you comfortable sharing on Facebook.

Your own common sense is going to be one of the best helpers in avoiding privacy problems. Facebook status updates aren't the right place to post Social Security numbers or bank passwords. Similarly, if you're thinking about sharing something that, if the wrong someone saw it, could lead to really bad real-world consequences, maybe it's not meant to be shared on Facebook.

Know Your Audience

Before getting into specifics about all the privacy controls, you need to understand some basic parts of the Facebook vocabulary. These terms are related to how Facebook thinks about the people you may or may not want to share with. For most pieces of information, the privacy options are related to the audience who can see what you're sharing. Each is represented by its own icon:

✔ **Public or Everyone:** By setting the visibility of something you post or list to Public, you're saying that you don't care who, on the entire Internet, knows this information about you. Many people list their spouse on their Timeline, and, just as they'd shout this information from the treetops (and register it at the county courthouse), they set the visibility to Public. This is a totally reasonable setting for innocuous pieces of information. In fact, some information is always available as Public Information that everyone can see. This includes your name, current profile picture, gender, your username, and your cover image.

Now, just because everyone *can* see something doesn't mean everyone *does* see everything. Your posts, information, friendships, and so on, populate your Friends' News Feeds (assuming that your Friends can see this information), but never the News Feeds of people you're not Friends with (unless you allow subscribers to see your public posts). When I think about who will see the information I share as Public, I imagine someone like you searching for me by name and coming to my Timeline. Although (hopefully) that might be a lot of people, it isn't anywhere close to the number of people who use Facebook. By default, much of your Timeline and all your posts are publicly visible. This chapter covers how to change these settings if you want to.

✔ **Friends:** Any information for which you set visibility to Friends will be accessible only by your confirmed Facebook Friends. If you trust your Friends, this is a reasonably safe setting for most of your information. If you feel uncomfortable sharing your information with your Friends, you can use Custom privacy, or you can rethink the people you allow to be your Friends.

Think of friending people as a privacy setting all on its own. When you add someone as a Friend, ask yourself whether you're comfortable with that person seeing your posts.

✔ **Friends Except Acquaintances:** Even though I always recommend adding Friends only if you're comfortable with them seeing your posts, this setting forces me to acknowledge that sometimes you have not-quite-friends on your Friend list. These may be distant family members, professional contacts, old friends from way back when, or that super-friendly neighbor whom you maybe just wish wouldn't stop by quite so often. No matter who they are, you can add them to the Acquaintances list and then use this setting to limit what they can see about you.

✔ **Only Me:** This setting is basically a way of adding something to Facebook but then hiding it from being seen by other people. I can't think of many times I've found this setting useful, except when I start something like adding a photo album, and want to come back later to finish it, and don't want it to be seen until I've added all my tags and captions.

✔ **Custom:** If you have very specific needs, customized privacy settings may help you feel more comfortable sharing on Facebook. The Custom privacy option allows you to choose specific people (or lists of people) who can see something, or choose specific people (or lists of people) who can't see something.

✔ **Lists:** Lists are ways to sort your friends into various categories. There are two types of lists: Smart Lists that Facebook creates on your behalf, and lists that you create for yourself. For example, Facebook creates the Family list based on information you enter about your family relation-ships. I've created a "Dummies" list to keep track of the various editors and co-authors I've had over the years. Often, you may want to share something with one particular list of people, in which case, you can choose the name of that list as your privacy setting.

Privacy on the Go

Privacy on Facebook isn't a one-time thing. Because you are constantly adding new status updates, photos, and content to Facebook, constantly interacting with friends and reaching out to people, privacy is actually an ongoing affair. To that end, one of the most common places you should know your privacy options is in the Share box.

The *Share box* is the blank text box that sits at the top of your Home page and under your cover photo on your Timeline. It's where you go to add status updates, photos, links, and more to Facebook. The part of the Share box that's important for this chapter is the Privacy menu, right next to the Post button, as shown in Figure 5-1.

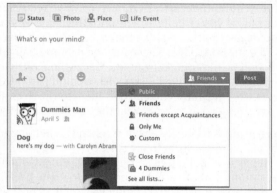

Figure 5-1:
Use the
Privacy
menu to
adjust pri-
vacy for an
individual
post.

Whenever you're posting a status or other content, the *audience,* or group of people you've given permission to see it, is displayed next to the blue Post button. The audience you see displayed is always the audience you last shared something with. In other words, if you shared something with the Public last time you posted a status, it displays Public the next time you go to post a status.

Hovering your mouse over this word turns it into a button. Click that button to reveal the drop-down menu. It shows a few options: Public, Friends, Friends Except Acquaintances, Only Me, and Custom. Additionally, if you use Friend Lists at all, commonly used ones appear below the usual privacy options (check out Chapter 6 for more about Friend Lists). Click the setting you want before you post your status, link, or photo. Most of the time, I share my posts with Friends. As a result, I don't actually change this setting that often. But if you do share something publicly, remember to adjust the audience the next time you post something.

Sometimes, you may find that you want to share something with only a portion of your friends. To do that, choose Custom from the Privacy menu. The Custom Privacy window appears, as shown in Figure 5-2.

Custom Privacy

✔ **Share this with** —————————

These people or lists: Friends ⬍

Friends of those tagged: ☑

Note: Anyone tagged can also see this post.

✖ **Don't share this with** —————————

These people or lists:

Save Changes   **Cancel**

Figure 5-2:
Customize
your privacy
down to the
person.

Custom Privacy here applies to the post you're creating, but this dialog box appears any time you choose Custom as a privacy setting for any type of information. Customized privacy has two parts: those who *can* see something and those who *can't*. The top portion controls the former and has four options:

- ✔ **Friends of Friends:** This means your friends and their friends can see whatever you post.

- ✔ **Friends:** This option allows only your friends to see what you post.

- ✔ **Specific People or Lists:** Choosing this option opens a blank text box. You can start typing a name or the name of a list of friends here. After you save these settings, only the people you've entered can see your post.

- ✔ **Only Me:** This option isn't one you'd typically use for a post, but you might use it later on if there's any information you want to store on your Timeline but you don't want to share with others.

Additionally, when you choose Friends of Friends or Friends, a check box allows you to choose whether the friends of any people you tag can see your post. Remember, tagging is a way of marking who is in a photo, who is with you when you check in someplace, or whom you want to mention in a post. For example, say that I'm going to spend a day at the park with one of my friends. I might post a status that says "Taking advantage of the nice weather with **Kate**." The name of my friend links back to her profile. By default, Kate's friends will be able to see this post, even if they aren't friends with me. If I deselect this box, Kate's friends will no longer be able to see that post.

The lower section of the Custom Privacy window controls who can't see something. Similar to the Specific People or Lists setting, the Don't Share This With section has a blank text box where you can type the name of people or lists of people. When you add their names to this box, they won't be able to see the content you post.

Whatever customized audience you create for one post will be the audience next time you go to post something. Make sure you check the audience the next time you post!

A post's privacy icon (Public, Friends of Friends, Friends, or Custom) is visible to anyone who can view that post. People can hover over that icon to get more information. Friend Lists appear as Custom privacy unless the viewer is a member of a list you shared the post with. Members of a default (Close Friends, Acquaintances) or a custom Friend List can see other people included on the list, but are unable to see the name of the list.

Changing privacy

After you post something, you can always change the privacy on it. From your Timeline, follow these steps:

1. **Hover your mouse over the privacy icon at the top of the post whose audience you want to change.**

   Every post displays the icon for Public, Friends, Friends Except Acquaintances, or Custom.

2. **Click the button to reveal the Privacy menu.**

   You'll see the usual options: Public, Friends, Friends Except Acquaintances, Custom, or specific Friend Lists.

3. **Click the audience you want.**

   A change to Public, Friends, Friends Except Acquaintances, or a specific Friend List is automatically saved. Changing to Custom requires you to make selections within the Custom Privacy window again.

Privacy Shortcuts

There are actually so many settings related to privacy on Facebook that it can sometimes feel overwhelming. That's why I am such a fan of the Privacy Shortcuts menu, which helps direct you to the settings you'll want most often by asking the questions you'll ask most often:

✔ Who can see my stuff?

✔ Who can contact me?

✔ How do I stop someone from bothering me?

To open the Privacy Shortcuts menu, click the lock icon next to your profile picture in the left sidebar (remember, you may have to hover over the left sidebar to expand it). The Privacy Shortcuts menu is shown in Figure 5-3. Click any of these three options to expand more privacy options.

Figure 5-3: You can find the answers to your most common privacy questions here.

Who can see my stuff?

You can adjust the privacy for each status or post you make, which means that over time you might find yourself asking, "Wait, who can see all of this? Who can see what I posted yesterday? Last week? What about if I post tomorrow?" Well, the answers can be found here. (The earlier "Privacy on the Go" section of this chapter covers the privacy options when you're sharing something.)

Facebook offers you one setting you can adjust here, named Who Can See My Future Posts. This is the exact same control that can be found in the Share box. It's described this way to emphasize that whatever you select here will be the default going forward, until you change it again. Click the little arrow to change this setting. You will see the same options you see from the Share menu: Public, Friends, Friends Except Acquaintances, Only Me, and Custom.

Additionally, the Who Can See My Stuff section offers you two links to help you double-check and understand what people can see. The first is a link to Activity Log, which is a granular summary of everything you've done on Facebook and who can see that thing. It ranges from the status updates you write to the content you like or comment on. As you look through your Activity Log, you can change who can see it, or remove the content entirely. I go over how to navigate and edit your Activity Log in more depth in the "Privacy Tools" section later in this chapter.

Finally, the Who Can See My Stuff section offers you a link to another privacy tool, the View As tool. This tool allows you to look at your Timeline as though you are another person. I like to use this to double-check what people see when they search for me on Facebook — in my case, they mostly see my biographical information and none of my posts.

Who can contact me?

A common Facebook problem that sends people scurrying to their privacy settings is getting a message or Friend Request that they don't want to get. It might be from a spammer or just someone you don't know (there was a whole point in time when I regularly got messages from people in Turkey asking if I would be their friend). This section is to help you control which messages you see and who can send you Friend Requests.

The first option in this section provides the filtering options for your Messages Inbox. I cover messaging in detail in Chapter 8, so for the purposes of understanding this setting, keep in mind that Facebook Inbox automatically sorts your messages to prioritize ones from friends. The two filter options are

- ✔ **Basic Filtering:** This is the default filter option. It shows you messages from friends, as well as messages from people Facebook thinks you might know. That could be friends of friends or other people Facebook's algorithms have determined you might know. These messages will all appear in your Inbox.

✔ **Strict Filtering:** This filter option means the messages from friends of friends and people you may know go to a separate section of your Inbox where you're not as likely to see them.

Regardless of what you choose, some messages will always go to the Other Messages section of your Inbox: messages Facebook thinks might be spam or those in which you have no connection whatsoever to the person sending it. The Strict filtering option just means you never get a message from someone you don't know in your main box.

The second control in this section concerns who can send you Friend Requests. There are only two options: Everyone and Friends of Friends. Everyone means that everyone who searches for you or finds your Timeline can add you as a friend. Friends of Friends means someone has to be friends with one of your friends before he's allowed to request you. As a personal anecdote, when I worked at Facebook, I received a lot of Friend Requests from people who wanted me to pass a message along to the CEO or something like that. I found this irritating, so I changed this setting to just Friends of Friends. Recently, however, I moved to a new city, and I realized the people I met were unable to add me as a friend. I changed my setting back to Everyone to make it easier for friends to find me.

How do I stop someone from bothering me?

Sadly, sometimes a friendship isn't really a friendship. If someone is bothering you, harassing you, bullying you, or in any way making your Facebook experience terrible, blocking might be the solution to the problem. Blocking is different than unfriending someone because someone who is not your friend might still wind up interacting with you on Facebook. For example, if you have mutual friends, you might wind up both commenting on the same post. Blocking someone means that as much as possible, neither of you will even know that the other person is on Facebook. You won't see each other's comments, even if they're on the same person's photo. They won't be able to send you messages, add you as a friend, or view your Timeline (all things they would likely be able to do even if you unfriended them).

If you're the parent of a teen, this can be a very handy setting to know about. Unfortunately, bullying can sometimes spread to Facebook from the classroom, and blocking can be a useful tool in terms of keeping your child safer on Facebook.

Privacy Settings

In addition to the privacy shortcuts, there are several more granular privacy settings located within the Settings page. You can get to these settings from the Privacy Shortcuts menu (click the link on the bottom that says See More Settings).

The Privacy Settings and Tools section of the Settings page is shown in Figure 5-4. The left side of the Settings page is a menu of different settings you can adjust here. The settings that are relevant to privacy are in the second section: Privacy, Timeline and Tagging, and Blocking. Additionally, I go over the Apps and Ads settings sections because people commonly have questions about how their information is used in these locations.

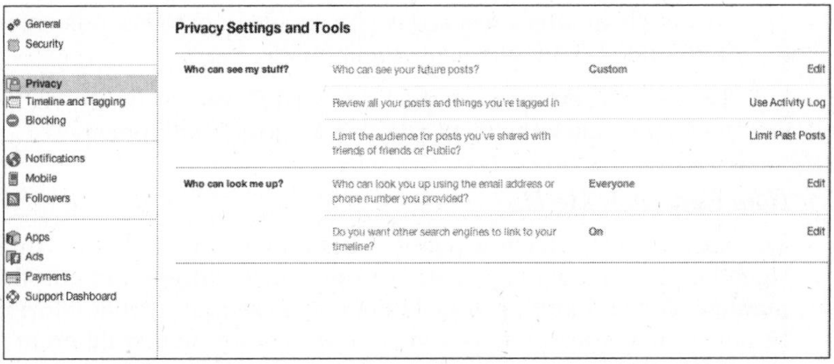

Figure 5-4:
Start here to
set privacy
options.

Privacy

The Privacy section of the Settings page is shown in Figure 5-4. It's broken into two sections: Who Can See My Stuff? and Who Can Look Me Up?

Who Can See My Stuff?

The Who Can See My Stuff section should look mostly familiar if you read the section on privacy shortcuts. There are three settings here, two of which are redundant with the Privacy Shortcuts menu.

✔ **Who can see your future posts?** This setting shows you your current setting for when you create posts. This is who can see all your future posts (unless you change it). You can change this setting by clicking the Edit link on the right side of the page. A sample share menu appears where you can select a new privacy setting.

✔ **Review all your posts and things you're tagged in.** This setting provides a link to Activity Log. Activity Log is a granular list of absolutely everything you've done on Facebook. I cover how to use Activity Log in the "Privacy Tools" section later in this chapter.

✔ **Limit the audience for posts you've shared with Friends of Friends or Public.** This setting is one you probably won't need too often, but it could come in handy once in a while. Remember, this setting is needed only if at any point, you shared posts with Everyone or with Friends of Friends. If you've shared only with Friends (or an even smaller subset of people), this setting won't change anything. Use it to change the privacy settings of all items that were previously public to be visible only to friends.

This setting might be useful if, for example, you're job hunting and you don't want potential employers to find your public posts about the most recent election (because that shouldn't matter in how they judge you as an applicant). Once you make this change, it can't be undone. In other words, those posts will always be visible only to Friends unless you go back and individually make them public.

To use this setting, click the Limit Past Posts link on the right side of the page; then click the Limit Old Posts button that appears.

Who Can Look Me Up?

This section concerns how people can find you on Facebook. When you signed up for Facebook, you entered an e-mail address and possibly a phone number. The first setting asks if people who search by that information will be able to find you. If you're someone who has a slightly different name than your real name on your Timeline (for example, if I were to go by Carolyn EA on Facebook rather than my actual name, Carolyn Abram), I absolutely recommend leaving this setting set to Everyone. Limiting it limits your potential friends' ability to find you.

To change this setting, click Edit on the right side of the page and use the Privacy menu to select whether Everyone, Friends of Friends, or only Friends can search for you by e-mail or phone number.

The second setting here concerns search engine indexing. Search engines like Google or Bing use web crawlers to create indexes they can search to provide results to users. So when someone searches for your name on Google, by default, a link to your Facebook Timeline appears. If you deselect this setting, that will no longer be true.

To change this setting, click edit on the right side of the page and deselect the check box labeled Let Other Search Engines Link to Your Timeline. A pop-up window will ask if you're sure you want to turn off this feature. Click the Confirm button.

Even if you deselect the search engine indexing check box, people will still be able to search for you by name on Facebook itself. With the exception of someone you have blocked, people will always be able to search for you and get to your Timeline from Facebook Search.

Timeline and tagging

The Timeline, as I describe in Chapter 4, is basically where you collect all your stuff on Facebook. That means photos, posts, posts Friends have left you, application activity, and so on. Your Timeline allows you to look through your history and represent yourself to your Friends.

Tags on Facebook are a way of labeling people in your content. For example, when uploading a photo, you can tag a specific friend in it. That tag becomes information that others can see as well as a link back to your friend's Timeline. In addition, from your Friend's Timeline, people can get to that photo to see her smiling face. You can tag people and pages in status updates, photos, notes, check-ins at various places, comments, and really any other type of post. And just like you can tag friends, friends can tag you in their photos and posts.

This section of the settings page allows you to control settings related to people interacting with you on your Timeline and tagging you in posts. For controlling the privacy on things you add to your Timeline, you use the Privacy menu in the Share box. The Timeline and Tagging Settings section is shown in Figure 5-5.

Figure 5-5: Edit your settings for tags.

	Timeline and Tagging Settings			
General				
Security				
	Who can add things to my timeline?	Who can post on your timeline?	Friends	Edit
Privacy		Review posts friends tag you in before they appear on your timeline?	Off	Edit
Timeline and Tagging				
Blocking	**Who can see things on my timeline?**	Review what other people see on your timeline		View As
Notifications		Who can see posts you've been tagged in on your timeline?	Friends of Friends	Edit
Mobile				
Followers		Who can see what others post on your timeline?	Friends	Edit
Apps	**How can I manage tags people add and tagging suggestions?**	Review tags people add to your own posts before the tags appear on Facebook?	Off	Edit
Ads				
Payments		When you're tagged in a post, who do you want to add to the audience if they aren't already in it?	Friends	Edit
Support Dashboard		Who sees tag suggestions when photos that look like you are uploaded?	Friends	Edit

Who Can Add Things to My Timeline?

This section focuses on other people adding things like photos, posts, or tags to your Timeline.

✔ **Who can post on your Timeline?** In addition to being a place where you add posts, your Timeline is a place where your Friends can leave you messages or posts. If you don't want your Friends leaving these sorts of public messages (if you're using Facebook for professional or networking reasons, for example), you can set this to Only Me.

By default, only Friends can post on your Timeline. This setting means no one can post to your Timeline except you.

To change this setting, click Edit on the right side of the setting and use the drop-down menu that appears to select Only Me.

✔ **Review posts Friends tag you in before they appear on your Timeline.** Timeline Review allows you to review the tags people have added of you before they are displayed on your Timeline. In other words, if I tag you in a photo, that photo won't appear on your Timeline until you log in to Facebook and approve the tag.

To change this setting, click Edit on the right side of the setting and use the drop-down menu that appears to toggle between Enabled and Disabled. By default, tags of you are automatically approved, and this setting is set to Disabled.

Who Can See Things on My Timeline?

There's a difference between *adding* things to your Timeline, which the preceding settings control, and simply *looking* at your Timeline, which the settings in this section control. Three settings here concern what people see when they look at your profile.

✔ **Review what other people see on your Timeline.** This isn't so much a setting as a link to the View As privacy tool (which I cover in detail in the "Privacy Tools" section later in this chapter). The View As tool allows you to look at your Timeline as though you're someone else, thus double-checking that your privacy settings are actually working.

✔ **Who can see posts you've been tagged in on your Timeline?** After you've approved tags (or if you leave Timeline Review off), you can still decide who can see the content in which you're tagged on your Timeline. In other words, if your Friend tags you in a photo, you can control who sees that photo on *your* Timeline. The idea behind this setting is that, although you will never post anything embarrassing to your Timeline, a Friend might (accidentally, I hope) do so. Making sure that not everyone can see that post (except other, more understanding friends) cuts down on any awkwardness.

To change this setting, click the Edit link on the right side of the page and then use the drop-down menu that appears to choose who can see this information.

✔ **Who can see what others post on your Timeline?** Another way to control the "embarrassing friend on your Timeline" problem is to limit who can see the posts your friends leave.

To change this setting, click the Edit link on the right side of the page and use the drop-down menu that appears to select who can see these posts.

How Can 1 Manage Tags People Add and Tagging Suggestions?

Although tagging has been mentioned in many of these Timeline settings, these settings refer to very specific use cases of tagging that you maybe never thought about before.

✔ **Review tags people add to your own posts before the tags appear on Facebook.** This setting controls tags your friends add to content you've uploaded. For example, if I upload a photo of 20 people to Facebook and don't tag anyone in it, my friends might choose to add tags. This setting lets me choose to review the tags my friends add before the tag is visible to other people.

To change this setting, click Edit on the right side of the page; then use the drop-down menu that appears to select whether Tag Review is Enabled or Disabled. By default it is Disabled.

✔ **When you're tagged in a post, whom do you want to add to the audience if they aren't already in it?** This setting sounds very complicated, and it is a little bit complicated. Say that I'm friends with Eric and Dave, but Eric is not friends with Dave (hmmm, this is starting to sound like a middle school math problem). Now, say that Eric adds a photo of me (meaning he has tagged me in it), and his privacy settings share that photo with his friends. Because Dave and Eric aren't friends, Dave cannot see that photo unless this setting allows my friends to be added to the audience of that photo.

To change this setting, click Edit on the right side of the page and use the drop-down menu that appears to select who is added to the audience of a post you're tagged in. There are only three options for this setting: Friends, Only Me, and Custom. By default, this setting adds your friends to the audience of a post you're tagged in.

✔ **Who sees tag suggestions when photos that look like you are uploaded?** Facebook employs some facial recognition software to help people tag photos. So if a Friend is uploading 50 photos and you appear in 30 of them, Facebook might recognize your face and suggest to your friend that you be tagged in those 30 photos. This is to save your friend time while he's adding photos, and to encourage people to add more tags to Facebook. You can choose not to appear in the suggestions Facebook gives your friends by disabling this setting.

To change this setting, click Edit on the right side of the page and use the drop-down menu that appears to select whether Friends or No One will see tag suggestions.

Blocking

Most of your privacy settings are preventative measures for making yourself comfortable on Facebook. Blocklists are usually more reactive. If someone does something on Facebook that bothers you, you may choose to block him or block certain actions he takes from affecting you. The Blocking section of the Settings page is shown in Figure 5-6. You can manage five blocklists here: Restricted List, Block Users, Block App Invites, Block Event Invites, and Block Apps.

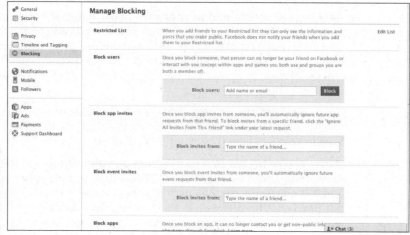

Figure 5-6:
Edit your blocklists here.

Restricted List

The Restricted List is a list you can create that's not quite as serious as blocking someone outright but that is also slightly more serious than simply adding the person to your Acquaintances list. For example, say that you receive Friend Requests from Veronica and Logan. You accept the Friend Requests and add Veronica to the Acquaintances list, and Logan to the Restricted list. Whenever you add a post that is visible to Everyone, both can see it. When you add a post that is visible to Friends Except Acquaintances, neither can see it. However, when you add a post that is visible to Friends, Veronica will be able to see it, but Logan won't be able to. Make sense?

To add someone to this list, click Edit List on the right side of the page. A pop-up window appears, as shown in Figure 5-7. If you've already added people to this list, they appear here, and you can remove them from the list by hovering over their pictures and clicking the x that appears in the right corner of the photos.

Figure 5-7:
Add people
to the
Restricted
List.

To add people to the list, follow these steps:

1. **Click the button in the top left of the box named On This List.**

   A menu of two options appears: Friends and On This List.

2. **Click Friends.**

   A grid appears showing all your friends listed alphabetically by first name.

3. **Select friends to add to the restricted list by clicking their pictures or by searching for them by name in the upper-right corner and then clicking their pictures.**

4. **When you're done, click the Finish button in the lower-right corner of the box.**

Block Users

Blocking someone on Facebook is the strongest way to distance yourself from someone else on Facebook. For the most part, if you add someone to your Block list, he can't see any traces of you on Facebook. You won't show up in his News Feed; if he looks at a photo in which you're tagged, he may see you in the photo (that's unavoidable), but he won't see that your name has been tagged. When you write on other people's Timelines, your posts are hidden from him. Here are a few key things to remember about blocking:

✔ **It's almost entirely reciprocal.** If you block someone, she is just as invisible to you as you are to her. So you can't access her Timeline, nor can you see anything about her anywhere on the site. The only difference is that if you blocked the relationship, you're the only one who can unblock it.

✔ **People you block are not notified that you blocked them.** Nor are they notified if you unblock them. If they are savvy Facebook users, they may notice your suspicious absence, but Facebook never tells them that they have been blocked by you.

✔ **You can block people who are your friends or who are not your Friends.** If you are friends with someone and then you block her, Facebook also removes the friendship. If, at some point in the future, you unblock her, you will need to re-friend her.

Blocking on Facebook doesn't necessarily extend to apps and games you use on Facebook and around the Internet. Contact the developers of the apps you use to learn how to block people within games and apps.

To add people to your blocklist, simply enter their names or e-mail addresses into the boxes provided. Then click the Block button. Their names then appear in a list here. Click the Unblock link next to their names if you want to remove the block.

Block App Invites

An *application* is a term used to describe pieces of software that use Facebook data, even when those applications weren't built by Facebook. As friends use apps and games, they may want you to join in on the fun and send you an invite to join them. This is all well and good until you find that certain people send you wayyyy too many invites. Rather than unfriend or block the overly friendly person who's sending you all those invitations, you can simply block invitations. This option still allows you to interact with your friend in every other way, but you won't receive application invites from him or her.

To block invites from a specific person, just type the person's name in the Block Invites From box, and click Enter when you're done. That person's name then appears on the list below the text box. To remove the block, click Unblock next to that name.

Block Event Invites

Similar to App Invites, you may have friends who are big planners and love to invite all their friends to their events. These may be events that you have no chance of attending because they're taking place across the country, and your friend has chosen to invite all his friends without any regard for location. Again, your friend is cool; his endless unnecessary invitations are not. Instead of getting rid of your friend, you can get rid of the invitations by entering his name here.

To block event invites from specific people, just type their names into the Block Invites From box, and click Enter when you're done. Their names then appear on the list below the text box. To remove the block, click Unblock next to their names.

Block Apps

Occasionally, an app behaves badly once you start using it. By "behave badly," I mean things like spamming your friends or using your information in ways that make you uncomfortable. If an app is doing so, you can block it to prevent it from contacting you through Facebook and getting updated Facebook information about you.

To block an app, type its name in the Block Apps text field and press Enter. The name of the app appears on the list below the text box. To remove the block, click Unblock next to its name.

Apps

An *app* is a term used to describe pieces of software that use Facebook data, even when those applications weren't built by Facebook. You may use apps as games, websites, and useful tools, all of which make use of the data you already share on Facebook. To make it easier to get people using these applications, they import the data from Facebook. I cover the specifics on using applications in Chapter 14. For now, keep in mind that the apps you see on this page are those you chose to interact with. You won't see random applications appear here without you giving them some permissions first.

This section, shown in Figure 5-8, is where you go to edit how apps, games, and websites interact with your Timeline.

Figure 5-8: App settings.

Apps You Use

The Apps You Use section shows all the apps you've used, in the order of those used most recently. Apps you use require direct permission from you to begin accessing your data and posting to your Timeline. Next to each app's name in this list is the audience that can see that app on your Timeline. Across from each app is an Edit link, which when clicked, reveals a menu of settings about that particular app (see Figure 5-9).

Just above the list of apps is a small setting that asks whether you want to Use Apps, Plugins, Games, and Websites on Facebook and Elsewhere. By default, this setting is On. If you don't want to use any applications ever, you can turn it off. I don't recommend turning it off, personally, because apps can be fun and useful, both on Facebook and across the web.

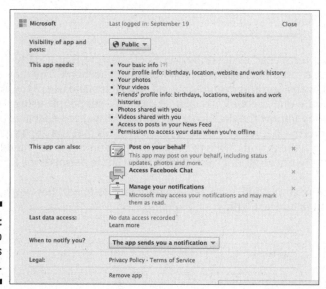

Figure 5-9:
Edit App
settings
here.

There are several sections of information about each app. Some of these sections have options you can change, and others are merely informative.

- ✔ **Last Logged In:** This lists the last time you logged into the app and used it.

- ✔ **Visibility of App:** The Privacy menu here has the same options as any other Privacy menu. You can choose who can see your activity within an app. For example, I keep my Kickstarter app visible to friends because I like them to know what projects I'm supporting. I make my Hulu app visible to Only Me because I'm ashamed of how much reality television I watch.

- ✔ **This App Needs:** This list of information shows you what Timeline information the app requires to function. For example, the Fandango app requires my likes and my friends' likes. Most likely, it uses this information to recommend movies I might like to see. If you ever see a piece of infor-mation on this list that doesn't make sense (like if Fandango required access to all my photos, that would confuse me), it might be a hint that the app isn't a reputable one. You could then choose to remove the app or block it.

✔ **This App Can Also:** This section might not be present for all apps. This reflects any special permissions you may have granted to an app. Special permissions are things like access to Facebook Chat or adding posts on your behalf. You can remove a permission by clicking the x next to it in this section.

Certain permissions are required by apps if you want to use them. That means you can't take the permission away unless you choose to remove the app entirely.

✔ **Last Data Access:** This shows the last piece of information the app accessed about you and when it accessed that info.

✔ **When to Notify You?** Apps may send you notifications about activity your friends have taken or other info you might want to know about. You can choose to let applications send you notifications whenever it wants, or never.

✔ **Legal:** These links take you to the app's Privacy Policy and Terms of Service.

✔ **Remove App:** At the very bottom of this information section is a link you can click to remove an app. Removing an app revokes the permissions you have given it in the past and means it won't be able to access any of your private information going forward.

Apps Others Use

Even if you don't use applications, your friends may. Similar to the way that you may not add photos to Facebook but your friends may add and tag photos of you, your friends may also pass on information about you to applications. You can restrict what applications can see by using the check boxes pictured in Figure 5-10.

Figure 5-10: What can your friends share with apps and games?

Instant Personalization

Instant Personalization is a Facebook feature that basically lets certain Facebook partners access your public Facebook information using browser information, as opposed to using the permission dialog boxes that most apps use before they get access to any information. These partners are websites like Bing, Yelp, and Pandora. You can turn off Instant Personalization by clicking Edit on the right side of the page and deselecting the Enable Instant Personalization on Partner Websites check box. You may be presented with a pop-up window with a video first. You can watch the video or just close the window to continue on to change your setting.

Old Versions of Facebook for Mobile

If you've never used Facebook on a mobile phone or are certain you're using the most recent Facebook app on an iPhone or Android phone, this setting doesn't apply to you. But if you're using a version of Facebook for Mobile that doesn't allow you to change your privacy for each post you create, you can use this setting to control who sees posts you make from your phone. Click Edit on the right side of the page and use the Privacy menu that appears to make your selection.

Ads

The Ads section of the settings page has two settings, both of which require a lot of explanation. The first setting, called Third Party Sites, is perhaps the most confusing because it's a setting that does nothing. Fundamentally, it asks if Facebook can share your information with other sites. Except, currently, Facebook doesn't share information with any other sites.

When Facebook does show ads on other sites (which it does), it does so in such a way that your data remains on Facebook's servers and doesn't get shared with anyone else. So when Facebook asks if you want to share this information with your friends or with no one, it only applies if, in the future, Facebook changes its policy.

To change this setting (which, remember, at the moment, changes nothing), click Edit on the right side of the page and use the drop-down menu that toggles between Only My Friends and No One.

The second setting is called Ads & Friends, and it actually does do something. Facebook pays its bills not by charging you money, but by showing you ads, and charging advertisers for that privilege. Facebook differentiates its ads from other ads on the Internet by pointing out that their ads are "social." In other words, if my friend likes something, there's a good chance I will like it, too. So in its ads, whenever possible, Facebook includes social information. You can see an example of this in Figure 5-11.

Figure 5-11:
Two ads —
one has
social infor-
mation, one
does not.

Personally, I'm comfortable with my friends seeing things that I've liked, or public events I've attended, or places I've checked in, being paired with an ad for that thing, event, or place. If you aren't comfortable with this, that's okay, too; you can prevent it from happening here.

To prevent your friends from seeing any information about you next to an advertisement, click Edit on the right side of the page. Use the drop-down menu that appears (below all the text) to toggle between Only My Friends and No One. Click Save Changes when you're done.

Even if you don't change this setting, only your Friends ever see information about you next to ads. If we're not Friends, you'll never see a notice that "Carolyn Abram likes this movie" next to an advertisement for a popular film.

Timeline Privacy

In addition to the content you post — which was covered earlier in the "Privacy on the Go" section — you can control the information that you've entered in the About and Interests sections of your Timeline.

All about privacy

This information, such as where you went to school or your relationship status, changes infrequently, if ever. You can edit the privacy for this content in the same place you edit the information itself. To get there, go to your Timeline and then click the Update Info button in the bottom-right corner of your cover photo.

The About page has several sections, each representing a different infor-mation category. So, for example, all your work and education information appears in the Work and Education section. Click the Edit button in the upper-right corner of a section to access additional editing options for that category. Next to each piece of information, a privacy icon appears signifying who can see that piece of information. By default, most of this information is set to Public and visible to Everyone, although contact information is visible only to Friends by default.

Figure 5-12 shows me editing the privacy for a piece of information — in this case, my current city in the Living section of my About page. Clicking the privacy icon to the right of the field displays the Audience Selector. When you've finished changing your settings for any particular category, remember to click Save wherever it appears.

Figure 5-12: Edit privacy for every piece of information on your Timeline.

Timeline information is one of the places where the Only Me setting might come in handy. For example, lots of people don't like sharing their birthdays on Facebook, but Facebook requires you to enter a birthday when you sign up. By making it visible only to you, it effectively hides your birthday from everyone.

Click Save Changes when you're done editing privacy settings. Otherwise, the new settings won't stick.

Interested in privacy

If you're looking at your About page and continue scrolling down past all the information sections, you come to the Interest sections. Interests are sorted into categories like Movies, Music, Books, and so on. For your TV Shows section, for example, you can add TV shows that you've watched, TV shows that you want to watch, and TV shows that you like. Each time you add a TV show to the list of shows you've watched or want to watch, you can also control who sees that you've added that particular show to that list. Figure 5-13 shows me editing who can see that I've watched the BBC show *Sherlock*. I opened this Privacy menu by clicking the privacy icon beneath the image representing the show.

Figure 5-13:
Selecting
who
can see
what I've
watched.

Additionally, I can control who can see what TV shows I like. Unlike the
Watched and Want to Watch sections, where I can edit this individually, I
decide who can see *all* the shows I've liked. To edit who can see what you've
liked, follow these steps:

1. **Make sure you're looking at the correct section on your screen.**

   In this case, I'm looking at the TV Shows box.

2. **Click the pencil icon button in the upper-right corner of the box.**

   A menu of options related to this section appears.

3. **Click Edit Privacy.**

   A pop-up window opens.

4. **In the section of the box labeled Likes, click the Privacy menu.**

   This opens the Privacy menu with familiar options: Public, Friends,
   Friends Except Acquaintances, Only Me, Custom, or Lists.

5. **Choose whom you want to see the TV shows you have liked.**

6. **Click Close to save the changes.**

Privacy Tools

Okay, that was a lot. A lot of settings, a lot of information. What if you don't
want to worry about these small settings and who tagged what when? What if

you just want to make sure that your Timeline looks the way you want to your friends and that people who aren't your friends can't see anything you don't want them to see? Well, the good news is that the View As tool allows you to do just that, and the Activity Log tool allows you to keep track of everything that's been happening recently and to make any needed adjustments without trying to figure out which setting, exactly, needs to be changed.

View As

You can get to the View As tool from the Privacy Shortcuts menu. Click the lock icon next to your name in the left sidebar to open the menu up. In the Who Can See My Stuff? section, click the link to View As.

Clicking that link brings you to your Timeline. Except, it's probably not the way you usually see your Timeline. The black bar running across the top of the page lets you know that you're currently viewing your Timeline as someone who is not your friend (also known as, everyone in the Public bucket of people). You can click through to the various sections of your Timeline. (Photos tends to be a section that people like to check, double-check, and triple-check.)

Note that no matter how much you've hidden your information and posts, everyone can see your cover photo and profile picture, gender, current city, and Friend List. Anything else the public can see can be hidden, if you so choose.

In the black bar on top of this view of your Timeline, there's a white bold link labeled View as Specific Person. If you want to check on, for example, what acquaintances or people you've added to your Restricted list can see, click this link and enter a friend's name into the text box that appears. If you're surprised by what that friend can see, you can go change the privacy on any content you don't want her to see. (If you've forgotten how to change the privacy on a post, head back up to the "Privacy On the Go" section.)

Activity Log

As you've probably noticed, a lot happens on Facebook. You take all sorts of actions: liking, commenting, posting, and so on. And people take all sorts of actions that affect you: writing on your Timeline, tagging you in photos, and inviting you to join groups. If you want to know, line by line, everything that could possibly be seen about you by someone on Facebook, Activity Log is for you.

You can get to Activity Log from a few places. You can get there from the Privacy Shortcuts menu or from your own Timeline. On your Timeline, simply click the Activity Log button, located under the right corner of your cover photo. This takes you to Activity Log (see Figure 5-14).

Figure 5-14:
Here's everything you've done on Facebook recently.

When you're looking at Activity Log, notice that there's a menu on the left for viewing only certain types of posts. For example, you can choose to view all the posts you've been tagged in, or all the photo posts, or all the app-related posts.

When you're looking at an individual line item, you see several columns of information. First is an icon and sentence explaining what you did (or what a Friend did). This might be something like "Carolyn wrote on Dana's Timeline" or "Carolyn was tagged in Dana's photo." Then there is a preview of that post, photo, comment, or whatever it is related to. For example, if you commented on a photo, the preview will show you that photo and the comment that you made.

To the right of the preview is an icon representing who can see that item. Hover your mouse over the icon to see text explaining who can see it. This might be the usual privacy options, or it might be members of a group you belong to, or in the case of a post to a Friend's Timeline, it will be that person's friends. For posts that you create, you can change the audience by clicking the icon, which opens the Privacy menu.

However, you'll find you can't change the privacy on lots of content. For example, a comment on someone else's post isn't something you can change the audience for. If you realize a comment you made or something you liked is visible to more people than you'd want, your only option is to delete that content.

You can delete content using the final icon to the right side of each item in Activity Log. This little pencil icon can be found all over the site and generally indicates that you can edit something. When you hover over the icon here, it explains that the item is allowed on Timeline. This means that people may see that item — possibly as its own post, possibly as a summarized item in recent activity, possibly in an app box — when they visit your Timeline. Clicking the Edit button reveals a menu of options for changing whether something appears on Timeline. For some items, such as likes or comments, the only option is to unlike the content or delete the comment. For others, like posts you've made or posts you've been tagged in, there are more options that allow you to hide something from the Timeline or edit it on your Timeline (these are the same options that appear when you go to edit or highlight something on your Timeline).

When I say something is visible on Timeline, I also mean that your Friends might see that item in their News Feed.

Personally, I find Activity Log useful in that it helps me understand all the ways I participate on Facebook and all the things my friends might see about me and my life. But I've found that I don't actually change the privacy or the Timeline settings on items here all that often.

Remembering That It Takes a Village to Raise a Facebook

Another way in which you (and every member of Facebook) contribute to keeping Facebook a safe, clean place is in the reports that you submit about spam, harassment, inappropriate content, and fake Timelines. Almost every piece of content on Facebook can be reported. Sometimes you may need to click an Options link to find the report link.

Figure 5-15 shows an example of someone reporting an inappropriate photo.

The various reporting options that you see may vary, depending on what you're reporting (a group as opposed to a photo, for example). These reports are submitted to the Facebook User Operations team. The team then investigates and takes down inappropriate photos, disables fake accounts, and generally strives to keep Facebook clean, safe, and inoffensive.

Figure 5-15:
Reporting
inappropri-
ate content.

When you see content that you don't like — for example, an offensive group name or a vulgar Timeline — don't hesitate to report it. With the entire Facebook population working to keep Facebook free of badness, you wind up with a pretty awesome community.

After you report something, Facebook's User Operations team evaluates it in terms of violating Facebook's Statement of Rights and Responsibilities. This means that pornography gets taken down, fake Timelines are disabled, and people who send spam may receive a warning or even have their account disabled. However, sometimes something that you report may be offensive to you but doesn't violate the Statement of Rights and Responsibilities and, therefore, will remain on Facebook. Due to privacy restrictions, User Operations may not always notify you about actions taken as a result of your support, but rest assured that the team handles every report.

Peeking Behind the Scenes

Facebook's part in keeping everyone safe requires a lot of manpower and technology power. The manpower involves responding to the reports that you and the rest of Facebook submit, as well as proactively going into Facebook and getting rid of content that violates the Statement of Rights and Responsibilities.

The technology power that I talk about is kept vague on purpose. I hope that you never think twice about the things that are happening behind the scenes to protect you from harassment, spam, and pornography. Moreover, I hope that you're never harassed or spammed, or accidentally happen upon a pornographic photo. But just so you know that Facebook is actively thinking about user safety and privacy, I talk about a few of the general areas where Facebook does a lot of preventive work.

Protecting minors

This section is purposefully vague to avoid becoming *Gaming Facebook's Systems For Dummies*. In general, I want you to note that people under the age of 18 have special visibility and privacy rules applied to them. For example, when a user under the age of 18 (in the United States) posts something and chooses Public from the Privacy menu, that post won't truly be public until she turns 18. Until then, that post will be visible only to friends of her friends.

Other proprietary systems are in place that are alerted if a person is interacting with the Timelines of minors in ways they shouldn't, as well as systems that get alerted when someone targets an ad to minors. Facebook tries to prevent whatever it can, but this is where some common sense on the part of teens (and their parents) can go a long way toward preventing bad situations.

You must be at least 13 years old to join Facebook.

Preventing spam and viruses

Everyone can agree that spam is one of the worst parts of the Internet, all too often sliming its way through the cracks into e-mail and websites — and always trying to slime its way into Facebook as well, sometimes in the form of messages to you, or Timeline posts, or groups, or events masking as something it's not to capture your precious attention.

When you report a piece of content on Facebook, "It's spam" is usually one of the reasons you can give for reporting it. These spam reports are incredibly helpful. Facebook also has a bunch of systems that keep track of the sort of behavior that spammers tend to do. The spam systems also keep track of those who message people too quickly, friend too many people, post a similar link in too many places, and do other such behaviors that tend to reek of spam. If you end up really taking to this Facebook thing, at some point you may get hit with a warning to slow down your poking or your messaging. Don't take it too personally, and just follow the instructions in the warning — this is the spam system at work.

Preventing phishing

Phishing is a term that refers to malicious websites attempting to gain sensitive information (like usernames and passwords to online accounts) by masquerading as the sites you use and trust. Phishing is usually part of spamming: A malicious site acquires someone's Facebook credentials and then messages all that user's friends with a link to a phishing site that looks like Facebook and asks them to log in. They do so, and now the bad guys have a bunch of new Facebook logins and passwords. It's a bad cycle. The worst part is that many of these Facebook users get locked out of their own accounts and are unable to stop the spam.

Just like spam and virus prevention, Facebook has a series of proprietary systems in place to try to break this cycle. If you do have the misfortune to get phished (and it can happen to the best of us), you may run into one of the systems that Facebook uses to help people take back their Timelines and protect themselves from phishing in the future.

The best way to protect yourself from phishing is to get used to the times and places Facebook asks for your password. If you just clicked a link within Facebook and suddenly there's a blue screen asking for your information, be suspicious! Similarly, remember that Facebook will never ask you to e-mail it your password. If you receive an e-mail asking for something like that, report it as spam immediately.

If you want to stay up-to-date with the latest scams on Facebook, or want more information about protecting yourself, you can like Facebook's Security Page at `www.facebook.com/security`. This provides you with ongoing information about safety and security on Facebook.

One Final Call to Use Your Common Sense

No one wants anything bad to happen to you as a result of something you do on Facebook. Facebook doesn't want that. You don't want that. I definitely don't want that. I hope that these explanations help to prevent anything bad from happening to you on Facebook. But no matter what, *you* need to take part in keeping yourself safe. In order to ensure your own safety on Facebook, you have to make an effort to be smart and safe online.

So what *is* your part? Your part is to be aware of what you're putting online and on Facebook. You need to be the one to choose whether displaying any given piece of information on Facebook is risky. If it's risky, you need to be the one to figure out the correct privacy settings for showing this information to the people you choose to see it — and not to the people you don't.

Your part is equivalent to the part you play in your everyday life to keep yourself safe: You know which alleys not to walk down at night, when to buckle your seatbelt, when to lock the front door, and when to toss the moldy bread before making a sandwich. Now that you know all about Facebook's privacy settings, you also know when to use the various privacy options, and when to simply refrain from posting.

I'm having a privacy freakout; what do I do?

I cannot tell you how many times I've gotten a frantic e-mail from a family member or friend saying something like, "Oh my gosh, my friend just told me that his friend was able to see these photos that I thought only my friends could see and now I'm freaking out that everyone can see everything; do you know what to do?"

The first step is to take a deep breath.

After that, the next best thing to do is to go to the Privacy Shortcuts menu and click the View As tool.

That allows you to click around your Timeline as though you're someone who isn't your Friend. If you think that person is seeing too much, I recommend using the Limit the Audience for Past Posts setting on the Privacy section of the Settings page. This pretty much changes anything that used to be visible to more than just friends to be visible only to Friends. After you do that, usually you can begin the process of adjusting your settings so that, going forward, you won't have any more freakouts.

Part II
Connecting with Friends on Facebook

In this part . . .

- ✓ Finding friends
- ✓ Interacting via comments, likes, and sharing
- ✓ Sending messages
- ✓ Managing groups
- ✓ Visit www.dummies.com/extras/facebook for great Dummies content online.

Chapter 6

Finding Facebook Friends

In This Chapter

▶ Understanding what *friending* someone means

▶ Finding friends on Facebook in various ways

▶ Organizing and controlling your Friend List(s)

Hundreds of sayings abound about friendship and friends, and most of them can be boiled down into one catch-all adage: friends, good; no friends, bad. This is true in life and also true on Facebook. Without your friends on Facebook, you find yourself at some point looking at a blank screen and asking, "Okay, now what?" With friends, you find yourself at some point looking at photos of a high school reunion and asking, "Oh, dear. How did that last hour go by so quickly?"

Most of Facebook's functionality is built around the premise that you have a certain amount of information that you want your friends to see (and maybe some information that you don't want *all* your friends to see, but that's what privacy settings are for). So, if you don't have friends who are seeing your posts, what's the point in sharing them? Messages aren't that useful unless you send them to someone. Photos are made to be viewed, but if the access is limited to friends, well, you need to find some friends.

On Facebook, the bulk of friendships are *reciprocal,* which means if you add someone as a friend, he has to confirm the friendship before it appears on both Timelines. If someone adds you as a friend, you can choose between Confirm and Not Now. If you confirm the friend, *Congrats!* You have a new friend! And if you ignore the friend, the other person won't be informed.

If you're low on friends at the moment, don't feel as though you're the last kid picked for the team in middle-school dodge ball. There are many ways to find your friends on Facebook. If your friends haven't joined Facebook, invite them to join and get them to be your friends on Facebook as well as in real life.

What Is a Facebook Friend?

Good question. In many ways, a *Facebook Friend* is the same as a real-life friend (although, to quote many people I know, "You're not real friends unless you're Facebook friends"). These are the people you hang out with, keep in touch with, care about, and want to publicly acknowledge as friends. These aren't people you met on Facebook. Rather, they're the people you call on the phone; stop and catch up with if you cross paths at the grocery; or invite over for parties, dinners, and general social gatherings.

In real life, there are lots of shades of friendship — think of the differences between acquaintances, a friend from work, an activity buddy, and best friends. Facebook gives you a few tools for negotiating these levels of friendship, which I cover in the Managing How You Interact with Friends section of this chapter. But by default, most friendships are lumped into a blanket category of "friend."

Here are the basics of what it means to be friends with someone on Facebook, though you'll notice that each of them comes with a few caveats on how it can be adjusted by either person in the friendship.

✔ **They can see all the stuff on your Timeline (like your posts and other information) that you have set to be visible to Friends.**

Remember, this is what happens by default. You can actually control which friends can see which posts more specifically by learning about your privacy options (which you can do in Chapter 5), and about Friend Lists, which I go over later in this chapter.

✔ **They see new posts you create in their News Feeds on their Home pages.**

Again, the information your friends see in their News Feed depends on the audience you've chosen to share each post with. It may also depend on your friends' News Feed settings.

✔ **You can see their posts and other information on their Timelines.**

This, of course, depends on their own privacy settings, but in general, you'll be able to see more as a friend than you did before you became friends.

✔ **You see new posts from them in your News Feed on your Home page.**

This depends on your friend's sharing settings, but more importantly, you can control whose posts you see in your News Feed through managing your own News Feed settings and preferences. I cover how to do this later in this chapter.

✔ **You'll be listed as friends on one another's Timeline.**

This is a small detail, but it's important in understanding the difference between becoming friends with someone and simply subscribing to someone's posts. Lots of people, especially public figures or people who have a business of some sort, allow you to subscribe to their posts without becoming friends. In these cases, you see their posts on your Home page, but they won't see your posts unless they choose to subscribe to you.

Adding Friends

Facebook has some unique verbiage that it has created over time. One of the most important Facebook verbs is "to friend." *Friending* is the act of adding someone as a friend. You may overhear people use this casually in conversation: "Oh, you won't believe who finally friended me!" And now, you too, will be friending people.

Sending Friend Requests

Now that you know what a friend is, it's time to send some requests, and maybe even accept some pending ones. For the purposes of this example, I searched for the Timeline of Dummies Man using the Search box in the blue bar on top. I cover using Search to find friends later in this chapter, so for now just remember that as you type, Facebook tries to autocomplete what you're looking for, meaning search results will appear below the Search box as you type, as shown in Figure 6-1.

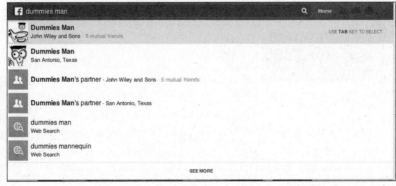

Figure 6-1: The search results for Dummies Man.

When you see the person you think you want to add, click on her face; this takes you to her Timeline. At the bottom-right corner of her cover photo is an Add Friend button. To add this person as a friend, all you need to do is click the Add Friend button. You can see this button in Figure 6-2. Clicking this button sends a Friend Request. When she accepts, you'll become friends.

Figure 6-2: A Timeline before I become a friend.

You won't be friends with someone until she confirms your Friend Request. After she confirms, you're notified by a red flag appearing above the notifications icon in the blue bar on top.

So what does your potential friend see after you send a request? That is a brilliant segue into the next topic, accepting Friend Requests.

Accepting Friend Requests

When you receive a new request, a little red flag appears over the Friends icon in the big blue bar on top of each page. You may also be notified in your e-mail or on your phone. Figure 6-3 shows an example. The number in the red flag indicates how many Friend Requests are waiting for you.

Figure 6-3: Someone wants to be your friend!

Clicking this icon opens the Friend Requests menu, as shown in Figure 6-4.

Figure 6-4: Click Confirm or Not Now.

To accept the Friend Request, click the Confirm button. You now have a friend. To reject the request, click Not Now.

When you click Not Now, Facebook may ask you whether you know that person outside of Facebook. In other words, is this a Friend Request from someone you know or someone you don't know? If you click No — meaning, "I have no idea who this person is" — Facebook prevents that person from friending you again in the future. If you click Yes, meaning "Yes, I know this person but I'm not sure I want him looking at my stuff," Facebook hides the request. In other words, you can go back to it in the future and confirm it at that time.

To get back to hidden Friend Requests, open the Friend Request menu and click See All at the bottom of the menu. This takes you to a page where all your outstanding requests (including hidden ones) appear. You can then confirm or permanently delete a request.

You can also access hidden requests by going to the Timeline of the person who sent the request. There, the Add Friend button is replaced with a button to accept the Friend Request. Click the button to become official Facebook friends.

Some people worry about clicking that Not Now button. If you're not sure what you want to do, you can always leave the request untouched. But never hesitate to click Not Now for someone you really just don't want to be friends with. Facebook won't notify her that you ignored her request.

Choose your friends wisely

Generally, you send Friend Requests to and confirm Friend Requests from only people you actually know. If you don't know them — *random Friend Requests* — click Not Now. Accepting a Friend Request from random people has a tendency to ruin the Facebook experience — it puts random content in your News Feed, exposes your own content to people you don't know, and is generally a bad practice. Remember the lecture you got about choosing good friends when you were in high school? It's every bit as true now.

If there are people you don't know personally but find interesting (such as a celebrity or public figure), you may be able to subscribe to their posts without becoming friends with them (more on that in the "Following" section near the end of this chapter). If that's not a possibility, you could add them as friends and then add them to your Acquaintances or Restricted Friend List, if you use these lists to control your privacy.

It's quality, not quantity

Another common misperception about Facebook is that it's all about the race to get the most friends. This is very, very wrong. Between the News Feed and privacy implications of friendship, aim to keep your Friend List to the people you actually care about. Now, the number of people you care about — including the people you care about the most and those you care about least — may be large or small. I don't think it matters how big or small your list is as long as the people you care about most are on it. In fact, one of the reasons for a number of the Friend List management tools that I cover in this chapter is because, over time, people's Friend Lists tend to bloat.

As you change jobs or cities or start a new hobby, you add more and more friends, but that doesn't displace the fact that you care about friends from your past. The Friend List management tools aim to help you keep track of the people you care about most, and not get distracted by the more distant friends.

Finding Your Friends on Facebook

How do you get to the people you want to be your friends? Facebook is big, and if you're looking for your friend John, you may need to provide some more detail. Facebook has a couple of tools that show you people you may know and want as your friends, as well as a normal search-by-name functionality for finding specific people.

If only real life had a Friend Finder

Friend Finder is a tool that matches e-mail addresses from your e-mail address book to people's Timelines on Facebook. Because each e-mail address can be associated with only one Facebook account, you can count on such matches finding the right people.

With your permission, Friend Finder also invites people who don't have a Facebook account but whose e-mail addresses match those in your address book to join Facebook. Sending invites this way causes Friend Requests to automatically be sent to those people. If they join based on an invite you send, they find a Friend Request from you waiting when they join.

To use Friend Finder, you need to give Facebook your e-mail address and e-mail password. Facebook doesn't store this information. It just uses the information to retrieve your contacts list that one time.

Chances are that you came across Friend Finder when you first set up your account. The following steps make several assumptions — namely, that you use web-based e-mail (Hotmail, Gmail, Yahoo! Mail, and so on), that you haven't used Friend Finder recently, and that the address book for the e-mail has a bunch of your friends in it. I cover other options, such as a client-based address book, later in this chapter.

Here's how to use Friend Finder:

1. **Click the Friends icon on the big blue bar on top.**

    The Friend Request menu opens.

2. **At the top-right corner of the menu, click the Find Friends link.**

    Figure 6-5 shows the Friend Finder. Below it, you may also see a list of People You May Know (not shown in figure), which I cover later in this chapter.

3. **Select the e-mail or instant message service you use.**

    This may be Windows Live Hotmail, AOL, iCloud, or any number of other e-mail services.

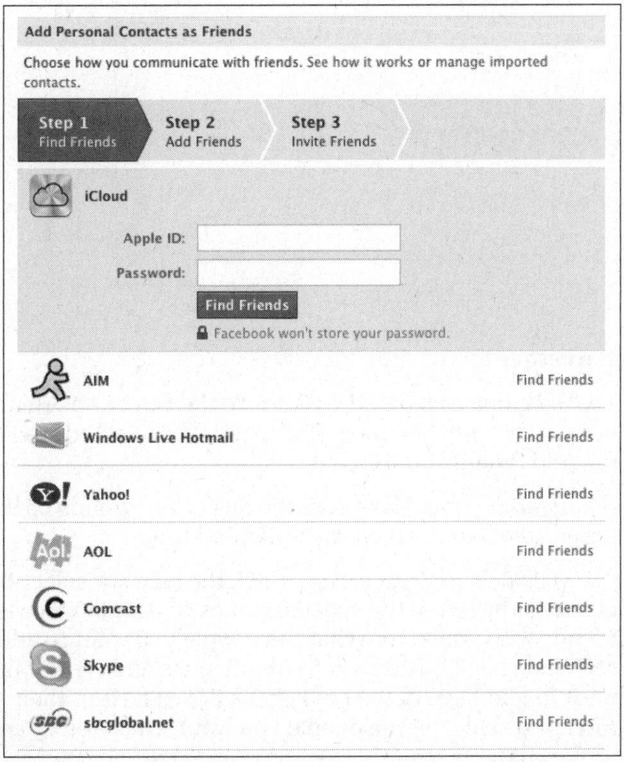

Add Personal Contacts as Friends

Choose how you communicate with friends. See how it works or manage imported contacts.

| Step 1 Find Friends | Step 2 Add Friends | Step 3 Invite Friends |

iCloud

Apple ID: [   ]

Password: [   ]

Find Friends

🔒 Facebook won't store your password.

AIM	Find Friends
Windows Live Hotmail	Find Friends
Yahoo!	Find Friends
AOL	Find Friends
Comcast	Find Friends
Skype	Find Friends
sbcglobal.net	Find Friends

Figure 6-5:
An unfilled
Friend
Finder.

4. Enter your e-mail address in the Your Email field.

5. Enter your e-mail password (not your Facebook password) in the Email Password box and then click Find Friends.

These instructions are meant for first-time users of the Friend Finder. If you've used it before, or if you're currently logged in to your webmail client, you may see some fields prefilled or additional pop-up prompts asking you for your permission to send information to Facebook. Don't worry if what you see on the screen doesn't match the figures here at the beginning.

If Facebook finds matches with the e-mails in your address book, you see a page that looks similar to Figure 6-6. (If Facebook doesn't find any friends, go to Step 6.) These people are the ones Facebook thinks you may know.

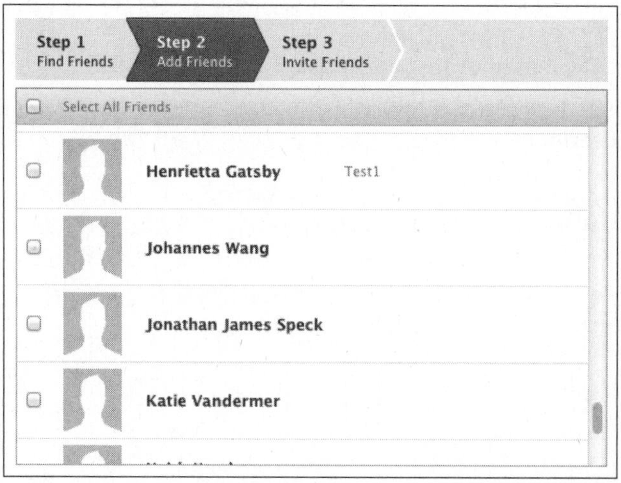

Step 1 Find Friends	Step 2 Add Friends	Step 3 Invite Friends

☐ Select All Friends

☐ Henrietta Gatsby   Test1

☐ Johannes Wang

☐ Jonathan James Speck

☐ Katie Vandermer

Figure 6-6: The friend selector portion of Friend Finder.

6. Decide whether to

- *Add everyone as a friend.* Make sure the Select All Friends check box (in the grey bar above the results) is selected, and then click the Add Friends button.

- *Not friend anyone.* Make sure the Select All Friends check box is deselected, and then click the Skip button.

- *Add specific people as friends.* Click the faces or select the check boxes to the left of the specific names of people you want to be friends with. Make sure that the people you want to add have selected check boxes next to their names and the people you don't want to add have deselected check boxes next to their names. After you select all the people you want, click Add Friends.

Everyone you select receives a Friend Request from you.

After you click either Add as Friends or Skip, you land on the Invite Friends portion of Friend Finder. Here you find a list of contact names and e-mail addresses. These e-mails or phone numbers are those that don't have matches on Facebook.

7. **(Optional) Invite people to join Facebook and become your friends.**

   Similar to adding friends, you can

   - *Invite all these contacts.* Make sure the Select All/None box is checked and click Send Invites.

   - *Invite none of these contacts.* Make sure the Select All/None box is unchecked and click Skip.

   - *Invite some of these contacts.* Select the Invite Some Friends option and then use the check boxes to the left of their e-mail addresses to choose which ones you want to invite to join Facebook. Selected check box = invite sent; deselected check box = no invite sent.

   After you make your selections, click Send Invites or Invite to Join. If you don't want to send any invitations, click Skip.

After taking all these steps, I hope you manage to send at least a few Friend Requests. Don't be shy about adding people you know and want to keep up with; it's not considered rude to add people as your friends. Your friends need to confirm your requests before you officially become friends on Facebook, so you may not be able to see your friends' Timelines until those confirmations happen.

If the whole experience yielded nothing — no friends you wanted to add, no contacts you wanted to invite — you have a few options. You can go through these steps again with different e-mail addresses. You should probably use any e-mail address that you use for personal e-mails (from where you e-mail your friends and family). If that's not the problem, you have more ways to use Friend Finder.

Import an address book

If you're someone who uses a *desktop e-mail client* — a program on your local computer that manages your e-mail (such as Microsoft Outlook or Entourage), create a file of your contacts and import it so that Facebook can check it for friend matches. The way to create your contact file depends on which e-mail client you use. Here's how to get the right instructions:

1. **From the Friend Finder, select the Other Tools option.**

   It's at the bottom of the list of Friend Finder options.

2. Click Upload Contact File, the first blue link.

If you're using a Mac, you may see a blue button named Find My Mac Address Book Contacts. In addition, both Mac and PC users should see a blue Upload Contacts button below a gray Choose File button.

At this point, unless you've already done so, you need to create a contact file. If you don't know how to do that, click the How to Create a Contact File link above the gray Choose File button. A list of different e-mail programs appears with instructions for most desktop e-mail programs, as well as a few websites.

3. Click Choose File.

A window appears allowing you to select the file from your computer's hard drive.

4. Select a file and click Open.

The upload begins automatically. After your contacts are compared with Facebook's records, you'll be taken to Step 2 of the Friend Finder, Add Friends.

5. Decide whether to

- *Add everyone as a friend.* Make sure the Select All Friends check box is selected, and click the Add Friends button.

- *Not friend anyone.* Make sure the Select All Friends check box is deselected, and click the Skip button.

- *Add specific people as friends.* Click the faces or select the check boxes to the left of the specific names of the people you want to be friends with. Make sure the people you want to add have selected check boxes next to their names and the people you don't want to add have deselected check boxes next to their names. After you select all the people you want, click Add Friends.

Everyone you select receives a Friend Request from you.

After you click either Add as Friends or Skip, you land on the Invite Friends portion of Friend Finder. Here you find a list of contact names and e-mail addresses. These e-mails or phone numbers are those that don't have matches on Facebook.

6. (Optional) Invite people to join Facebook and become your friends.

Similar to adding friends, you can

- *Invite all these contacts.* Make sure the Select All/None box is selected and click Send Invites.

- *Invite none of these contacts.* Make sure the Select All/None box is deselected, and click Skip.

- *Invite some of these contacts.* Select the Invite Some Friends option, and then use the check boxes to the left of their e-mail addresses to choose which ones you want to invite to join Facebook. Checked box = invite sent; unchecked box = no invite sent.

After you make your selections, click Send Invites or Invite to Join. If you don't want to send any invitations, click Skip.

People you may know

After you have a friend or two, Facebook can start making pretty good guesses about others who may be your friends. Facebook primarily does this by looking at people with whom you have friends or networks in common. In the People You May Know box, you see a list of people Facebook thinks you may know and, therefore, may want as friends. People You May Know boxes appear all over the site — on the Find Friends page, on your Home page, and sometimes on your Timeline or on the right side of a group. Usually the boxes include a list of names, profile pictures, and some sort of info like how many mutual friends you have or where the other person attended school. These little tidbits are meant to provide context about how you might know that person.

Anytime you find yourself looking at the People You May Know list and you do, in fact, know someone on the list, simply add that person as a friend by clicking the Add Friend button or link by the person's name. If you're not sure, you can click a name or picture to go to that person's Timeline and gather more evidence about whether and how you know that person. Then you can decide whether to add that person as a friend. If you're sure you don't know someone, or if you do know someone but are sure you don't want that person as your Facebook friend, mouse over the person's picture and click the X that appears. After you do that, she stops appearing in your People You May Know list. As you add or remove people from the list, more pop up to take their places. This fun can last for hours.

Find classmates and co-workers

Friend Finder works by looking for large groups of people you might want to become friends with. A common assumption is that you'll want to become friends with people you've gone to school with and worked with over the years. To find these people, follow these steps:

1. **Click the Friends icon in the big blue bar on top.**

   The Friend Requests menu appears.

2. **At the top of the menu, click the Find Friends link.**

   The Friend Finder page appears.

3. **Click Other Tools (usually found at the bottom of the list of options).**

A menu of possibilities based on information you've filled out on your Timeline appears.

4. **Click any of the Find Coworkers From or Find Classmates From links.**

All these links go to the same place, which is a page for browsing people on Facebook.

5. **Use the check boxes on the left side of the page (shown in Figure 6-7) to look for people from your various jobs or schools.**

Selecting a check box displays people from that school or company. You can also look for people from your hometown, current city, or workplace by entering a mutual friend's name.

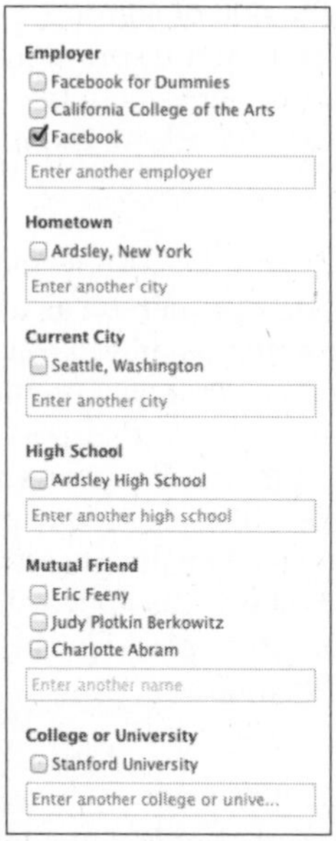

Employer
- ☐ Facebook for Dummies
- ☐ California College of the Arts
- ☑ Facebook
- Enter another employer

Hometown
- ☐ Ardsley, New York
- Enter another city

Current City
- ☐ Seattle, Washington
- Enter another city

High School
- ☐ Ardsley High School
- Enter another high school

Mutual Friend
- ☐ Eric Feeny
- ☐ Judy Plotkin Berkowitz
- ☐ Charlotte Abram
- Enter another name

College or University
- ☐ Stanford University
- Enter another college or unive...

Figure 6-7:
Use the check boxes to find your friends.

When you select more than one check box, it actually shows you *fewer* people because now Facebook is looking for people who both worked at Mom's Pizza *and* went to Hamilton High School. To find more people, select only one check box at a time.

You can actually browse for people in cities, companies, and colleges other than the ones you've listed on your Timeline. Look for the empty boxes that say Add Another, and type the school, city, or company where you think you know people.

Find what you're looking for: Search

Friend Finder is a great way to build your Friend List quickly without a lot of work. After you build it a bit, though, what if you find other people who may want to be your friends? Facebook Search offers you the capability to seek out certain friends by name.

The Search box in the blue bar on top lets you search a whole lot of things on Facebook: pages, groups, events, even things your friends have liked. But most of the time, you use it to search for people. It may be people you're already friends with and you just want to go to their Timelines. Sometimes it will be people you aren't friends with yet but whom you want to reach out to.

Basic Search can be a little confusing because Facebook autocompletes the names that you type and assumes you're trying to get to your friends' Timelines. If you're the type of person who is used to pressing the Enter key to begin a search, this can lead you landing on friends' Timelines when you meant to search for someone _else_ named James.

You'll wind up using Search two basic ways. The first way is if the name of the person you're looking for (or at least someone with the same name) appears in the autocomplete menu. You can accomplish that sort of search following these steps:

1. **Begin typing the name you're looking for in the Search box.**

   Pay attention to the people who appear in the autocomplete menu. Facebook displays first your friends and then friends of friends. There's a good chance that you may find the person you're looking for in this menu.

2. **If you see the name in the autocomplete menu, use your mouse or arrow keys to highlight the person you're looking for.**

3. **Click the name or press Enter.**

   This brings you to the person's Timeline, where you can verify that you know the person and add him as a friend.

If you don't see the person you're looking for, don't despair; you can get more results:

1. **Type the person's full name in the search box.**

2. **Click See More at the bottom of the search menu.**

   The search menu expands to reveal new options for search. So, if you type Jane Smith and then click See More, you can now either search People Named Jane Smith, Pages Named Jane Smith, or Places Named Jane Smith.

3. **Click the People Named *<Friend's Name>* option.**

   A blue friend icon is next to this option. A search results page appears with larger previews of people's profile pictures and Timeline info. The right side of the page also has options for narrowing your search using fields such as Gender, Employer, Current City, and so on.

4. **Use the fields on the right side of the page to zero in on your actual friend.**

   This might be information like where your friend works or where she's from.

5. **When you find the person you're looking for, add her as a friend.**

Managing How You Interact with Friends

After you do all the work of finding and adding your friends, at some point, you may find that things are feeling a little out of control. Chances are you may be seeing posts from someone you find uninteresting; you might not be sure who, exactly, can see your own posts anymore. At this point, it's a good idea to get acquainted with the way Facebook automatically helps you end the madness, as well as some of the more specific and manual things you can do.

Friend Lists

Friend Lists (capital L) are subsets of your giant list of friends (lowercase l). Confused yet? Friend Lists are a way of organizing your friends into lists to make your Facebook experience even easier and more personalized to you and your types of friends. Organizing your friends into Friend Lists allows you to do the following:

✔ **Share different types of information with different sets of friends.** For example, your best friends may get to see your party photos, and your family may get to see your wedding photos. This is a custom privacy setting you can use all over Facebook.

✔ **See a version of News Feed that shows only updates from people in that list.** You can make sure that you can easily zero in on updates from a certain group of people, which may be your family, or friends from college, or both. You can choose to view only News Feeds from those people.

➤ **Use Friend Lists in Chat.** You can show yourself as online or offline to different groups of people, or easily scan for certain types of friends currently online, such as social friends if you're looking for a dinner date or carpool friends if you need a ride. I tell you more about this topic in Chapter 8.

The options for how you create Friend Lists are virtually limitless. Your lists can be for silly things (Girls' Night Out Girls), real-world needs (Family), or general bucketing (co-workers).

Smart Lists

Smart Lists are the lists that Facebook makes on your behalf. These lists are created automatically based on your interactions with your friends and shared characteristics of your friends. Here are some common Smart Lists:

➤ **Close Friends:** Facebook creates this list based on things like people you interact with a lot on Facebook, people you appear in a lot of photos with, and so on.

➤ **Acquaintances:** The opposite of the Close Friends list. This list is meant to be a place where you can cordon off the people you don't know as well. They may be perfectly nice people, but they aren't necessarily the people you want to share everything with. In fact, one of the default privacy options when you post something from the Share box is Friends Except Acquaintances, which is Facebook's way of saying, "Share this with my *real* friends only."

➤ **Restricted:** This list is for people you want to add as friends but don't want to see posts that are visible to friends. In other words, people on this list see only posts that you choose to make public.

➤ **Family:** Based on information you've entered about your family, they may show up on this Smart List.

➤ **<*Your High School*>:** If you've caught up with a lot of old friends on Facebook, a Smart List might be created so you can post photos from the reunion or share memories just with them.

➤ **<*Your college/university/workplace*>:** Similar to a high school list, depending on the information your friends have listed on their profiles, additional Smart Lists may be created for these groups. For example, I have Smart Lists for Stanford (where I was an undergraduate), CCA (where I was a graduate student), and Facebook (where I used to work).

Although Facebook is smart, it's not perfect. Although these lists will be mostly accurate, you may find that you have to do some editing to them. The accuracy of the lists may also depend on how you want to use your lists. For example, you may want your Family list to make it easy to share with just your immediate family and, therefore, need to remove the more distant members.

Or you want it to be a giant family reunion all the time, in which case, you need to add some of the third and fourth cousins once removed to the mix.

To edit a Smart List, follow these steps:

1. **From the Home page, look on the right side of the page for the News Feed menu.**

2. **Click the down arrow to expand the News Feed menu once and then click the See All link at the bottom of the menu to expand it even further.**

   All your lists appear, along with links to categories of News Feeds you can look at, such as Music and Photos.

3. **Click the list you want to edit.**

   Doing so takes you to that list's News Feed. On the right side of the page is an On This List section, where you can check out the current members of the list.

4. **To add people to a list, type their names in the text box in the On This List section.**

   Facebook autocompletes as you type. Select your friends' names when you see them.

5. **To remove people from a list, click Edit in the upper-right corner of the On This List section.**

   A menu appears with options for changing what you see in this view.

6. **Click Add/Remove.**

   A pop-up window displays the names and pictures of all members of the list.

7. **Hover over the person you want to remove.**

   A small X should appear in the upper-right corner of the person's picture.

8. **Click the X.**

   Repeat Steps 7 and 8 for each person you want to remove.

9. **Click the Finish button when you're done.**

You can edit who is on a Smart List at any point in time.

Creating your own Friend Lists

Smart Lists can usually help you figure out whom you want to share your own posts with. But sometimes you may want a specific list that Facebook can't figure out. This might be a sub-sub-group, like all the people you played Frisbee with in college. In these cases, you can create your own list.

To create a Friend List, follow these steps:

1. **From the Home page, look on the right side of the page for the News Feed menu.**

2. **Click the down arrow to expand the News Feed menu once and then click the See All link at the bottom of the menu to expand it even further.**

   This brings you to a list of all the different ways you can view News Feed, including seeing only certain types of stories or only stories from certain lists.

3. **Click the Manage Lists option (the last item in the list).**

   The Manage Lists page appears. In other words, a page that lists all your lists.

4. **Click the Create List button in the upper-right corner.**

   The Create New List window appears, as shown in Figure 6-8.

Figure 6-8: Creating a Friend List.

5. **In the List Name box, type the name of your list.**

   Maybe something like **Dummies** for the Dummies Team.

6. **Add friends who belong on this list by typing their names in the Members box.**

   Facebook autocompletes as you type. Press Enter when you highlight the correct friend's name.

7. **Click Create.**

   Now, wherever Friend Lists appear on Facebook, including where you set privacy, you have access to the new list you just created.

Friend Lists you create are private, so even if the list you're messaging is known in your mind as *Annoying Co-Workers,* all that your annoying co-workers see is a list of names. Members of Smart Lists are able to see the name of a list they've been added to.

Updating lists on the go

After you create and start using your lists, you can continuously add people to them at the same time you add them as friends.

When you're the one sending a Friend Request, follow these steps to also add the person to a particular Friend List:

1. **From his Timeline, after you've added him as a friend, click the Friend Request Sent button.**

   A menu appears asking you if you want to add that person to any of your Friend Lists. By default, your most commonly used lists will appear at the top.

2. **Click the list you want to add your friend to.**

   You may need to select Add to Another List to see your full menu of lists.

If you're the one receiving the Friend Request, you can follow these steps to add someone to a list as you accept the request:

1. **From the Friend Request menu, click Confirm.**

   This adds the person as a friend. The Confirm button changes to a Friends button.

2. **Click the Friends button that appears.**

   A menu appears with some options about News Feed, in addition to lists you may want to add the friend to.

3. **Click the list you want to add this person to.**

   You may need to select Add to Another List to find the list you want.

If at any point you remember, *Hey, I meant to add So-and-So to the Whatchamacallit list,* simply visit that person's Timeline and click the button that says Friends at the lower-right of the cover photo. The menu covered in the preceding steps appears, which you can use to add So-and-So to the right list.

Groups

Groups are, in many ways, a more public version of Friend Lists. Instead of your friends not knowing which list they're on, friends are always notified when they're added to a group. In turn, they can add their friends to the group if they think the information shared there is relevant to them. Groups are extremely useful for sharing information that only a specific group of people might care about. For example, a funny video from a family gathering that perhaps only members of your crazy family will understand is a good candidate to be shared via a family group. I cover Groups in great detail in Chapter 9.

News Feed options

In addition to News Feed views, you can use News Feed options to help you control which friends' posts you see when you log in to Facebook. For example, if one of your friends changes her profile picture back and forth between two photos all week long, it might start to clutter up your News Feed. Similarly, I've heard lots of complaints about reading political screeds you disagree with during the election season. From your News Feed and from your friends' Timelines, you can control how much you see of your friend in your News Feed. You can also be very specific, talking about the sort of posts you want to see from them (Yes to photos, No to status posts, for example). Chapter 7 covers controlling your News Feed and which posts you see from which people in great detail.

Following

Occasionally, next to the Add Friend button on someone's Timeline, you'll see an additional button named Follow. Following people on Facebook is a way of getting updates from them in your News Feed without actually becoming their friend. Usually people follow people like journalists or public figures because they don't really want to expose their posts to someone who, let's face it, doesn't really know them.

Following someone is as easy as — actually, it's easier than — adding someone as a friend. Navigate to that person's Timeline and click the Follow button. To unfollow her, click that same button (it now says Following) to open a menu of options. Select the Unfollow option (the last item on the menu).

If you're someone who plans on posting lots of public updates or are a public figure (locally or nationally), you can allow people to follow you instead of becoming your friend (they'll also be able to add you as a friend, but you won't have to accept their requests for them to see your posts). Follow these steps to allow people to follow you:

1. **Click the upside-down triangle in the upper-right corner of the big blue bar on top.**

   A menu of options appears.

2. **Select the Settings option.**

   The Account Settings page appears, which has a menu running down the left-hand side.

3. **Select Followers from the left menu.**

   The Follower Settings page appears.

4. **Check the box labeled Turn On Follow.**

   Congrats! People can now follow your public posts. Once you opt into this feature, more settings appear on the page. These settings allow you to specify how followers can find and interact with your Timeline. This is also where you can connect a Twitter account so your tweets will also be imported to Facebook.

Unfriending

It happens to everyone: After a while, you start to feel like a few people are cluttering up Facebook for you. Maybe you just feel like you have too many friends, or maybe you and a friend have legitimately drifted apart. Maybe you had a big falling-out and just need a break. Don't worry; Facebook friendships are not set in stone. You can *unfriend* just like you friend people.

To unfriend someone, do the following:

1. **Go to the person's Timeline.**

2. **Click the Friends button.**

   A menu appears that is for assigning people to Friend Lists. The last item in this list is Unfriend.

3. **Click the Unfriend link.**

   A window pops up asking if you're sure you want to remove this friend.

4. **Click the Remove from Friends button.**

   Take a moment of silence. Okay, that was long enough.

People aren't notified when you unfriend them, but people who care about you (that is, family, close friends) have a tendency to notice on their own that, hey, you're not in their list of friends anymore. This can sometimes lead to awkwardness, so it might be worth using your privacy settings to further limit these people's knowledge of your life *before* you unfriend them.

Lots of people go through periodic friend-cleaning. For example, after changing jobs or moving, you may notice that you want to keep in touch with some people from that chapter in your life; others, you just don't. Unfriend away.

Chapter 7

Keeping in Touch with News Feed and Timelines

*R*eaching out to *all* the friends you care about to find out what's going on in their lives is a lot of work. That's one of the reasons why, in a pre-Facebook world (talk to a 14-year-old — he won't believe such a thing existed) people frequently lost touch with friends as they moved through their lives. Calling each friend once a week, or even once a month, was time-consuming. In this happy, shiny, post-Facebook world, however, keeping in touch with friends is much easier.

The main way people keep in touch on Facebook is through News Feed, the constantly updating list of stories about content people are posting to their Timelines. I talk about News Feed at length in this chapter, and also about the ways you interact with what you see there. News Feed isn't just about reading the posts you see there; it's also about comments, likes, and the occasional foray to visit a friend's Timeline. Additionally, if you're ever feeling a bit nostalgic, Friendship Pages is a virtual scrapbook that may just bring tears to your eyes.

Your Daily News . . . Feed

News Feed is the centerpiece of your Home page. When you log in to Facebook, you see the familiar blue bar on top and the left sidebar, but mostly you see News Feed.

So what is News Feed? It's primarily a collection of stories by and about your friends. If that doesn't clarify things, here are some definitions for the definition.

- ✔ **Collection:** Depending on the number of friends you have and how often you (and they) use Facebook, the little robots at work creating News Feed may show you different things. You may see everything your friends have done or shared, or you may see only a fraction of your friends, and only a fraction of the things they do and share. Luckily, the robots are open to suggestions and there are lots of ways to change and influence what you see.

- ✔ **Stories by your friends:** Most of your News Feed will be posts people have made to their Timelines. Things like people updating their status and posting photos, links, and videos. These are things your friends actively want to share with you, so Facebook puts them right on your Home page.

- ✔ **Stories about your friends:** Lots of this book is dedicated to all the things you can *do* on Facebook. You can add friends, like Pages, and RSVP to events. These sorts of actions that your friends may take also appear as stories in News Feed.

You may wander out to the front step in your robe and slippers every morning, searching for the paper to let you know what's happened in the world. Many people log in to Facebook first thing in the morning to find out what their friends have been up to since they last checked. News Feed is like a newspaper centered around you and your friends.

Your News Feed may also include public posts from people you follow or Pages you like.

Anatomy of a News Feed story

Figure 7-1 shows a sample News Feed story. In this case, it's a status update from a friend.

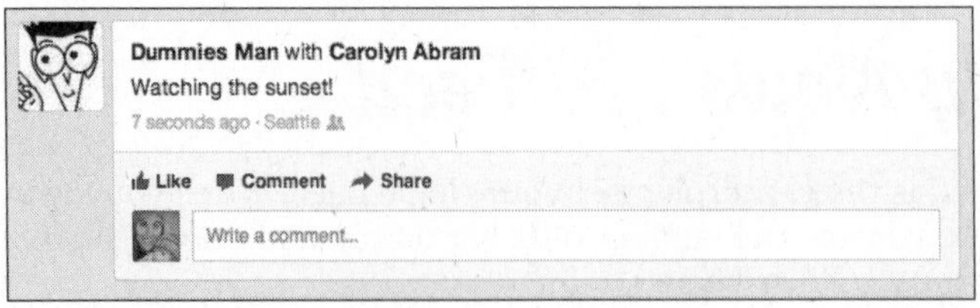

Figure 7-1:
Just your
average sta-
tus update.

> **Dummies Man** with **Carolyn Abram**
> Watching the sunset!
> 7 seconds ago · Seattle 👥
>
> 👍 Like   💬 Comment   ➡ Share
>
> Write a comment...

Even in this tiny example, there are six significant parts of the story:

- **Name and profile picture:** The first part of any story is who it's about or who wrote it. Both the name and picture are links to that person's Timeline. In addition, if you hover your mouse over a person's name, you'll see a miniaturized preview of the person's Timeline and buttons to message him and give him gifts.

  Hovering your mouse over any bolded text in a News Feed story generates a preview for a Timeline, Page, or interest with specific buttons for adding friends, liking, or subscribing.

- **Content:** In Figure 7-1, it's the actual status, but depending on the content, this might be a preview of an article, or a video, or a photo album. It could also be a location where someone has *checked in,* or marked her location via GPS, using her phone. The content is the part of the story that is the most important.

- **Tags:** Tags are a way of marking who is with you when you post something to Facebook. I'm using it here to include any of the additional info that may be appended to a post — location information, information about things you're doing, thinking, or feeling. Tags in posts are bolded. You can hover your mouse over these tags to view more info about that person, Page, place, or thing.

- **Timestamp:** The little gray text at the bottom of the post tells you how long ago this post was added. In posts about photos, the timestamp often appears at the top of the post instead of the bottom.

- **Privacy Info:** The gray icon next to the timestamp represents whether your friend has shared this post with everyone (Public), just friends (Friends), or some other group of people (Custom). Hover over the icon to see who else can see the post.

- **Like, Comment, and Share:** These links allow you to interact with your friends about the content they've posted. In addition, you can see how many people have already liked a post, and you can see any comments that have been made beneath the post itself. Clicking Share allows you to repost that content to your Timeline so your friends can see it in their News Feeds. In Figure 7-1, no one has yet liked or commented on the post.

Common story types

News Feed is made up of all sorts of stories. Although the basic anatomy is the same, here are some of the common story types you might encounter:

- **Status updates:** The status update post appears in Figure 7-1. Status updates are the short little posts that your friends make about what's going on in their lives.

✔ **Links:** Figure 7-2 shows a post sharing a link. This is one of the chief ways I get my news: Friends share links to articles, and the previews are so interesting to me I have to read the whole article. Click the links (or the article's title) to go to the articles.

✔ **Photos:** Figure 7-3 shows a post about photos. When people add photos or are tagged in photos, it creates this type of post, with information about who was tagged and a sample of the photos that were added. Click the photos to see bigger versions and browse the entire album.

Figure 7-2:
Use your
status to
share links
to articles.

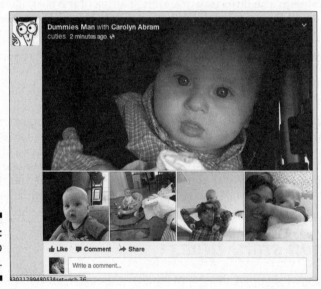

Figure 7-3:
A photo
story.

✔ **Videos:** Figure 7-4 shows a video story. Clicking the Play button opens the video viewer overlay where the video will begin to play. Videos from other sites, such as YouTube, often play right there in your News Feed.

Figure 7-4:
A video
story.

✔ **Timeline Posts:** Figure 7-5 shows a Timeline post story between two friends. The first person wrote the message on the second person's Timeline.

Figure 7-5:
A Timeline
post
between
friends.

You see Timeline post stories only when you're friends with both of the people involved. You won't see stories about a friend posting on a non-friend's Timeline.

✔ **Group and event posts:** When people post to a group or event you're a member of, it may show up in your News Feed. These stories look very similar to the Timeline posts; the second friend's name is simply replaced with the group or event name.

✔ **Check-ins/Check-in tags:** A check-in is something that you can do from either your mobile phone or the Share box on News Feed or Timeline. It allows you (or your friends) to use GPS to mark, on Facebook, where you are. Check-ins are often accompanied by mobile photo uploads or status updates. For more about check-ins, see Chapter 12.

✔ **Likes:** Like stories are usually just quick little stories that let you know what Pages your friends have liked recently. The Pages are linked so you can click right through to check them out yourself.

✔ **Read/Watch/Listen:** Certain services and websites, such as the book-reading site Goodreads, may be allowed to automatically post specific actions people take on their site to Facebook. See Chapter 14 for more information about how these applications work. Figure 7-6 shows an automated News Feed post from Goodreads.

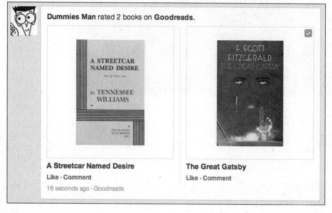

Figure 7-6: What are your favorite books?

✔ **Friendships:** Friendship stories might be about just two people becoming friends or about one person becoming friends with lots of different people.

✔ **Changed cover and profile pictures:** These stories often look very similar to a regular photo story. Click through to look at the new photos on your friends' Timelines in their full-sized glory.

✔ **Events:** Stories about events (usually letting you know which friends have RSVPed *yes* to an event) include a link to the event, so if you're looking for someplace to go, you can say *yes,* too. Only public events show up here, so if you've added a private event, don't worry about people who weren't invited seeing it in News Feed.

✔ **Most Shared:** If you follow certain Pages that post a lot of content and many of your friends share and reshare that content, you might find these sorts of compiled story in your News Feed. A sample is shown in Figure 7-7. Because I follow three different news sources *(NPR, The Economist,* and *The New York Times),* I can hover my mouse over any of their icons to see the most shared stories from their respective Pages.

✔ **Sponsored and suggested:** Suggested and sponsored stories are ads. Ads are what keep Facebook free to use, so there's no way to remove them. These ads are hopefully relevant to you and your life and may even help you find Pages or services you find interesting.

Figure 7-7:
Check out
the most
shared
articles from
your favorite
publications.

Adjusting News Feed

News Feed is designed to learn about what you like and who you care about and to show you stories accordingly. Of course, there are limits to how well a machine can figure these things out, so a number of tools are at your disposal to help you see more of what you like, and less of what you don't.

News Feed views

News Feed takes up the bulk of your Home page. To the right of News Feed is a skinnier column where you may see reminders or ads. In addition, at the top of that right column is the News Feed menu where you can choose to see different News Feed *views*. Each view of News Feed allows you to control who and what appears in that view. To expand the News Feed menu, click the down-pointing arrow at the bottom of the box that's labeled News Feed. Figure 7-8 shows an expanded News Feed menu.

Figure 7-8:
The News
Feed menu
lets you
select
different
views.

	News Feed	
★	Close Friends	5
👥	All Friends	20+
♫	Music	
🎮	Games	
📰	Following	20+
🕐	Most Recent	3
🔤	Groups	3
	See All...	

Much like the menu option in your left sidebar, the views of News Feed may appear in a different order depending on your own Facebook habits. You may also have to click the See All option at the bottom of the News Feed menu to view all your options:

- ✔ **All Friends:** News Feed doesn't necessarily show you all your friends. The program pays attention to the stories you seem to care about most and over time culls stories from people you aren't as close to. If you do want to look at what *everyone* is up to, you can view All Friends.

- ✔ **Close Friends:** The Close Friends view is pretty much the opposite of the All Friends view. While News Feed tries to show you the people you care about most, it also tries to update fairly constantly, so it may show you posts from people who are a little less close to you. Additionally, certain story types might not appear in News Feed from close friends; for example, a photo story about a less close friend may show up in News Feed over a story about a close friend RSVPing to an event. The Close Friends view of News Feed shows you just stories from your closest friends. While looking at this view, you can also edit which friends belong on the Close Friends list from the On This List section on the right side of the page.

- ✔ **Following:** When you like a Page, you automatically start *following* its posts, which means the posts that Page makes may appear in your News Feed. In addition, certain public figures may enable the capability for you to follow their posts without becoming their friend. This view of News Feed just shows you posts from the people and Pages you follow.

- ✔ **Photos/Music/Games (not all pictured in Figure 7-8):** These options each show you just one *type* of story. A view of only photos, or only stories related to music your friends are listening to or like, or only stories related to games you and your friends may be playing.

- ✔ **Most Recent:** This view of News Feed is sorted solely by how recently something happened. Normal News Feed tends to show you the newest things at the top, but may show you something that happened a little further back in time if it thinks this will be particularly interesting to you. The Most Recent view shows you only the latest happenings with your friends.

- ✔ **Lists:** Chapter 6 goes over the process of creating and using Friend Lists. These groupings of your friends appear in your News Feed menu so you can focus just on stories from your high school friends, or from your family, or from any other list you've created.

Hiding stories

While you can use News Feed views to look at a different version of News Feed, you can also influence what News Feed shows you by hiding stories you don't like. Hiding stories (and subsequently hiding all stories from certain people) sends a signal to News Feed that it will try to learn from. If you're constantly hiding stories about people checking in to locations, it will stop showing you so many of those stories. Hiding stories also comes in handy if there's a single story that you find annoying and you just don't want to look at anymore.

To hide a story, follow these steps:

1. **Hover your mouse over the story you want to hide.**

   A small gray downward-pointing arrow appears in the upper-right corner of that story.

2. **Click the gray arrow.**

   A menu of options appears: Hide, Report/Mark as Spam, Follow Post.

3. **Select Hide.**

   The story immediately disappears and is replaced with two lines of text. There are two links in bold: **Unhide** and **Hide All Stories from *<Friend Name>*.**

4. **(Optional) If you realize you actually do want to see a story, click the Unhide link.**

   The story reappears in your News Feed.

5. **(Optional) If you never want to see this person's stories appear in your News Feed, click the link to Hide All Stories.**

If you choose to hide people from your News Feed entirely, there may come a day when you want to unhide them. To do so, follow the preceding steps on any story in News Feed. After you have hidden all stories from a friend, a link appears to Edit News Feed Options. Click this link to bring up a list of all the people and Pages you've hidden from News Feed. Scroll through the list and click the X next to any name you no longer want hidden (in other words, click X next to names you'd like to see in News Feed again). Click Save when you're done.

Settings for friends

Whenever you add a friend, you start seeing some of that friend's updates in your News Feed. And depending on the friend, what you see about him might be perfect. But that "depending on" is a pretty big "depending." You might like one friend's statuses but hate seeing photos of her baby all the time. You might feel like someone else is posting way too often and your News Feed is cluttered with his constant status updates. Or you might want to make sure you don't miss a single thing your best friend does. You can actually control these settings from a friend's Timeline.

To adjust News Feed settings for a friend, follow these steps:

1. **Go to her Timeline.**

   You can get there using Search or by clicking her name anywhere you see it around the site. Once you're on your friend's Timeline, look for the button on her cover photo that says Friends.

2. **Click the Friends button.**

   A menu of options appears. By default, the Show in News Feed option is selected. You can remove your friend from News Feed entirely by selecting Show in News Feed, which will remove the check mark. Assuming you want to see something from your friend, though, proceed to Step 3.

3. **Select Settings from the menu.**

   The News Feed settings menu appears, asking which updates you want to see from that person. You can control what you see by both quantity and type.

4. **Decide how much you want to see from your friend.**

   You can choose to see

   - *All Updates:* All updates really does mean everything, so if your friend is particularly active on Facebook, your News Feed may be overrun with her stories.

   - *Most Updates:* Most friends are set to Most Updates by default. This means News Feed determines which stories from this person to show you.

   - *Only Important:* Important updates are really the big things: an engagement or kid, or maybe a post that seems to be getting a lot of attention from other friends. If you want to see drastically less of a person, this usually does the trick, without the danger of you missing any big news.

5. **Decide whether there are any types of stories you particularly want to see.**

   The bottom part of the News Feed settings menu shows types of stories that appear in News Feed (it may seem similar to the list of stories I detail earlier in this chapter). By default, all types are selected, because News Feed assumes you like variety. Select any story type to remove the check mark next to it.

On Facebook, everyone has the option to turn on *following* for his posts. This means that followers can receive that person's public posts in their News Feed without becoming friends. It is a settings that's handy for public figures and people who might want to share some things very broadly and other things more privately.

Most people don't allow following, which is why when you go to someone's Timeline, you just see a button to add her as a friend. If someone allows followers, you will see an additional button that says Follow. Click that button to start getting that person's posts in your News Feed.

After you're following someone, you can edit News Feed settings for him just as though he were any other friend. Navigate to his Timeline, click the Following button, and select Settings from the menu that appears. This brings up the exact same News Feed settings you see in the preceding section. Make your choices about quantity and type of posts you want to see.

Additionally, when you like a Page, you automatically start following its posts as well. Unlike following a regular Timeline, you either get updates from Pages or you don't. From a Page's Timeline, hover over the Liked button to bring up a menu of options. By default, the Show in News Feed option is checked. Select it again to uncheck it and prevent stories from that Page from appearing in your News Feed.

Allowing followers

You have the option of adding a Follow button to your own Timeline to enable non-friends to receive your public updates in their News Feeds:

1. **Open the Account menu by clicking the small down-pointing arrow in the big blue bar on top.**

2. **Select Settings from the menu that appears.**

   The Settings page appears. Items on the left side of this page allow you to edit different types of settings.

3. **Select Followers on the left side of the page.**

   The Followers section of the Settings page appears.

4. **Select the check box to Turn On Follow.**

   A series of other settings related to being followed appear:

   - *Follower Comments:* Here you can control which people can comment on your posts.

   - *Follower Notifications:* Choose which people interacting with your posts generate notifications.

   - *Username:* Set up a username so people can quickly type a URL into their browsers and go straight to your Timeline.

   - *Twitter:* If you already use Twitter to post short updates, you can automatically import them into Facebook here.

If you had previously turned off the capability for your Facebook Timeline to be found via search engines like Google or Bing, you'll see an additional setting here called Follower Search. Checking this box turns back on your capability to be found in searches people do outside of Facebook.

Ticker

If your browser window is wide enough to support the expanded sidebar on the left, when you are on your Home page, you may see *ticker stories* appear right above the Chat search box. Ticker stories are the latest happenings with your friends (and Pages). They may show up in your News Feed or they might not; it's simply another way for Facebook to show you up-to-the-minute news.

Hover your mouse over a ticker story to expand a preview of the story, as shown in Figure 7-9. The preview has most of the same information as a typical News Feed story, including links to like, comment, or share the story.

Figure 7-9:
An expanded ticker story.

Good Timelines Make Good Neighbors

Your News Feed pulls posts that your friends make into one place so you can read them all at once. But sometimes you want to read all about just one person. Fortunately, all their posts have been collected on their Timelines. Figure 7-10 shows a sample Timeline. Timelines are covered in detail in Chapter 4, but it's worth talking about them again here, not just as something you have on Facebook, but as something your friends have on Facebook.

The Timeline is kind of like a News Feed all about one person. The links, videos, photos, and statuses she's posted all appear here, organized from newest to oldest by year and month, as well as posts her friends have left for her.

Figure 7-10:
Timeline,
a digital
scrapbook
of Facebook
activity.

People post on their own Timelines with different intentions and frequencies (and subsequently, wind up appearing in your News Feed in varying amounts). Here are some of the types of information different people may tack up on the Timeline:

- **Major life milestones:** Timelines come with specially allocated spaces for the big stuff: a recent move, a college graduation, a new job, or a wedding engagement. People can add past milestones at any time.

- **Detailed account:** On the other end of the extreme, you get people who tell the stories of their lives through the sum of all the little things. These are the friends who post to their Timelines about their daily activities, thoughts, feelings, and plans. You know when they're relaxing at home, and when they're out to lunch; you know when they're about to leave work, and when they get stuck in traffic. You know when they have a piece of popcorn stuck between two teeth, and you'll be relieved to know when they get it out.

- **Something to share:** Some people reserve their Timelines as a place to disseminate generally useful or enjoyable information to their friends. These people may post a link to an article they read or upload interesting mobile photos. They post news articles or write detailed accounts of things that just happened to them that others would find useful to know.

- **Meet up:** Some people use their Timelines as a way to meet up with friends. They post when they're hanging out at a park or planning to visit a new city. If a friend is nearby and happens to read the post, the two of them can have a serendipitous adventure together.

- **Go public:** You may see promotional posts on the Timelines or Pages of celebrities or brands. Bands may remind their fans about an upcoming tour or album release. A company may let people know about an upcoming contest in which fans may want to participate.

Timelines wind up being one of the places you are most likely to reach out to a friend. Usually leaving a Timeline post or a message that is visible on a Timeline is a way of tapping a friend on the shoulder to remind him you're there. Sometimes people have entire conversations on each other's Timeline.

To post on your friend's Timeline, follow these steps:

1. **Go to her Timeline.**

   Unless she has changed her Privacy settings, she has a Share box at the top of her Timeline, just as you have in yours.

2. **Click the type of post you want to leave.**

   You can post just text by clicking into the text box that says Write Something. You can click Photo to post a photo or video.

3. **Type your comment to your friend.**

4. **(Optional) Add any tags or location information to your post using the appropriate icon at the bottom of the Share box.**

5. **When you're done, click Post**.

Although there aren't any rules about when you can or can't post on someone's Timeline, one convention that has evolved over time is the Happy Birthday Timeline post. Because people get reminded of birthdays on Facebook, it's pretty easy to pop on over to your friend's Timeline and write a quick "Happy Birthday!" in honor of his day. It makes for a pretty sweet day on the receiving end as well.

Unlike the posts you write for your own Timeline, you don't have specific privacy controls on the posts you leave on friends' Timelines. They may be seen by mutual friends (in their News Feeds) or by someone visiting your friend's Timeline. If you're worried about who's going to see what you're writing, you may be better off sending a private message.

Sharing Is Caring

You've probably noticed the word *share* being used a lot on Facebook. In addition to the Share box at the top of your News Feed and Timeline, Facebook has a specific Share feature, designed to make it easy to post and send content that you find both on Facebook and on the web.

Perhaps you've already noticed the little Share links all over Facebook. They show up on albums, individual photos, events, groups, News Feed stories, and more. They help you share content quickly without having to copy and paste.

If you're looking at content on Facebook that you want to show someone, simply click the Share link near it. This opens a pop-up window with a Share box inside, as shown in Figure 7-11.

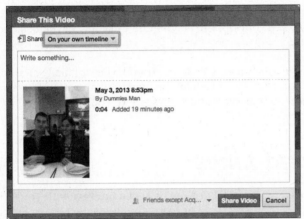

Figure 7-11: Share here.

The Share box has a drop-down menu for choosing where you want to share the content. You can share

- ✔ **On Your Own Timeline:** This option posts the content to your Timeline the same way you post a link or a photo from your Share box. This means it will go into your friends' News Feeds as well.

- ✔ **On a Friend's Timeline:** This option is the same as copying and pasting a link into a post you leave on your friend's Timeline (but it's much easier than all that copy/paste nonsense).

- ✔ **In a Group:** This option allows you to post the content to a group you're a member of. You can find more about sharing with groups in Chapter 9.

- ✔ **On a Page You Manage (for Page owners only):** If you're the admin of a Page — a Timeline for non-people — you can share things as a post from your Page.

- ✔ **In a Private Message:** This accomplishes the same thing as copying and pasting a link into a message to a friend. In other words, only the friend you send it to will see the link, whereas sharing via the Timeline means anyone viewing your friend's Timeline can also see the link. I talk about messages in Chapter 8.

If you're choosing to share on your own Timeline, you can click the privacy drop-down menu next to the Share button to set privacy on the post.

After you choose how you want to share the item, you can write something about what you're sharing. If you're sharing an article, you can edit the preview that appears in the post. The Share box shows you the preview, and you can hover over the headline and teaser text to highlight them. Click the highlighted text to begin editing the preview. You can also choose a thumbnail to accompany most shared links. Use the arrow keys next to the words Choose a Thumbnail to see your options. If you don't like any of them, select the No Thumbnail box.

If you click Share on a friend's post, the friend who originally shared it is given a credit. So if you reshare an article, the post that your friends see will say Via *<Friend's Name>* so that everyone knows where you found it.

Comments and Likes

In addition to leaving a Timeline post, you can interact with your friends on Facebook by commenting on or liking the things they post. Frequently, people post things that you want to respond to. You may read an article they posted and want to respond to the viewpoint with one of your own. Their photos may be so beautiful that you just have to tell them. To comment on anything on Facebook, follow these steps:

1. **Click Comment.**

   The comment box expands. Frequently, this box is already expanded, in which case you can simply go on to Step 2.

2. **Click in the text box that appears.**

3. **Type what you want to say.**

4. **When you're finished, press Enter.**

Frequently, comment *threads,* or a series of comments, can become like an ongoing conversation. If you're responding to someone who commented above you, type the @ symbol (Shift+2) and start typing the name of the person you want to respond to. You'll be able to select her name from an autocomplete list that appears as you type.

After you comment on something, you'll be notified about subsequent comments so that you can keep up on the conversation. If you decide, on second thought, that maybe you didn't really want to say that thing, you can always delete your comment by hovering your mouse over it and clicking the X that appears. You can do the same when someone comments on something you've posted and you don't like what she says.

Liking

Sometimes, a status or photo or link is just good. You might not have a brilliant comment to make, or you might just feel a little lazy. A great example of this is news about someone's engagement. That's awesome, you might think. And then you look and notice about 50 comments saying simply, "Congrats!" Because, while the engagement is empirically good, there's not much to say beyond "Congratulations" or "I'm so happy for you" or "Mazel Tov!" That's where liking comes in. Liking is just a fast way for you to let your friends know that you're paying attention and you like what you're seeing.

To like something, simply click the word *Like* below or next to the item. Your friend will be notified that you like it. If you didn't mean it, really, click Unlike and your like will be taken away.

Liking Pages

You can like almost anything on Facebook. You can like a photo or a status; you can even like a comment on a photo or status. But there's a slight difference between liking this sort of content and liking Pages.

Pages are sort of official Profiles that companies, bands, and public figures make to represent themselves on Facebook. They mostly work like Timelines (the key differences are covered in Chapter 13), except instead of friending or following Pages, you like Pages.

This sort of liking has one big implication you should be aware of. It means you may start seeing posts and updates from the Page in your News Feed, alongside stories from your friends. These sorts of updates can be really interesting and cool if you're into the particular company or brand (for example, Old Spice Guy or *The New York Times*). If they start to bother you, you can always hide that Page from your News Feed.

Commenting, liking, and sharing across the Internet

If you're a reader of blogs, you may notice that the Comment and Like links and icons appear in lots of places. For example, at the top of blog posts on Jezebel, a Gawker Media blog, a little Like button counts the number of people who have liked any particular post, as shown in Figure 7-12.

Figure 7-12:
Like this
post? Let
the blog
authors
know.

You can like posts on any website you're viewing, and those likes will be recorded on your Timeline and may appear in your friends' News Feeds. Through *Social Plugins,* Facebook allows other website developers to enable certain Facebook features like the Like button on their own websites. If you're currently logged in to Facebook, you may start noticing these buttons all over the Internet. This is a really quick way to let your Facebook friends know about the most interesting content you've come across online.

Other websites have Share links that generate the same Facebook Share box that you find on Facebook itself. So from an entirely separate website, you can choose to post to a friend's Timeline, your own Timeline, to a group, or to a message thread.

Similarly, some blogs use Facebook comments as their primary commenting system. Figure 7-13 shows an example from TechFlash, a technology blog.

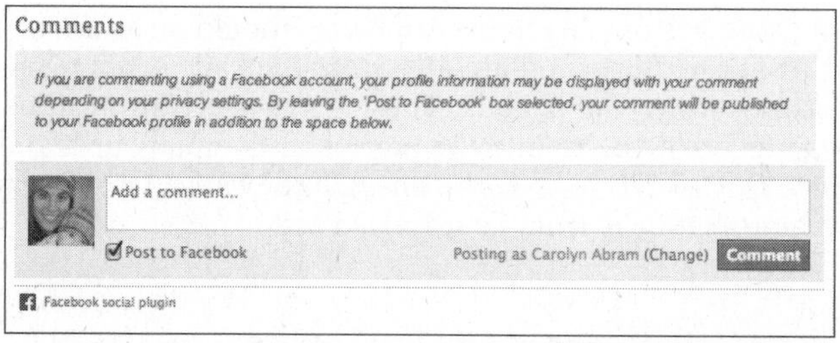

Comments

If you are commenting using a Facebook account, your profile information may be displayed with your comment depending on your privacy settings. By leaving the 'Post to Facebook' box selected, your comment will be published to your Facebook profile in addition to the space below.

Add a comment...

☑ Post to Facebook   Posting as Carolyn Abram (Change)   [Comment]

Facebook social plugin

Figure 7-13:
Care to
comment?

The preview in Figure 7-13 should look familiar: It's you, your Timeline picture, and a space for you to add a comment. It's just not on Facebook; it's on a different website. The way you comment is exactly the same, and in this case, you can choose whether you want your comment to be posted back to your Facebook Timeline by selecting or deselecting the Post to Facebook box.

Tracking the Past with Friendship Pages

After you've been on Facebook for a while, you'll likely find that you've littered your closest friends' Timelines with posts, tagged photos, and invitations. Facebook offers a quick way to see all the communication you've shared with an individual friend over time with the Friendship Page feature.

A Friendship Page collects the Timeline posts and replies you've shared with a friend, photos in which you're both tagged, a listing of event invitations to which you've both responded, and the list of mutual friends you share. The Friendship Page even supplies a default cover photo and profile picture. It's basically a version of Timeline that's about two people, instead of one person.

To see the Friendship Page you share with one of your friends, follow these steps:

1. **Navigate to your friend's Timeline by entering his name in the Search box or clicking on his name wherever you see it.**

2. **From his Timeline, click the gear icon in the lower-right corner of his cover photo.**

3. **Click See Friendship in the drop-down menu that appears.**

   Facebook automatically generates the Friendship Page, as shown in Figure 7-14. It looks much like your personal Timeline, including a cover photo and profile picture (you can actually edit the cover photo if you'd like). Posts you've left for each other or tagged each other in appear from newest to oldest in the right-hand column. Mutual friends, photos in which you both appear, and Pages you both like appear in the left column.

Figure 7-14:
The Story
of Us.

Giving gifts to Facebook friends

If you pay attention to reminders about your friends' birthdays, you may notice small links to give your friends gifts. Facebook Gifts have been around in many forms over the years. Right now, they specialize in making it easy to give your friends real gifts without troubling you with the addressing/mailing/shipping part of the process.

Click the prompts or the Give Gift button on your friend's Timeline to open the gift shop window. There, you can browse through gift options by type. You can give either

✔ Digital gifts like gift cards that will be delivered via e-mail.

✔ Real gifts, in which case Facebook will take care of contacting your friend for a shipping address.

After you select a gift, you can choose an e-card to accompany delivery, as well as a date on which you'd like to notify your friend. You can also choose for a post to be made to your friend's Timeline about the gift. When you post a gift to your friend's Timeline, your mutual friends may see it in their News Feeds.

Gifts are a fun option to have, but don't feel obligated to give gifts! A Happy Birthday post on someone's Timeline is often celebration enough. If you were thinking of sending a gift anyhow, though, consider Facebook Gifts a way of doing it more easily.

Chapter 8

Just between You and Me: Facebook Messages

In This Chapter

▶ Realizing how Facebook's messaging systems differ from other systems

▶ Discovering how to send messages to friends

▶ Chatting with friends instantly

Chances are that you're someone who communicates with other people online. You may use e-mail all the time or use instant messaging programs like AIM or Skype. If you have a smartphone, you probably check e-mail and text messages on it as well. Facebook has similar functionality and integrates into all these programs. In other words, Facebook Messages stitches together e-mail, texting, and instant messaging with a Facebook twist.

One special component of Facebook's messaging system as opposed to other systems is that you no longer have to remember e-mail addresses, screen names, or handles. You just have to remember people's names. The other benefit is that your entire contact history with specific people is saved in one place. The basic aspect of Facebook Messages is the more traditional message, so I start there in this chapter. After that, I go over the Inbox and what's special about it compared to your other Inboxes. Then I talk about Facebook Chat before I finish up with a few advanced messaging features like importing e-mail and getting text message notifications set up.

Sending a Message

Figure 8-1 shows the basic New Message window. I generated this one by clicking the Messages shortcut in the big blue bar on top (it looks like two overlapping word bubbles) and clicking the Send a New Message link from the menu. The New Message window then opened.

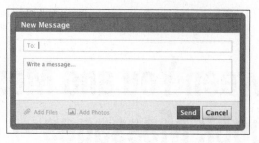

Figure 8-1:
Send a new
message.

This dialog box has only two fields for you to fill out: a To field and a message box where you type the text of your message. If you're used to using e-mail, this may strike you as a little odd because it doesn't have a Cc, Bcc, or subject line.

One trait of e-mail is how much it mirrors the formal letters people used to write, whereas now, we all spend a lot of time writing quick notes to the people we see the most. Except for work messages, most of our e-mails are sent to our spouses ("Don't forget dinner with the Joneses tonight") and our friends ("What are you up to this weekend?"). Given that Facebook is all about friends, and very rarely used for work, you're not very likely to require that subject line.

Messaging friends

To address your message, simply start typing the name of the friend you're messaging into the To field. Facebook autocompletes with the names of your friends as you type. When you see the name you want, highlight it and click or press Enter. You can type more than one name if you want to have a conversation with more than one person at the same time.

You can send a message to people's e-mail addresses if they aren't yet on Facebook (although if they aren't yet, it's truly their loss). Simply type the full e-mail address into the To field. Separate multiple e-mail addresses with commas.

Type your message into the message box. There are no rules around what goes here. Messages can be long or short, fat or skinny, silly or serious — whatever you have to say. If you want to add a link to a website or article to a message, you can copy and paste it into the message box. Facebook then generates a preview of the article so your friend has more info before clicking the link. This is very similar to the way the Share box works when you add a link to a post or status update, except instead of sharing the link with all your friends, you're sharing it with just the people you're messaging.

Two icons beneath the message box (refer to Figure 8-1) represent features that are entirely optional and infrequently used, but just in case, here's what they are:

- ✓ **Add Files:** Much as it does in many e-mail programs, the paperclip icon signifies attaching files to a message. Clicking the icon opens an interface for searching and selecting files from your computer's hard drive. You can attach photos, videos, documents, and so on.

- ✓ **Add Photos:** Though you can attach photos by clicking the Add Files button, if you want Facebook to generate a preview of them for your intended recipients (as opposed to having to download and then open them) use the Add Photos button. This will again open an interface for searching and selecting photos from your computer's hard drive.

When you're done writing your message, just click Send and be on your way. Your friends will receive the e-mail in their Facebook Messages Inbox, and Facebook notifies them with a little red flag on their Home page. Depending on their account settings, they may also receive an e-mail in their e-mail Inbox letting them know about a message in their Facebook Inbox (yes, it's a little redundant).

Messaging non-friends

You can message friends on Facebook or people not on Facebook via their e-mail addresses. You can also message a person who is on Facebook even if she's not a friend (if that person's Privacy settings allow it). This is particularly helpful when you encounter someone on Facebook whom you'd like to say something to, but are not sure whether you want to add her as a friend. For example, you may want to make sure someone is the "right" Jane Smith you went to high school with before you add her as a friend. I've heard lots of stories of lost wallets getting returned to people found through a Facebook message.

Because of the way the Messages Inbox works, messages from non-friends are often treated slightly differently than messages from friends. This means your recipient might not necessarily see your message right away.

You've Got Mail!

Chances are if you send out a message, pretty soon you'll get a reply. Depending on your settings and whether you're logged in to Facebook, when you receive a new message, you see either a new chat window open up (like you're receiving an IM) or a little red flag on your Home page over the Messages icon in the big blue bar on top. Click the flag to open the Inbox preview; then click the message preview to be taken to a full conversation.

On Facebook, the series of messages between two people is a *conversation* or *thread.* This is because when you look at a message, it doesn't stand alone;

rather, it is added to the bottom of all the messages, chats, and texts you have ever sent each other through Facebook.

Anatomy of a conversation between you and a friend

In Figure 8-2, you can see a conversation between my friend Amy and me.

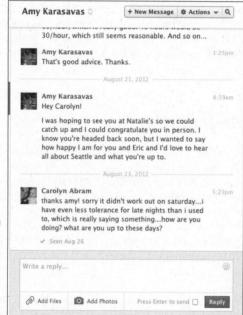

Figure 8-2:
Carolyn
and Amy
converse on
Facebook.

The most important thing to notice is that the most recent message is on the bottom of the page. Unlike News Feed or Timeline, you scroll up to see older messages. In this case, if you keep scrolling up, you'll see an ongoing conversation that started three years ago, when Carolyn and Amy first became Facebook friends.

Although the part of the conversation captured in Figure 8-2 relates to us missing a chance to catch up at a party, topics in this conversation have ranged from team logos to information about various coffee shops where the two of us could meet. Unlike e-mail, which is sorted by *what* you're talking about (the subject line), Facebook only sorts by *whom* you're talking to.

You may not always be messaging a friend from your computer. You may message a friend from your phone or chat via Facebook Chat (which I cover later in the "Chat" section of this chapter). No matter where the message is sent from, it's recorded in this ongoing conversation. Small icons representing a mobile phone, a chat bubble, or an e-mail envelope designate where each message came from, but in reality, that's not important. What's important is *whom* you're talking to.

At the bottom of your conversation, below the most recent message, is the message composer. The message box is the same as the one just covered in the Sending Messages section; however, the To field is missing because whom the message is to is already clear. The conversation is with Amy, so any messages sent are going to Amy.

The smaller options are the same, and there is one additional option at the bottom of the conversation. This is definitely a good one to know: Press Enter to Send.

The Press Enter to Send option (refer to Figure 8-2) allows you to send messages simply by pressing Enter. Some people love this; other people hate it. To turn it on, check the Press Enter to Send box. If you need a paragraph break in whatever you're writing, press Shift+Enter. Deselect the box to turn it off. When it is turned off, a Reply button appears. You can then click that button to send your message.

At the top of your conversation page are three buttons, as shown in Figure 8-2: the New Message button, the Actions button, and a Search button (the magnifying glass).

The New Message button opens a blank conversation with a blank To field and an empty message box.

Clicking the Search icon (the magnifying glass) opens a Search box you can use to search the entire conversation for something. Trust me, after a few back and forths between you and your friend, when you need to remember something she said a while ago, this comes in handy.

In the upper-right corner of the message reply box is a light gray smiley face. Click it to open a menu of the emoticon options Facebook offers. Emoticons are things like smiley faces and hearts.

The Actions button features a drop-down list, as shown in Figure 8-3, with the following options:

- **Mark as Unread:** Choose Mark as Unread to mark the conversation as having unread messages (makes sense, right?). After you choose this option, the main Messages Inbox appears, and the conversation is highlighted in blue.

Figure 8-3:
Actions to
choose for
your con-
versation.

✔ **Open in Chat:** Opening a message thread in Chat allows you to send messages back and forth with your friend while you're browsing Facebook. It opens a small chat window (covered later in this chapter) at the bottom of the screen. You can then chat with your friend even when you leave the Inbox.

✔ **Forward Messages:** Choose Forward Messages to send some or all messages from this conversation to other people. This option allows you to select certain messages via check boxes so that you don't accidentally send the whole conversation to another friend.

✔ **Delete Messages:** Like forwarding a message, this option allows you to delete some (or all) of the messages from any given conversation. After a message is deleted, you can never get it back.

Just because you've deleted a message doesn't mean your friend has deleted it. So if you send some private information and then delete the message, your friend can still see that information unless he deletes it as well.

✔ **Delete Conversation:** Deleting a conversation removes the entire history of messages from your Inbox. This is the digital equivalent of shredding a box of letters.

✔ **Mute Conversation:** Muting is usually used in group conversations that, over time, are more annoying than useful to you. For example, if you're in an ongoing conversation with some old friends to catch up, but then the conversation turns to a local meet-up that you won't be able to make, rather than having chat windows open up or notifications appear each time someone else proposes a new date and time, you can choose to mute the conversation.

Check in every once in a while, and if the conversation grows more relevant, you can unmute it by clicking the Actions button and choosing Unmute from the options.

✔ **Move to Other:** The Other Inbox is for messages that aren't as important as your messages from friends. If a conversation with someone doesn't really deserve top billing among the messages you really care about, you can relocate it to the Other Inbox, which I discuss in the "The Other Inbox" section, later in this chapter.

When you're looking at a conversation in the Other Inbox, this option will be Move to Inbox.

✔ **Archive:** Choose Archive to send your conversation to the archives. Remember, this moves the conversation out of your main Messages Inbox until a new message is sent.

✔ **Report Spam or Abuse:** Unfortunately, like any method of communication, Facebook is not immune to spam, harassment, or abuse. If you see a message that is clearly spam, even if it's from a friend, you can report it to try and prevent the spam from spreading further. After you choose to report something, there are three options:

  • Mark this conversation as spam and move it to the Spam folder.

  • Report individual messages from a hacked friend as spam and delete them.

  • Report conversation participant(s) for harassing or threatening me.

✔ **Keyboard Shortcuts:** This option provides a menu of keyboard shortcuts that do . . . nothing. As far as I can tell, it's a practical joke on the part of Facebook. Well played, Facebook. Well played, indeed.

✔ **Feedback:** This option takes you to the Help Center, where you can submit specific feedback to Facebook for improvements to Messages.

Anatomy of a conversation among many people

You can message more than one person at a time. Doing so creates a new conversation among all the people you message. Everyone can see and reply to the message. So if you send a message to Mike, Jenny, and Steve, a new conversation is created. When you're looking at that conversation, you can see all the messages that have been sent by all the people involved. Figure 8-4 shows a conversation among several friends.

Much like the individual conversation, you can read this exchange from top to bottom, with the most recent message appearing at the bottom of the page. You can scroll up to read earlier messages.

Below the most recent message is a box for replying. The main thing to remember about group conversations is that you cannot reply individually to members of the conversation. When you reply, all members of the conversation see your reply.

Figure 8-4:
A group of friends conversing.

As you're reading, you can see who said what by looking at the names and profile pictures identifying each message. Each message is separated and has a timestamp so you can see when it was sent. At the top of the page, just like with a one-on-one conversation, is the New Message button, the Actions button with a drop-down list, and a Search button for searching through the content of the conversation.

Along with options to mark messages as unread, forward messages, archive messages, delete messages, report spam, and move to the Other Inbox, the Actions drop-down list for group conversations offers a few more options not included for individual conversations:

- ✔ **Create Group:** If you find yourself talking with the same set of people all the time, you may want to create a group for a richer set of options for sharing. Groups make it easier to share and talk about things like links and documents. To learn more about how to use groups for sharing, check out Chapter 9.

- ✔ **Add People:** If you feel that someone has been left out of the conversation, or if you suddenly realize he should be part of the conversation, choose this option to add him. You're asked to enter the name(s) or e-mail(s) of the person you want to add. The person added can see the entire conversation history, even though he wasn't added until the middle of the conversation.

- ✔ **Leave Conversation:** If a conversation isn't interesting to you anymore, choose this option to leave it. If you do leave a conversation, the other people on the thread will see a small notice that you have left.

Inbox

After you're comfortable sending and receiving messages to and from your friends, it's time to find out about the Inbox, where all your messages are collected for easy viewing at any time. Facebook's Inbox is organized a bit differently from traditional e-mail Inboxes. Most significantly, messages you receive from people you aren't friends with and are unlikely to know are separated from the conversations you're having with friends.

To understand how Facebook Messages works, take a look at how your Messages Inbox is organized on the page. First, navigate to the Messages Inbox from your Home page by clicking the Messages icon (it looks like two overlapping word bubbles) on the left menu. You may have to hover your mouse over the left-hand menu to expand it. Figure 8-5 offers a snapshot of the Dummies Man Inbox.

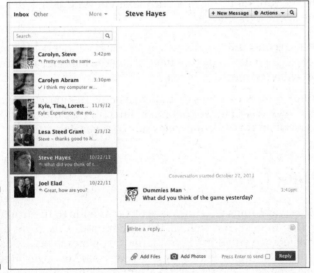

Figure 8-5:
Welcome to
Facebook
Messages.

The main portion of this page, the center area, is where conversations appear. As you click different conversations on the left, the contents of that conversation — messages, photos, links, and files — appear in the main portion of the screen.

The left side of your Inbox displays your messages. Each conversation gets its own line in the Inbox. Like your e-mail Inbox, these conversations are organized from most recent near the top to older ones toward the bottom of the page. As you scroll down, Facebook will continue to load your conversation history right back to the very first message you ever sent on Facebook.

Figure 8-6 shows a close-up of two conversation previews. The bottom one is a conversation among many people. You can see the text of the most recent message and the profile picture of the most recent sender. The top one is a one-on-one conversation with a single friend. On the right side of each is the conversation's timestamp. And below the name of the person or people you're talking to is a preview of what was most recently said.

Figure 8-6:
Conversation
previews
in the
Messages
Inbox.

Carolyn Abram   3:30pm
✓ i think my computer w...

Kyle, Tina, Lorett... 11/9/12
Kyle: Experience, the mo...

When you hover your mouse over a particular conversation, two icons appear in the lower-right corner:

- The **little circular button** allows you to mark a conversation as read or unread. The button appears filled when the message is unread and unfilled when the message is read.

- The **little X icon** allows you to archive a conversation. *Archiving* conversations allows you to move them to a different part of your Inbox until a later time, when they become relevant to you again.

The Other Inbox

Facebook Messages brings your messages from friends to the front of your Inbox. The Other Inbox is for, well, all that other stuff. This might include messages from people you don't know, large group messages, and so on. In many ways, the Other Inbox is exactly like your main Messages Inbox. The conversations are organized by person. Conversations with unread messages are highlighted in blue. When you click through to view a message, you'll see the most recent messages at the bottom, as usual.

You can change your filtering options to adjust how often messages are sent to the Other Inbox. You have two options for filtering messages:

- **Basic Filtering:** This is the default filtering option for your Facebook Inbox. It works by showing you all the messages you receive from friends, as well as the messages you receive from people Facebook thinks you might know. (Facebook determines whom you might know based on factors like mutual friends or schools you both attended.) Messages from people you don't know are sent to the Other Inbox.

✔ **Strict Filtering:** If you find you're getting messages that are effectively junk — you don't really know the people who are sending them, or you don't find the content important or interesting — you may want to consider turning on Strict Filtering, which shows you *only* messages from friends and sends all other messages to the Other Inbox.

You can adjust your filtering choice from the Privacy Shortcuts menu on any page. In the left sidebar, click the lock icon next to your name, which opens the Privacy Shortcuts menu. When you click the Who Can Contact Me? section, you can choose either Basic or Strict Filtering.

If you have a conversation in Other Messages that you want to be more prominent, click into the conversation, click the Actions button to open the drop-down list, and choose Move to Inbox. All the other options are the same as the conversations in your main Messages Inbox.

Searching the Inbox

If you're as popular as I suspect you are, your messages add up over time. And if you don't want to go scrolling through tons of messages to find the one you're looking for, you need a faster way to get to the information you want. That's why at the top of the Messages Inbox, you'll notice a Search box. You can search for people's names or for the content of messages.

For example, say you want to find the address of a park where you're meeting with some friends to play Frisbee and you organized this whole outing through Facebook Messages. You can search for the name of the friend(s) on the conversation. As you do so, Facebook tries to autocomplete your friend's name and shows you snippets of recent conversations with her. Alternatively, you can type *Frisbee* in the Search box and press Enter. When Facebook can't find any messages sent by a person named Frisbee, click the Search Messages link to get a list of results from conversations where the word Frisbee appeared.

Chat

Sometimes you've got something to say to someone, and you've got to say it now. If that someone is not sitting right next to you, try sending her an instant message through Facebook Chat. Chat allows you to see which friends are online at the same time you are and then enables you to send quick messages back and forth with any one of those people, or have multiple simultaneous conversations with different friends.

Facebook doesn't discriminate when it comes to the way you talk to your friends. Whether a message or a chat, it all goes into your conversation history in your Messages Inbox.

You'll find Chat in the bottom-right corner of any page on Facebook.

Receiving and sending chats

Chat is meant to be quick and easy to use. Receiving chats is simply a matter of being online. When a friend sends you a chat, a small window pops up next to the Chat bar in the bottom right of your screen, as shown in Figure 8-7.

Figure 8-7: Someone chatted with you!

To send a chat message back, simply click into the text field at the bottom of the chat window, start typing, and press Enter when you're done. Your message appears below your friend's, just as it does with most IM services. Each new chat window lines up next to the other open ones. You can close those that aren't currently active by clicking the X in the blue bar at the top of the individual chat window.

Because Chat and regular messages are integrated, when you begin a new chat with someone, your chat history is populated with your historical conversations, so your chat window tends to look a lot like a message thread.

To start a new chat with someone, you just need to select his name from the Chat menu. This opens a chat window that you can type in.

Chat options

At the top of each chat window is a blue bar displaying the name of the person you're chatting with and two or three icons. The one you might or might not have is the video icon, which is covered shortly. The two you will definitely have are the gear and X icons.

The X, farthest to the right, simply allows you to close the chat window at any time. Don't worry about losing the contents of your conversation. Everything said is saved in your Inbox.

The gear icon, when clicked, opens a menu of options. These options include the following:

- ✔ **Add Files:** Just like when you're sending a message from the Inbox, you can select this option to search your computer for files you want to share.

- ✔ **Add Friends to Chat:** If you're discussing something with a friend and think that you need the opinion of someone else, you can add her to the chat, which opens a new group chat window.

- ✔ **Turn Off Chat for <*Friend*>:** Friends may be more likely to chat with you when they see that you're online. If any friend in particular is popping up a little too often, you can turn off chat for that individual person. From that point on, she will no longer see you in the Chat menu.

- ✔ **See Full Conversation:** Selecting this option brings you back to the Inbox view of your entire conversation history.

- ✔ **Mute Conversation:** Just like with the Inbox, you may find a chat thread growing annoying or irrelevant. You can mute the conversation to stop being notified whenever someone replies.

- ✔ **Clear Window:** If you find yourself wading through too much history at a time, selecting this option gives you a blank slate of a chat window. This won't delete the contents permanently, though. Your full message history is still saved in your Inbox.

- ✔ **Report as Spam or Abuse:** If you're getting odd messages from a friend promoting something he wouldn't normally promote, there's a chance his account was *phished,* meaning someone who shouldn't have gained access to it. Report the spam messages to protect yourself, your friend, and other users from having the same thing happen to them.

Chatting with a bunch of people

To get a group chat going, follow these steps:

1. **Begin a chat with a friend by selecting her name from the Chat menu.**

   This opens a chat window.

2. **Click the gear icon to open the Chat Options menu.**

3. **Select the Add Friends to Chat option.**

   This opens a text box at the top of your existing chat window.

4. **Type the name of the friend you want to add into this text box.**

   Facebook autocompletes as you type. As soon as your friend's name appears, you can select it. You can add more than one friend at this time if you want.

5. **Click Done.**

   This opens an entirely new chat window for the group conversation. All messages sent in that Chat menu are sent to all participants.

This chat window has an additional icon, the Groups icon of overlapping people. Click this icon at any point to add even more participants to your group chat.

Video Chat

Video Chat is a fairly new addition to Facebook, which is why you may or may not see the video camera icon at the top of each chat window. Facebook's Video Chat is actually powered by Skype, an Internet telephone service. If you see the video icon, you can initiate video chat with a friend. Keep in mind that you can video chat with only one friend at a time. Here's how to begin a video chat:

1. **Begin a chat with a friend by selecting his name from the Chat menu.**

   This opens a chat window.

2. **Click the video icon to begin video chat.**

   If you've already set up video calling, this step begins the call. A pop-up window appears, letting you know that Facebook is calling your friend.

   If you haven't yet used video calling, a pop-up window appears, asking you if you want to set up video calling.

   If you aren't asked to set up video calling, skip to Step 4.

3. **Click Set Up or Install.**

   This initiates a file download. Each web browser and operating system may have slightly different instructions. In general, you need to save the file to your hard drive and run it to complete the setup.

   After the setup is complete, a new pop-up window appears telling you that Facebook is calling your friend. In the future, you'll be able to skip Step 3 and go straight to Step 4 when you want to use Video Chat.

4. **Wait for your friend to pick up.**

   When he does, a video of him appears in a new window above Facebook. A video of you (what your friend is seeing) appears in the upper corner of this window.

5. **To end the call, close the window.**

Video Chat assumes both people have webcams either built in or installed in their computers. If you don't have a webcam, Video Chat isn't really for you.

Group chat

A Facebook group is a way for a group of people to connect and share in the same place on Facebook. Creating and using groups is covered in detail in Chapter 9. But it bears mentioning here that one of the useful features of

Groups is the capability to start message threads and chats with the members of your group.

To start a group chat, follow these steps:

1. **Navigate to the group's page on Facebook.**

2. **On the right side of the group page, click the link that says Message.**

   This opens a window that allows you to select from the group's members.

3. **Select the group members you want to be part of the chat.**

   Click the faces of all the people you want included in the message thread. If you want everyone included, click Select All at the bottom of the window.

4. **Click the Start Chat button.**

   A chat window opens at the bottom of the screen. Use it as you would any chat window.

Anatomy of the Chat menu

The Chat menu is actually built into the left sidebar, which you can expand by mousing over the left side of any Facebook page. (Depending on the width of your web browser, this menu may always be open.) The top part of the left menu is for navigating to parts of Facebook you use most frequently. The bottom part is the Chat menu, shown in Figure 8-8.

Figure 8-8:
The Chat menu.

By default, the Chat menu displays the friends you message and chat with most often, in alphabetical order. A green dot next to their names means they are active on Facebook. A mobile phone icon next to their names means they have downloaded the Facebook app for iPhone or Android and can receive your message on their phones. No icon means they aren't currently logged in or have turned off Chat. Messages you send to them will go to their Messages Inboxes.

At the bottom of the Chat menu is a Search bar. To quickly find the friend with whom you want to chat, or to see if that friend is even online, start typing that friend's name in the Search box at the bottom of the Chat menu. As you type, the list of online friends narrows to only those with names that match what you've typed. After you see the friend you were looking for, click the name to start chatting.

At the bottom of the Chat menu is the gear icon that signifies an Options menu. Here are the three options available for you to adjust your chat experience:

✓ **Chat Sounds:** If Chat Sounds is on (signified by a check mark next to this option), you will hear a sound every time you receive a new chat.

✓ **Advanced Settings:** Selecting this option reveals a pop-up window of options, shown in Figure 8-9. These options help you control who can and cannot see you as online and available in Chat.

Figure 8-9:
Choose who
can chat
with you.

Three options are available here:

• **Turn On Chat for All Friends Except:** This option is selected by default. If there are just a few friends you don't want knowing when you're online, enter their names into the box below this option, and they won't be able to chat with you. Instead, messages from them will go straight to the Inbox.

• **Turn On Chat for Only Some Friends:** This is the option if you really don't want to talk to anyone except your nearest and dearest via Chat. When you select this option, you then enter the names of people or Friend Lists that will be able to see that you're online.

- **Turn Off Chat:** This option means no one will see that you're online or be able to send you instant messages via Chat. Instead, messages sent to you will go to the Inbox.

✔ **Turn Off Chat:** This is the same as the "Turn Off Chat" option found in the Advanced settings. Lots of people like to use Chat some times but not at other times (for example, I turn Chat off when I'm working from home). This option lets you easily toggle Chat on and off.

Messaging on the Go

Facebook integrates its messaging system seamlessly with its smartphone apps. It even has an app just for messaging: Facebook Messenger. You can see the same message three different ways in Figure 8-10. The first is a message in the Message Inbox, the second is in a Chat window, and the third is using the Facebook Messenger app for iPhone.

Figure 8-10: The same conversation, viewed three ways.

Notice that in each view, you see the same conversation, with slight adjustments to allow for the amount of screen real estate you get.

The Facebook Messenger app is pretty simple. It displays the contents of your Inbox: a list of conversations from most recent at the top to oldest at the bottom. You can tap any conversation to open it and read it. When you're looking at a conversation, tap into the text box at the bottom of the screen to open a keyboard for typing a new message.

What's a poke?

Since Facebook began, the most common question I've heard is, "What's a poke?" And since that time, the answer has been, "I don't really know." I can tell you what it *does,* but I can't tell you what it *is;* it can mean something different to everyone. In some cases, poke is a form of flirtation. Other times, poke may mean a genuine *thinking-of-you.* Some people do it just to say, "Hi."

Say your wife pokes you (maybe her poke means, "Take out the trash, honey"). The next time you log in to Facebook, you will receive a notification that you have been poked.

When you click that notification, you're taken to the Pokes page, which once again informs you

that you have been poked by your wife. Next to this information are two options: You can either select Poke Back or click the X. Poking back means she'll see the same notice you got the next time she logs in (except with your name instead of hers). Clicking the X next to the Poke Back option simply removes the notice from the Pokes page. If you sense the potential for an endless loop, you sense right.

To poke someone, go to that person's Timeline. Click the gear icon in the lower-right corner of his cover photo to open an Options menu. Select Poke from that menu. That was it; you just poked him.

To start a new conversation, when you're looking at your Inbox, tap the new message icon (it looks like a pencil inside a box) in the bottom-right corner of the screen. This opens a New Message screen, where you can enter the names of the people you want to message and the message itself. This should feel eerily similar both to sending a text message and to sending a message on Facebook.

If you're using an app like Facebook Messenger on your phone, you will likely be notified on your phone each time you get a new message. You can adjust these settings from the app itself. If you want to know more about using Facebook from your mobile phone, check out Chapter 12.

Chapter 9

Sharing with Facebook Groups

*B*y now, you've probably individually found and linked yourself to your friends. Hopefully, you've also started sharing with them by posting statuses and photos and links, and you're seeing your News Feed fill up with much of the same. All that is great, but as you share certain things, you may find yourself thinking, "Really, only people from work will care about this article" . . . or . . . "Really, only the people in my parents' support group will find this funny." Now, you could elect to use Friend Lists to choose who can see these posts. But chances are, you also want those people to talk about it with you. *Groups* are a way to truly interact with a group of people, almost as though you were sitting in the same room.

Groups can be large or small. They may have very active participants or have many people who just sit back and watch for relevant info. Some groups may involve ongoing forums; others may exist only to achieve a goal (for example, planning a big event), and the conversations will peter out over time. Groups can be open to anyone in the world to join, or they can be more private affairs that require invites to join. This chapter covers how to use the features of groups, as well as the many options that come with using, creating, and managing groups.

Evaluating a Group

When someone adds you to a group, a notification is sent to your Facebook Home page. The next time you log in, you'll see a little red flag over the notifications icon (the globe icon in the big blue bar on top). When you click, it will tell you what the group is and who added you; then you can go check out the group and make sure you want to be a part of it.

When looking at a group, you'll find a lot to pore over, as you can see by the sample group shown in Figure 9-1. Some pieces of the group will look familiar — for example, the Share box and the recent posts from group members in the center of the page. Other parts are unique to groups, such as the photos at the top of the page and the tabs for different sections of the groups.

Figure 9-1:
Checking
out a group.

You can get to any particular group from your Home page by clicking its name in the left sidebar. (Remember, you may have to hover your mouse over the left sidebar to expand it.) Groups you look at frequently should be in the top section; you may have to click the See More link to see a full list of your groups. Click the name of the group you want to visit.

When you first visit a group, before doing anything else, make sure you want to be a part of that group. Although I'd like to think I'd join any group that would have me, I, for example, wouldn't want to join one that's about garnering support for a cause I don't believe in.

Although your notification may explain that you were invited to join the group, these invitations work by adding you to the group until you decide to leave it. It's sort of like saying "RSVP regrets only" on an invitation to a party.

The first thing I look at when I join a group is the group name and who added me. Usually that's enough for me to know if I belong there or not. For example, if a friend from my parenting group adds me to a November/December Parents group, I know I want in. When a more distant friend adds me to the I Love Puppies group, I may do a bit more research to see if I want to be a member.

So, if I'm unsure about wanting to be part of a group, I check out the recent posts in the center of the page. These posts are ones that group members have shared directly with this group. In other words, say that I post a funny photo of my husband mowing the lawn with the baby on his back. If I post it from my Timeline or from my Home page, all my friends will see it. It won't appear in the Recent Posts section of any of my groups. If I post it to my New Moms group, only group members will see it, and it will appear in the group's recent posts section.

Looking at the recent posts tells me a lot about what to expect from a group in the future. Are posts relevant to the group or not? Is there a lot of discussion or not? Am I interested in the posts I'm seeing? These are the sorts of things I think about when I'm deciding whether to stay in a group.

If the group was created only recently, you may not find very many posts yet. You can still learn a bit about the group by checking out the About section. On the right side of the group's page (next to the recent posts) is a box labeled About (see Figure 9-2).

Figure 9-2: About this group.

The About section shows you some of the basics of the group to help you understand what it's for and how it will work:

- ✔ **Privacy:** At the top of the About section is information about the privacy of the group. There are three types of groups:
  - *Open:* Open groups are publicly visible and available for anyone to join. In other words, anyone who uses Facebook will be able to see the posts and the members of that group.
  - *Closed:* Closed groups are only partially visible. Anyone on Facebook can see the name of the group and its members but won't be able to see the posts until becoming a member of the group. People are added to closed groups by other members, or they can request to join it.
  - *Secret:* Secret groups are the most private groups. No one other than those who have been added to it can see that it exists, who its members are, and the posts that have been made. If you're invited to join a secret group and you choose to leave it, you won't be able to add yourself again later on, because you won't be able to find it.
- ✔ **Info:** Any information the group creator enters will appear in the Info section of the group. Usually people use the space to describe what the group is about and how people ought to use it.

✔ **Members:** Next to the word About is the member count. Although the text is in gray, you can click it to be taken to the Members tab and peruse who belongs to the group. If it's a big group that's open and united around a big topic like a political cause, you may not know many of the members. If it's a smaller group united around a real-world, local activity, chances are you know more of them.

After you acquaint yourself with the group, you can decide whether you want to remain a member or leave the group. If you decide you want to leave, follow these steps:

1. **Click the gear icon.**

   It's located on the right side of the page, across from all the different tabs for the group. When you click it, a drop-down menu appears.

2. **Select Leave Group from the drop-down menu.**

   A pop-up window opens, asking if you are sure that you want to leave the group.

3. **Decide whether you want to prevent members of the group from adding you again by selecting or deselecting the Prevent Other Members of This Group from Re-adding You check box.**

   You can leave this check box selected, which means you'll never be able to be added to the group again; or if you think maybe in the future you might want to be part of the group, deselect this check box.

4. **Click Leave Group.**

More often than not, however, you'll usually decide to stay in the group, which actually brings you to the point of sharing and communicating with fellow group members.

If you're considering leaving a group because you're being inundated by notifications about new posts, you can instead just turn off notifications from that group. From the group, click the Notifications button at the top of the page. You can then select whether you want all notifications, notifications about friends' posts, or no notifications.

Sharing with a Group

The whole point of creating or joining a group is to enable communication, so get started communicating! Ways that you can get involved include posting to the group, commenting on others' posts, chatting with group members, and creating files or events.

What's the difference between a group and a Friend List?

That's a great question. Both groups and Friend Lists are used to share information with specific friends. The best way to think about the difference is in terms of who owns the member list.

✔ **Friend Lists** are owned entirely by you: You decide who gets to be on a Friend List. If you're looking at a certain list's view of News Feed, you're choosing to filter posts down to the posts from a specific group of people. If you don't want to see someone's posts when you look at your Close Friends feed, you can remove that person from the Close Friends list.

✔ **Groups,** on the other hand, are collectively owned. Generally speaking, all members can add other members, and all members can be equal contributors to the Recent Posts section of the group. If you don't like the posts from a group member, you can't prevent those posts from appearing.

The other main difference is that groups tend to have a discussion element. Just like a group of people showing up for a class or public forum or mixer in the real world, people show up in groups to talk about things.

Using the Share box

Posting to the group works the same way as posting from a Timeline or the News Feed. There is a Share box at the top of the Recent Posts section of the page. A few sections of the Share box appear for groups that *don't* appear on Timelines or in News Feeds: Ask Question and Add File.

The important thing to remember is that when you share something from a group, you're sharing it only with the members of that group. And if you're a member of a group, you also need to remember that you may not be friends with everyone in the group. In a big group, you may actually be sharing with many people who typically couldn't see the things you post.

Although the Share box works almost the same way across Facebook, all the options are briefly explained here within the context of groups.

Write Post

Posts are basically like status updates that you share only with the members of a group (unless the group is open, in which case anyone can see your post). You might post an update just to say "Hi" or to start a discussion with group members. To write a post, follow these steps:

1. **Click in the Share box (where it says Write Something at the top of the group page).**

After you click in the box, the Post button appears below the text box along with buttons to indicate where you are and which other Facebook members are with you.

2. **Type whatever you want to say in the box.**

   For the Dummies group, this might be something like "What do people think of the new groups?" or "Does anyone know how I can start group chat?" You can also post a link to a relevant article or website in this space. You can see a post in progress in Figure 9-3.

Figure 9-3:
What's on
your mind?

3. **(Optional) Add location information or tags to the post.**

   Clicking the person icon in the lower-left corner of the Share box allows you to add a tag to others when you write a post. Clicking the location icon allows you to add information about where you are when you write the post.

4. **Click Post.**

   Your post appears in the group, and group members may see it in their notifications and News Feeds.

If you want to share a link, usually some sort of article, video, or other online content that you want the group to see, simply type or paste the complete link to whatever you want to share, along with your thoughts or opinions, in the Share box.

Add Photo/Video

Sometimes, writing a post won't do for the current circumstances. For example, if I want my fellow dummies to know that I received the most recent edition of *Facebook For Dummies,* I could tell them by writing a post to the effect of "Hey, dummies, I got my copy of the new book." Or I could *show* them by posting a photo of my dog reading the new copy. To post a photo to a group, follow these steps:

1. **Click Add Photo/Video at the top of the Share box at the top of the group page.**

   The photo options appear, as shown in Figure 9-4.

2. **Decide whether you want to upload photos or a video or create an entirely new album.**

   Clicking either option expands an interface for selecting photos from your computer's hard drive. When you choose to upload photos, thumbnails are displayed in the Share box, and you can write one post to describe the collection of photos. When you choose to create an album, you're taken to the Create Photo Album interface, where you can add tags and captions to individual photos.

3. **Click Post.**

   The post appears in the group, and all members (depending on notification settings) are notified about your post. They can then comment and like what you're sharing.

If you want to upload a video, choose Upload Photos/Video and then select the video file from your computer's hard drive.

Ask Question

One of the added features of Groups is the Ask Question feature. Questions allow group members to gather information in a more efficient way than simply using a post and then sorting through the comments for the answers. The Ask Question feature mostly works by creating a poll that members can vote on from the Recent Posts section of the group. To ask a question and poll your group, follow these steps:

1. **Click Ask Question in the Share box at the top of the group page.**

2. **Type your question in the Ask Something box.**

3. **Click the Add Poll Options link beneath the text box.**

   This expands the poll options, as shown in Figure 9-5.

4. **Type your first option into the first Add an Option section.**

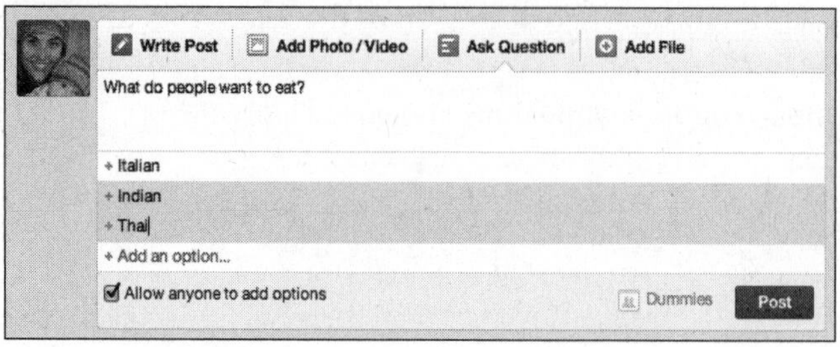

Figure 9-5:
You've got
questions?
Facebook
has
answers.

5. **Add more options until you're finished.**

   Facebook keeps adding more boxes as you fill up these first few, so just stop when you're ready.

6. **Choose whether people can add more options.**

   The Allow Anyone to Add Options check box controls this setting. Allowing this options means people can add more answers to a poll. For example, if before people could choose only Dog or Cat, group members may be able to add Hedgehog as an option. Depending on how big your group is, this choice may or may not be significant.

7. **Click Post.**

   The question then appears in the group and in members' notifications and News Feeds. They will be able to vote, like, or comment on the question.

Add File

Adding files is part of the Files and Docs feature of groups. If you're part of a group that has real-world things to accomplish — for example, a literary magazine to put out or a wedding welcome letter to create with your family — you can add files to help you collaborate on these documents. From the Share box, you can upload files from your computer or, if you use Dropbox (an online file storage and sharing site), from your Dropbox.

I cover the different ways to add and create files in the "Files and Docs" section, later in this chapter.

Reading and commenting on posts

After you create a post or see a post that someone else has created, that's when things really get interesting, because members of the group can start talking about it. On Facebook, that means commenting, liking, and following posts.

One unique feature of posts to Facebook Groups is that you can see who has read those posts. At the bottom of each post, look for a check mark icon.

Next to it, Facebook displays the number of people who have seen that post. If you hover over the number, you will see a list of names. These are the people who went to the group after you posted. It doesn't necessarily mean they've read your post in depth yet.

Below each post are two links of actions you can take:

✔ **Comment:** When you see something you have an opinion on, click Comment below the post and let everyone know. (This action means you'll be notified about all subsequent posts.) Often, you'll see a blank comment box already open beneath a post, just inviting you to chime in.

✔ **Like:** When you like anything on Facebook, the person who created that content is notified that you like it. It's an easy and quick way to say "Good job!" when you don't have an active comment to make.

Depending on your notification settings, you may be following all posts in a group, only ones from friends, or none at all. When you comment on a post or vote on a question, you automatically start following that post. Following a post means you'll be notified every time there's a new comment on that post, which can be awesome if you're actively talking about something with group members, or kind of annoying if there are too many people commenting. If that happens and the notifications are bothering you, you can always unfollow a post by taking these steps:

1. **Hover your mouse over the post you no longer want to follow.**

   A small down arrow appears in the upper-right corner of the post.

2. **Click the down arrow to open a menu of options.**

3. **Choose Unfollow Post.**

Just as you can unfollow a post you previously commented on, you can choose to follow a post you haven't commented on. If you want to read what others have to say, but don't have anything to add at this time, follow the preceding steps for the post you want to follow. Instead of an Unfollow Post option, you will see a Follow Post option. Select that option to be notified every time there's a new comment on that post.

Chat

One of the most exciting features of Groups is the capability to talk in real time with other group members, so you can do something like ask when people are leaving for that Ultimate game.

When you chat with group members, any member of the chat can add more people — even if they aren't in the group — to that chat. The people who are added can see the entire conversation, even parts that happened before they joined in.

To chat, follow these steps:

1. **Click the Message link on the right side of the page.**

   It's actually inside the About section. The link is black, not blue like most links. This pops open a Friend Selector box, as shown in Figure 9-6.

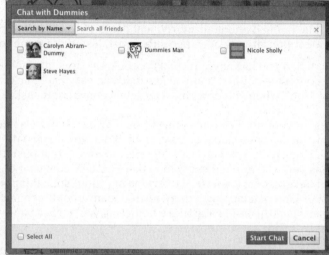

Figure 9-6:
Choose the
group
members
you want to
chat with.

2. **Choose whether you want to chat with all members of the group or just specific people.**

   For example, you might want to ask everyone if there's any interest in meeting for a drink after work, or you might have a very specific question for your two editors. You can start either of these conversations from the Friend Selector box.

3. **After you choose the people you want to talk to, click the Start Chat button.**

   A chat window opens at the bottom of your screen.

If you don't want to be bothered by conversations others start, you can always use the Options menu of the chat window to mute or leave the conversation. For more details on using Facebook Messages and Chat, check out Chapter 8.

Events

Your group may be based around an activity, so Facebook makes it easy for people to plan events for group members, whether it's a game of pick-up or a family reunion. To create an event, follow these steps:

1. **Click the Events tab (it's next to the Members tab underneath the member photos).**

    This takes you to the group's Event Calendar, which displays any upcoming group events.

2. **Click the Create Event button.**

    This opens the Create New Event pop-up window, shown in Figure 9-7. If you've read Chapter 11, about planning events, these fields should look familiar.

Figure 9-7:
Create an
event for
group
members.

3. **Fill out the event details.**

    This includes the event's name, location, date, and time.

    Notice that the privacy of the event is prefilled as the group name. If you want to change the privacy, you can do so by clicking the group name. However, because chances are that you're creating an event from the group because it's a group event, I recommend leaving the Privacy setting alone. By default, that means that only group members will be able to see the event and RSVP to it.

4. **Decide whether you want to invite all group members by selecting or not selecting the Invite All Members check box.**

    Regardless of what you choose, all members will be able to view the event and RSVP. However, if you leave the Invite All Members box selected, when group members are notified about the event, they will be told that you were the one who invited them.

5. **Click Create.**

    This brings you to the event's page, where you can add an event photo and keep track of RSVPs. (I cover this type of event maintenance in detail in Chapter 11.) As the event creator, you're automatically listed as attending. The post appears in the group's recent posts and in members' News Feeds.

To RSVP to a group event, follow these steps:

1. **Click the event's name in the Recent Posts section of the group.**

   This takes you to the Event Home page, which shows you more information about the event, including who has already RSVPed.

2. **Choose Join, Maybe, or Decline.**

   All these options are big blue buttons on the right side of the page. To find out more about how to interact with the event as it draws near, check out Chapter 11.

Files and Docs

Other features that are particularly helpful to groups representing real-world projects are Files and Docs. These are ways to create and share files among group members. *Docs* are more like wikis in that they are able to be edited by all members of the groups. *Files* are more like a file-sharing system that allows people to upload and retrieve files from user to user.

Docs

To create a document that all group members can see and edit, go to the Files tab of the group and click the Create Doc button. This brings you to the New Doc page, where you can enter a title and body text. Some basic formatting options are at the top of the body section, as shown in Figure 9-8. After you enter all your text, click the Create Doc button.

After you create a doc, any member of the group can view it, comment on it as though it were any other post, and also click Edit Doc next to it in order to change it. You can always find docs that have been created by clicking the Files tab. Find the document you want to change from the list of documents displayed on the screen and then click the Edit Doc link below its title. You can also leave comments on docs in order to let group members know what you liked or didn't like about them.

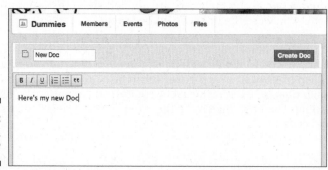

Figure 9-8:
What's up,
doc?

Docs are a *collaborative* way to write something: As with a wiki, anyone who is a member of the group can edit and delete docs that have been created. (A *wiki* is a website that anyone can make changes to. Probably the most famous example is Wikipedia.) So if you've written something you don't want changed in any way, keep it on your own computer.

Files

Like docs, files are shared among group members, but unlike docs, they cannot be edited within Facebook. Instead, members upload, download, and then reupload files they want changed. Or they simply upload files they want to share, and other group members are then able to download the files to their own computers.

From the Files tab, click the Upload Files button to add files from your computer. To download files that others have added, click the Download link to the right of the file.

Creating Your Own Groups

Now that you understand how to use groups, you may find an occasion to create your own group. As a group's creator, you're by default the *group administrator,* which means that you write the group's information, control its Privacy settings, and generally keep it running smoothly. You can also promote other members of the group to administrator. This grants them the same privileges so that they can help you with these responsibilities.

Here are the steps you follow to create a group:

1. **Expand the left side menu by hovering over it.**

2. **Click See More beneath the list of your most common destinations on Facebook.**

   This expands the left menu to show all the groups you belong to.

3. **At the bottom of the list of groups, click Create Group.**

   The Create New Group window appears (see Figure 9-9).

4. **Enter a group name into the Group Name field.**

   Choose something descriptive, if possible, so that when you add people to it, they'll know what they're getting into.

5. **Type the names of people you want to add to the group.**

   At this time, you can add only friends as members. Facebook tries to autocomplete your friends' names as you type. When you see the name you want, press Enter to select it. You can add as many — or as few — friends as you like. If you forget someone, you can always add him later.

Figure 9-9:
The Create
New Group
window.

6. Choose the privacy level for your group.

Groups have three privacy options:

- *Open:* Open groups are entirely available to the public. Anyone can join simply by clicking a Join button; anyone can see all the content the group posts. This type of group is best for a very public organization that wants to make it easy for people to join and contribute.

- *Closed:* By default, your group is set to Closed. This means that anyone can see the list of members, but only members can see the content posted to the group by its members. People can request to join the group, but admins (like you) need to approve those requests before the requesters can see group info.

- *Secret:* Secret groups are virtually invisible on the site to people who haven't been added to the group. No one except members can see the member list and the content posted.

People who have been added to the group can also add their friends, so if you're protecting state secrets, you might want to find a more secure method. I recommend carrier pigeons.

7. Click Create.

The window changes to the icon selection window, as shown in Figure 9-10.

8. Choose an icon from the options and click the Okay button.

Facebook tries to provide an option for lots of common group types; you can see some of the icons in Figure 9-10. If you can't find anything that represents your group, click Skip.

After you choose your icon and click Okay, you're taken to your group's Home page.

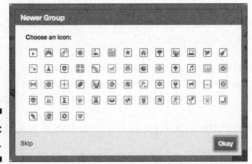

Figure 9-10:
Icon-o-rama.

Group Dynamics

Now that you know how to create, share, and navigate your way through a group, it's time to look at some of the long-term things to keep in mind as you join groups.

Controlling notifications

Sometimes, especially in larger groups, you may find yourself a bit overwhelmed by all the notifications. To control them, you just need to get comfortable with the Notifications Settings menu, which you access by clicking the Notifications button from a group's Home page. Clicking Notifications (it's on the right side of the page under the member photos) reveals a drop-down menu with three options, as shown in Figure 9-11.

Figure 9-11:
Control
notifications
here.

✔ **All Posts:** Because comment threads can often become very long and rambling, this option allows you to see when a new post is created, but not see comments on those posts unless you follow the post.

✔ **Friends' Posts:** In especially large groups, you might not be official Facebook friends with everyone in the group, so a good way to filter down to the material you're most likely to care about is to pay attention only to the things your friends post.

> ✔ **Off:** Some people may want to read the posts only when they choose to look at the group and not receive any notifications from this group. Selecting Off gives you that silence.

If you're being inundated by e-mail notifications but still want the notifications to appear on Facebook, you can change your e-mail notification settings from the Account Settings page. To adjust this setting, follow these steps:

1. **Click the upside-down triangle icon in the blue bar at top of any page.**

   A drop-down menu appears.

2. **Select Settings.**

   The Settings page appears. You can choose different types of settings from the menu on the left side of the page.

3. **Click Notifications on the left side of the page.**

   This opens all notifications settings. Look for the Email line in the How You Get Notifications section.

4. **Click Edit to the right of the Email option.**

   This expands to three options for e-mail notifications: All Notifications, Important Notifications, and Only Notifications about Your Account Security and Privacy.

5. **Select either Important Notifications, or Only Notifications about Your Account, Security and Privacy.**

   This step limits how many e-mail notifications you receive from Facebook.

If, after you change this setting, you're still getting e-mails about activity happening in a group, scroll to the bottom of one of the offending e-mails and click the Unsubscribe link. You will be asked to confirm that you want to unsubscribe from that type of e-mail. After you confirm, you'll no longer see e-mails about groups.

Searching a group

If your group is particularly active — meaning that lots of people are constantly posting content and commenting on things — you may have trouble finding something that was posted in the past. On the right side of the group's page under the member photos is a search icon (it looks like a magnifying glass). Click it to expand a Search box and search for the thing people were talking about at that time.

The search functionality here can be a bit limited, so sometimes posts will escape you entirely. The only way to find them is to keep scrolling back and back in the group's history.

Adding friends to a group

In most groups, most members can add more members at any time. This is a fast and easy way for groups to get all the right people in it even if the original creator isn't friends with everyone in the group. For example, if I'm friends with someone creating a group for our neighborhood association, but he isn't friends with my husband, I can easily add him to the group instead of him searching for my husband, adding him as a friend, and then adding him to the group. At any time, you can type a friend's name in the box on the right side of the group that says Add People to Group. Facebook autocompletes as you type. Press Enter when your friend is highlighted, and she will be notified that she has been added to the group.

Being a group administrator

If you're the creator of a group, you're automatically its *admin,* or administrator. Additionally, you can be added as an admin of someone else's group. After you have members in your group, you can use the group member list to remove (and even permanently ban) undesirable members, promote your most trusted members to administrators, or demote your existing administrators (if any) back to regular members.

To get started in your career as an admin, take a look at the Edit Group Settings page, shown in Figure 9-12. You get to this page by clicking the gear icon on the right side of your group's page (under the member photos). This expands a drop-down menu with several options. Select Edit Group Settings from the menu, which takes you to the Edit Group Settings page.

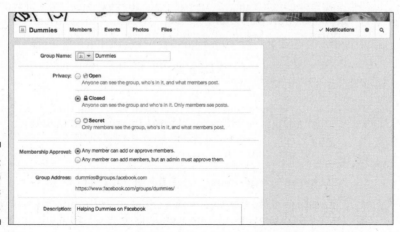

Figure 9-12: Edit Group Settings as an admin.

The Edit Group Settings page allows you to revisit some of the decisions you made when you were first creating your group, as well as adjust some settings that tend to be relevant only for people who are admins of large, open groups.

- **Name:** Edit the group name here (but I don't recommend pulling the rug out from underneath people by, say, changing a group name from Yankees Fans to Red Sox Fans).

- **Icon:** You can change your icon at any time from here.

- **Privacy:** The privacy level of the group can change here. Again, I don't recommend changing a secret group to an open group if people are sharing content they may feel is sensitive.

- **Membership Approval:** By default, any member of a group can add other members. You can change this option by requiring admins to approve new members.

- **Group Address:** If you want, you can create a group e-mail address and web address. Group addresses appear as something like `groupname@ groups.facebook.com` and web addresses appear as something like `www.facebook.com/groups/groupname`. E-mails sent to the group e-mail address are added as posts to the group wall.

- **Description:** The description of your group appears in the About section of the group the first time new members visit your group page. So this is a good place to set expectations for what the group is for and how you expect to use it.

- **Posting Permissions:** By default, all members of a group can post to it. But if you're the admin of a large group, you may want to change this setting so that only administrators can post. Keep in mind that this can really limit discussion!

- **Post Approval:** Similarly, if you want to make sure the content of a group is appropriate and relevant, you can choose to have admins approve posts before all group members see them.

Click Save when you're done editing your group's information; otherwise, all your hard work will be lost.

As an admin, you can remove and ban members from the group, as well as create other admins to help shoulder the burden of admin-hood.

To edit members, follow these steps:

1. **Next to the group's name, click the Members tab.**

   This takes you to the Members section of the group, the bulk of which is taken up by images of group members. If you are an admin, below each group member's name is a little gear icon.

2. **Click the gear icon below the name of the person you want to remove or make an admin.**

   A menu with two options appears: Make Admin or Remove from Group. You can see this in Figure 9-13.

Figure 9-13: Edit group members here.

3. **To make someone an admin, click Make Admin.**

   When someone is already an admin, you can remove her admin status by choosing Remove as Admin from this same menu.

4. **To remove someone from the group, choose Remove from Group.**

   You need to confirm this via a pop-up window that appears. If someone has been posting consistently offensive or abusive content, you can ban that person permanently by selecting the Ban Permanently check box; that person can never rejoin the group.

Reporting offensive groups

If you stumble upon an offensive group in your travels, you should report it to Facebook so that the company can take appropriate actions. To report a group, follow these steps:

1. **Click the gear icon on the right side of the group's Home page and then select the Report Group link.**

   A form appears in a pop-up window.

2. **Fill out the report by choosing a reason for the report.**

3. **Click Submit.**

Facebook removes any group that

✔ Contains pornographic material or inappropriate nudity.

✔ Attacks an individual or group.

✔ Advocates the use of illicit drugs.

✔ Advocates violence.

✔ Serves as advertisements or are otherwise deemed to be spam by Facebook.

Many groups on Facebook take strong stands on controversial issues, such as abortion or gun control. In an effort to remain neutral and promote debate, Facebook won't remove a group because you disagree with its statements.

Using Groups from Your Mobile Phone

If you use a smartphone, you can download the Facebook App for your phone, which allows you to use most Facebook features on the go, including Facebook Groups.

To get to a Facebook group from your mobile or tablet app, follow these steps:

1. **Tap the menu icon in the upper-left corner of the screen.**

   This expands the left-hand menu. Scroll down to look at the list of groups.

2. **Tap the name of the group you want to check out.**

   This brings you to the group's mobile Home page. It's actually not all that different from the regular view of groups. You see all the group's recent posts.

When you're looking at a post, you can tap on the post or the gray text at the bottom listing the number of comments to see all the comments that have been made. You can tap the Like button to like the post, or the Comment button to add your own comment. Tapping a photo focuses the screen on just the photo. You can then use your normal finger shortcuts to zoom in and out for a better view of that photo.

When you're looking at the group's recent posts, you can choose to add a post from your mobile phone by tapping the Post button at the top of the page. Tap the Photo button to post a photo from your phone. Just like creating a post anywhere on Facebook, you can add tags and location information.

See Chapter 12 for an in-depth discussion on using Facebook for mobile devices.

Part III
What to Do on Facebook

In this part . . .

- ✔ Adding photos and videos
- ✔ Managing schedules
- ✔ Connecting on the move
- ✔ Customizing Pages
- ✔ Using apps
- ✔ Visit www.dummies.com/extras/facebook for great Dummies content online.

Chapter 10

Filling Facebook with Photos and Videos

. . . .

In This Chapter

▶ Looking at friends' photos and videos

▶ Adding your own photos and videos to Facebook

▶ Adding photos and videos from your iPhone or other smartphone

▶ Understanding privacy for photos and videos

. . . .

Many Facebook users share the sensation of getting "lost" in Facebook — not in a bad way, but like you lose yourself in a good book. It starts simply enough. You're looking at News Feed; then you click an appealing photo, which leads you to an album you like, which leads you to a video from a friend's vacation, which leads you to another friend who has a ton of new updates about her life. And the next thing you know, your editor is tapping you on the shoulder and saying, "Did you finish writing that chapter about photos yet?"

Facebook Photos is the leading photo-sharing application on the web. This may sound surprising because entire sites are dedicated to storing, displaying, and sharing photos, whereas Photos is just one piece of the Facebook puzzle. But the fact that *all* your friends are likely on Facebook and using Photos makes it a one-stop shop for tracking all the photos of you, all the photos you've taken, and all the photos of your friends.

Additionally, Facebook Photos allows you to add and share videos. Though slightly less common, videos are pretty similar to photos. If you let them languish on your hard drive or on your mobile phone, nobody gets to enjoy them. Nobody gets to tell you how cute the photos of your baby are. No one lets you know that she likes your wedding video. When you share photos and videos, they can become even more cherished, even more valuable as keepsakes.

Viewing Photos from Friends

Just by opening up Facebook and looking at News Feed, you'll find yourself looking at lots of people's photos. You'll see photos a few different ways: in your News Feed, in the photo viewer, and in an album format.

Photos in News Feed

Figure 10-1 shows an example of how a single photo appears in News Feed. Most of the screen is taken up by the photo. Running across the top is the name of the person who posted it and any description she wrote about it. There is also info about when the photo was added and how it was added (via mobile phone, for example). Underneath the photo are links to Like, Comment, and Share the photo. Beneath those links is the count of how many likes the photo has already gotten, and any comments people have already made. You may even see a blank comment box, waiting for you to add your two cents.

Figure 10-1:
Looking at
a friend's
photo in
News Feed.

Clicking the photo expands the photo viewer, which is covered in the following section.

Figure 10-2 shows an example of a photo album preview in News Feed. It's similar to the single photo, but previews more of the photos from the album. The name of the album appears at the top of the post and tells you how many photos are in the album. Clicking any of the photos expands the photo viewer, and clicking the album title brings you to an album view.

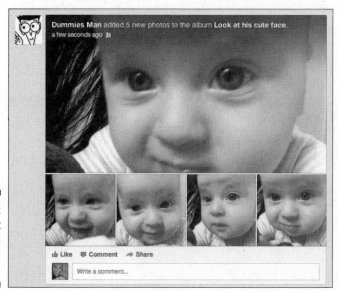

Figure 10-2: Looking at a friend's album in News Feed.

Photo viewer

The photo viewer is an overlay on top of Facebook that allows you to quickly browse photos (and videos, but I get to that topic in the "Working with Video" section of this chapter) and leave comments. Clicking a small version of a photo almost anywhere on Facebook expands the photo viewer and fades the rest of the screen to black, as shown in Figure 10-3. The left side of the viewer is where the photo appears, and the right side is where comments, likes, and info about the photo appear.

When you hover your mouse over the photo, more options show up in white on the photo. On either side is an arrow that allows you to navigate through a photo album. Clicking anywhere on the photo will also advance the album forward. At the bottom of the viewer, the following information appears:

- ✔ **<Album Name>:** The album's name is usually one your friend has created, like "Summer in February!" or a descriptive name generated by Facebook, such as "Mobile uploads."

- ✔ **Photo count:** The number of the photo you're on in the album (for example, 5 of 8) is also displayed.

- ✔ **Tag Photo:** Clicking this allows you to add *tags* or labels for those in the photo. I cover tags in upcoming section, "Editing and Tagging Photos."

✔ **Options:** Clicking this reveals a menu of options for things like down-loading the photo to your computer, reporting the photo, removing a tag, or making a photo your own profile picture.

✔ **Share:** Clicking this lets you post the photo to your own Timeline.

✔ **Like:** Same as with the Like link that appears on the right side of the viewer, selecting this option lets the person who added the photo know that you like the photo.

Figure 10-3:
The Photo
Viewer.

The album view

The album view is the grid of thumbnail photos that you see when you click the name of an album or click a View Album link. Most average screens can fit about 8 to 12 photos in this view, and as you scroll down the page, more and more photos appear until you reach the end of the album. Sometimes if people add a really large album, you may want to just skim an album view to see where the parts of the album are that interest you. Clicking on any one photo brings up the photo viewer.

At the top of the album view is the name of the album, some info about when and where the album was added, and any general info your friend has added about the album. Beneath the last row of photos, you can see who has liked the album or commented on it. Figure 10-4 shows an example album view.

Commenting on an album is different than commenting on a single photo. Leave a comment on an album to comment on the collection: "Looks like a great trip!" "Can't wait till we see the place ourselves." Comment on a single photo when you have something to say about that photo in particular: "Did you use a fisheye lens to get this shot?" or "Omg I was at this exact spot a year ago!"

Figure 10-4:
An album view of photos.

Viewing photos on your mobile device

Chances are that if you have a smartphone or a tablet computer like an iPad, you'll wind up looking at photos using the Facebook app. Looking at photos on these devices isn't too different from looking at them on a computer screen. Tapping a photo in News Feed expands the photo and fades the rest of the screen to black. Tap the photo once to see the options to like (tap the thumbs-up icon), comment (tap the comment bubble), or return to News Feed (tap the Done button). Tapping the count of likes or comments expands a screen where you can scroll through the comments people have made on the photo. You can page through photos in an album just like you page through photos you've taken on your phone, swiping a finger from the right to the left side of the screen. The two-finger method of zooming in and out also works on Facebook photos.

Viewing tagged photos and videos of yourself

When I say *photos and videos of yourself,* I'm referring to photos and videos in which you're *tagged.* Tags are ways of marking who is in a photo — the online equivalent of writing the names of everyone appearing on the back of a photo print. Tags are part of what make Facebook Photos so useful. Even if you don't add lots of photos, other people can add photos of you. Photos you've been tagged in might be scattered across your friends' Timelines, so Facebook collects all these photos in the Photos section of your Timeline. You can get there by clicking the Photos tab underneath your cover photo.

The Photos section defaults to showing Photos of *<Your Name>*. You can also view photos you've added or albums you've added. The Photos of *<Your Name>* section shows the most recently tagged photos at the top of the page. As you scroll down, you see older and older photos of yourself. This is a great place to take a trip down memory lane, and also to make sure that you're aware of all the photos of you that are out there.

If you've been tagged in a photo and you don't like that tag, you can always remove the tag. Then that photo will no longer be linked to your Timeline, and it won't appear in the Photos of You section of your Timeline either.

If there's a photo or video you don't want on Facebook at all, even after you've removed the tag, get in touch with your friend and ask him to remove it. If you think it is offensive or abusive in any way, you can also report the photo and ask Facebook to remove it.

Adding Photos to Facebook

Facebook is a great place to keep your photos and videos because it's the place where most of your friends will be able to see them. Whether that's a single photo you snapped on your phone or a big album detailing the latest family vacation, photos are most fun when you can share them and talk about them with your friends.

From the Share box at the top of News Feed, click the Add Photos/Video link to post photos. (You can also click the Photos link in the Share box at the top of your Timeline.) When you do so, you see something like Figure 10-5. This screen gives you options for how you want to upload your content.

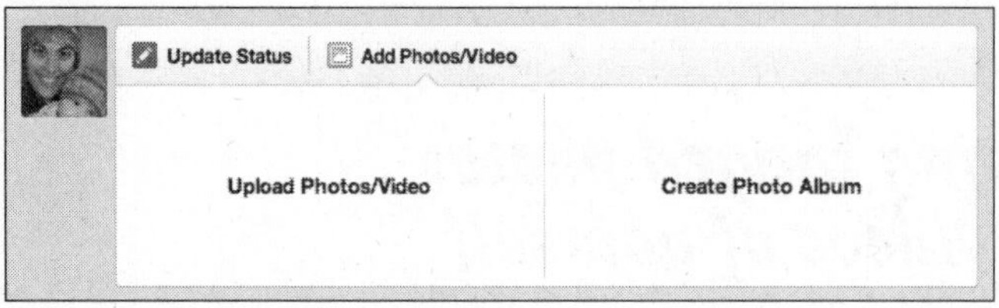

Figure 10-5:
Choose how you want to upload your photos.

You can choose from two options:

- **Upload Photos/Video:** Use this option if you have one photo you really want to share or a few photos that you want to share and don't want to organize into a true album. You also use this option for adding videos, covered later in this chapter.

- **Create Photo Album:** Use this option when you want to really show off a series of photos. Usually Albums are created to detail a particular event or period of time.

What's a tag?

Tagging — the part of Facebook Photos that makes the application so useful for everyone — is how you mark who is pictured in your photos. Imagine that you took all your photos, printed them, put them in albums, and then created a giant spreadsheet cross-listing the photos and the people in the photos. Then you merged your spreadsheet with all your friends' spreadsheets. This is what tagging does.

When you tag a friend, it creates a link from her Timeline to that photo and notifies her that

you've tagged her. Your friends always have the option to remove a photo tag that they don't want linked to their accounts.

Tagging is most commonly used in Photos, but you can also tag friends in videos, status updates, and even in comments. All these little tags allow your friends to know when you're talking about them (good things, of course) or want to talk with them about something.

Uploading a photo

If you have a few photos you want to quickly share, follow these steps to get them out to your friends:

1. **Click Add Photos/Video in the Share box on your Home page.**

   The photo options appear (refer to Figure 10-5).

2. **Click Upload Photos/Video.**

   A window appears allowing you to browse your computer's hard drive and select the photo you want.

3. **Click the photo you want to share to select it.**

   You can select more than one photo if you want.

4. **Click Open or Choose (the wording may depend on your browser and operating system).**

   This brings you back to Facebook. A thumbnail of that photo appears inside the Share box.

   Sometimes Facebook may be a little slow to add your photo. Blue progress bars may appear instead of thumbnails. You won't be able to post your photo until the photo has been added.

5. **Click in the Share box (where you see Say Something about This Photo) and type any explanation you think is necessary.**

6. **(Optional) Add tags, location info, and change the privacy of those photos from the options at the bottom of the Share box.**

If you've never changed your Privacy settings, by default, everyone on Facebook can see this photo if she navigates to your Timeline. I usually like sharing my photos with Friends Except Acquaintances (see Figure 10-6). Of course, you can always choose a custom group of people who can and cannot see the photo.

7. **Click Post Photos.**

This officially posts the photo to Facebook. People will be able to see the photos on your Timeline and in their News Feeds (provided they're allowed by your Privacy settings to see the photo). By default, this photo is added to an album called Timeline Photos, which is basically a collection of all the photos you've ever added individually.

You can also drag and drop photo files from your desktop straight into the Share box just like moving files around on your computer. Once you have dragged a photo into the Share box, you can add a comment, location, tags, and change privacy like normal.

Figure 10-6:
Fill out info while your photos upload.

Creating an album

Whereas a single photo can share a moment, an album can truly tell a story and spark conversations with your friends. To create an album, follow these steps:

1. **Click Add Photos/Video in the Share box on your Home page.**

The photo options appear (refer to Figure 10-5).

2. **Click Create Photo Album.**

This opens the same interface for exploring your hard drive that you used to upload a single photo.

3. **Select multiple photos by pressing the Ctrl or Command button and clicking the files you want.**

If you use a program like iPhoto to organize your photos, create an album there first; then navigate to it and select all those photos to add to Facebook. You'll save yourself some time trying to figure out whether you want to use IMG0234 or IMG0235.

4. **When you're done, click Open.**

The Upload Photos window appears (refer to Figure 10-6). The progress bar fills with blue as your photos are uploaded.

5. **Fill out Album Info.**

As your photos upload, you'll see three empty text fields at the top of the page. Click Untitled Album to add an album title, Where Were These Taken to add a location, and Say Something About This Album to add a description of the album. You can click the Add Date link to add the date the photos were taken, which is especially useful if you're adding photos from the past and you want them to show up way back on your Timeline.

6. **Decide whether you want your photos shown in standard or High Quality resolution via the check box at the bottom of the screen.**

High-resolution photos obviously look a bit better, but they also take longer to upload. Unless you're a pro photographer or using a truly professional-level camera, standard quality is usually sufficient.

7. **Choose who can see the album using the Privacy menu.**

The Privacy menu reflects the privacy setting from the last time you posted something. For example, if you last posted something publicly, the Privacy menu displays the globe icon and says "Public." As usual, the basic options are Public, Friends Except Acquaintances, Friends, Only Me, or a Custom set of people.

8. **(Optional) After your photos finish uploading, add descriptions to individual photos.**

The thumbnail of each photo has a blank space beneath it. Click into that space to add a caption or description of that individual photo.

9. **(Optional) Click on friends' faces to tag them. Type the name of the friend in the box that appears.**

The tagging box is shown in Figure 10-7. You don't have to tag friends in your album. However, tagging is highly recommended. It allows your friends to learn about your photos more quickly and share in discussing them with you.

Figure 10-7:
Who dat?

10. **Click Post Photos.**

    If Facebook's facial recognition software detects many photos of the same face, you may see a screen that shows you all the photos of that person and asks Who Is in These Photos? This allows you to make sure your friend is tagged in many photos without having to enter his name a zillion times. You may add tags here or skip to go to the album view of your album. After you get to the album view, you may rest assured that your album has been added to your Timeline and may appear in your friends' News Feeds.

Whew! That was a bit of a marathon. If you need a break or a drink of water, feel free to indulge. Then, when you're ready, jump to the "Editing and Tagging Photos" section to find out how to edit your album and the photos in it.

Adding photos from your iPhone

Lots of photos you see on Facebook are added when people are nowhere near a computer. Instead, they're the photos of things that happen while you're out and about. Things that are beautiful (spring blossoms!), or weird (how did this person lose only one high heel?), or just emblematic of your day (another cute photo of the baby).

If you add the Facebook app to your phone, iPhones and Android phones try to make it as easy as possible to send photos from your phone right to Facebook.

Here's a simple way to share photos if you're using an iPhone:

1. **From your photo gallery, tap the photo you want to share; then tap the Send icon at the bottom left of the photo.**

   A menu of options appears, including things like e-mail or text messages. If you previously installed the Facebook app, you should see the Facebook icon among the other options.

2. **Tap the Facebook icon.**

   A Facebook window for sharing that photo appears, as shown in Figure 10-8.

3. **(Optional) Use the keyboard to type any explanation the photo needs.**

Figure 10-8:
Don't
let your
photos go
unshared!

4. **(Optional) Tap Add Location to use GPS to share where you're adding the photo from.**

5. **(Optional) Tap the Privacy menu to change who can see this post.**

   Remember, by default, the audience you shared your last post with will be the people who can see this post.

6. **Tap Post in the upper-right corner of the Facebook window.**

   The photo is added to your Timeline as part of the Mobile Uploads album, and it may appear in your friends' News Feeds.

If you use an iPhone, you can download the Facebook Camera app specifically for taking and sharing photos. This app gives you tools like filters for your photos and makes it easy to look only at friends' photos.

Editing and Tagging Photos

After uploading a photo, you can still make changes to the way it appears on Facebook. If you added a whole album, you may want to add more photos or rearrange the order of the pictures. For any photo you added from a phone or just quickly from your computer, you may want to add tags, date, or location information. Doing all of this is relatively easy using the following common editing "tasks."

Editing albums

Editing an album usually consists of editing the album's information or settings. You may also want to edit specific photos within an album. For those types of edits, hop on down to the "Editing a Photo" section.

Edit album name, location, description, and privacy

From the album view, look above the top row of photos for an Edit icon, next to the Add Photos button.

This little pencil icon always indicates that you can edit something.

Click the Edit icon to bring up the Edit Album screen (see Figure 10-9). It should look familiar — it's pretty much the same screen you saw when you created the album.

Figure 10-9:
Edit your
album's info.

The fields at the top are the same as when you created the album: album name, description (Say Something . . .), location (Where Were These Taken), and a Privacy menu. Remember to click Done when you finish editing this information.

From the album view, you can also click the pencil icon next to the existing description to edit it.

Delete an album

While you're looking at the Edit Album screen, look for a button in the upper-right corner with a trash can icon on it. If you ever decide, in retrospect, that adding a particular album was a poor choice, you can click this button to remove the whole thing.

WARNING!

If you delete your photo album, all the photos in it will be gone forever, so make sure you want to get rid of it completely before you delete it.

Reorder photos in the album

Chances are that if you added your photos in bulk, they don't appear exactly in the right order. And it's awkward when the photos of the sunset appear first, and the photos of your awesome day of adventure come afterward. To reorder photos from the album view, follow these steps:

1. **Hover your mouse over the photo you want to move.**

2. **Click and hold the photo.**

3. **While holding the mouse button down, drag the photo thumbnail to its correct place in the album.**

   The other photos shift positions as you move your chosen photo (as shown in Figure 10-10).

4. **When the photo is in the spot you want, release the mouse button.**

5. **Repeat with the next photo until your whole album is organized correctly.**

No need to worry about saving. Facebook automatically saves the new order of your album.

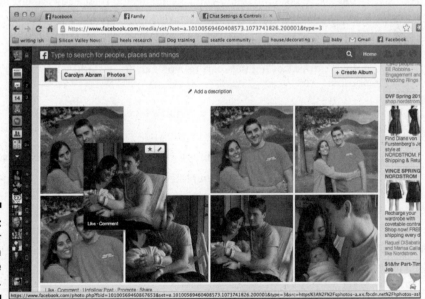

Figure 10-10: Make your album tell a story in the right order.

Add more photos

After you create a photo album, you can add more photos later. Sometimes, depending on how organized the photos on your hard drive are, you may want to add photos in batches anyhow. To add more photos, follow these steps:

1. **Click the Add Photos button in the upper-right corner of the album view.**

   This opens the interface for exploring your computer's hard drive.

2. **Select the photos you want to add.**

3. **Click Open.**

   The upload process begins, complete with a progress bar so you know how long the upload will take.

4. **Click the Done button after the upload is complete.**

   You're asked to tag the new photos you added.

Editing a photo

In addition to the actions you can take on an entire album, you can also take actions on individual photos within an album.

For all these possible photo edits, I assume you're already looking at the photo you want to edit in the photo viewer.

Add a tag to an individual photo

If you skipped adding tags earlier, you can always add your tags to individual photos.

1. **Hover your mouse over a friend's face.**

   The tagging box appears, as shown in Figure 10-11.

2. **Enter the name of the person you want to tag in the text box.**

   Facebook tries to autocomplete your friend's name as you type.

Figure 10-11:
Tagging a friend in a photo.

3. **Repeat Steps 1 and 2 until everyone in the photo is tagged.**

   Or stop after you tag a few people. You can always come back to this later.

Rotate a photo

Lots of times, photos wind up being sideways. It's a result of turning your camera to take a vertical shot as opposed to a horizontal one. You don't have to settle for this:

1. **Click Options at the bottom of the photo viewer.**

   This opens a menu of options related to that photo. Remember, you won't see this text until your mouse hovers over the photo.

2. **Click Rotate Left or Rotate Right from the menu.**

   You may have to click it more than once to actually get it properly oriented.

Add or change a description for an individual photo

Just like you can add a description to the album as a whole, you can add descriptions or captions to individual photos:

1. **Click the Edit button on the right side of the photo viewer.**

   A text box appears where you can edit the description.

2. **Enter your description in the text box.**

3. **(Optional) Add any tags you want about who was with you when the photo was taken.**

4. **(Optional) Add location information about where this photo was taken.**

   Facebook tries to autocomplete your location information as you type.

5. **When you're finished, click Done Editing.**

Delete a photo

Maybe you realized that all 20 group shots from the high school reunion don't have to go in the album, or that one photo has a whole bunch of crossed eyes. You can remove photos entirely from Facebook:

1. **Click the Options link at the bottom of the photo viewer.**

   A menu of options appears.

2. **Click Delete This Photo.**

   A pop-up window appears asking if you are sure.

3. **Click Confirm.**

   You're taken back to the album view, now with one less photo.

Automatic albums

Most of the time when you're creating a photo album, you decide what to title it and which photos go into it. There are a few exceptions to this rule. Facebook assembles certain types of photos into albums on your behalf. Most importantly, every time you change your profile picture or cover photo, Facebook adds it to the Profile Pictures or Cover Photos albums, respectively. Facebook creates albums of all your profile pictures and cover photos automatically.

You can access this album by clicking your current profile picture or cover photo from your Timeline. This takes you to the photo viewer, where you can click through your historical record of profile pictures. Even though Facebook created this album, you can still edit any part of it like any other album — you can caption, tag, reorder, and delete photos simply by clicking the photo you want to edit.

You can automatically turn any photo from this album back into your profile picture by clicking the Options link and selecting Make Profile Picture from the menu that appears.

Similarly, single photos that you add to your Timeline are collected into the Timeline Photos album. Photos that you add from your phone are added to a Mobile Uploads album. Videos (which I'm about to talk about) also are collected into a Videos album.

Working with Video

Too often, videos wither away on hard drives or cameras or even on mobile phones. The files are big, and they can be difficult to share or e-mail. Facebook seeks to make sharing videos easier. So film away and then let everyone see what you've been up to.

Viewing videos

You'll mostly encounter videos in your News Feed with a big fat Play button in the center. Simply click that button to watch the video. It expands the photo viewer overlay (yes, the photo viewer is what you use to view videos, calling it the Photo and Video Viewer is just too long), which makes the background darken and lets you focus on the video you want to watch. The video plays on the left side of the screen, and the right side displays the video's title, description, and tags, as well as links to Like, Comment, and Share the video. Any comments or likes that have already been made also show up on the right side of the screen.

While the video is playing, you can hover your mouse over it to see the progress bar and to display the various links you can click related to the video. These appear in white toward the bottom of the video, as shown in Figure 10-12.

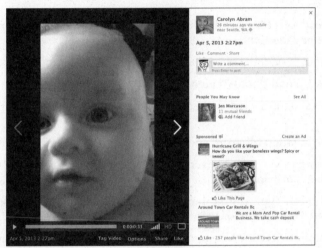

Figure 10-12:
A video on
Facebook.

Here are the components of the photo viewer when you are watching a video:

- **Progress bar, Volume, and Full Screen:** You can pause the video from the progress bar, as well as adjust the video's volume from the volume meter. Click the square icon to the right of the progress bar to expand the video and watch it on your entire computer screen.

- **Video Title:** The video's title is at the bottom left of the viewer. If video doesn't have a title, the date and time of upload are displayed.

- **Tag Video:** Click this link if you want to tag someone in the video.

- **Options:** Clicking this link expands a menu of options, including a Report option if you ever see a video you think shouldn't be on Facebook.

- **Share:** This link allows you to post a video to your own Timeline and share it with your friends.

- **Send:** This link allows you to send the video to friends attached to a message. When you send a video, the message and video go to your friend's Inbox.

- **Like:** Click this link to let your friends know that you like their videos.

Adding a video from your computer

Uploading a video to Facebook includes going out into the world, recording something, and then moving it from your camera onto your computer. I'm going to assume you've already done that part and are now back to being sedentary in front of your computer. Now, to upload a video to Facebook, follow these steps:

1. **Choose Add Photo/Video in the Share box at the top of your Home page or Timeline.**

   Options for adding photos and videos to Facebook appear.

2. **Click Upload Photos/Video.**

   This expands a window that allows you to navigate your computer's hard drive.

3. **Select a video file from your computer.**

   This brings you back to Facebook, where your video is appended to your post. A filmstrip icon indicates that you're adding a video, not a photo.

4. **(Optional) Type any explanation or comment into the Say Something About This Video box.**

5. **(Optional) Select who can see this video using the Privacy menu.**

   As usual, your basic options are Public, Friends Except Acquaintances, Friends, Only Me, or a Custom group of people.

6. **Click Post.**

   A blue progress bar appears at the bottom of the post. Uploading a video can sometimes take a while, so be patient. When it's ready, you'll be notified that your video is processing. This means that you need to wait a little while until your video is ready. You can use Facebook in the meantime or decide to edit the video's info, which is covered in the "Editing and tagging videos" section, later in this chapter.

Adding a video from your iPhone

Much like photos, many of the videos you want to share most are ones you take when you're out and about: someone attempting to park a car in a spot that's too small, your kid chasing a soccer ball, the bride and groom cutting the cake. More and more often, you may find yourself using your phone to record these videos.

You could move the video from your phone to your computer and then add it to Facebook, or you could skip the middleman and share it directly from your phone using the Facebook app:

1. **Tap the Photo option at the top of your mobile News Feed.**

   Your Photo and Video roll from your phone appears.

2. **Tap the video you want to add.**

   A preview of your video appears. You can play it here to make sure you want to share it.

3. **Tap the blue Pencil in Box icon at the bottom of the video preview.**

   The screen becomes the usual box you see when you add a status or other post, with a thumbnail icon representing the video. You can add a comment, a location, tags, and change the privacy option just like you do for any other type of post.

4. **When you're done, tap Post in the upper-right corner of the screen.**

   The video is then added to Facebook. Your friends will be able to see it on your Timeline and in their News Feeds (depending on your privacy settings, of course).

Editing and tagging videos

When I talk about editing videos that you've added, I don't mean the kind of fancy editing that editing software like Final Cut Pro might do. Rather, you're editing how these items are displayed and seen by your friends.

To get to the Edit Video screen, shown in Figure 10-13, click the Play button in the center of the video. This opens the Photo viewer overlay, where the video begins playing. On the right side of the viewer are three buttons: Tag Video, Add Location, and Edit. Clicking Edit turns the right side of the viewer into a series of text boxes where you can add information.

Figure 10-13:
The Edit
Video
screen.

Apr 5, 2013 2:27pm

Add a description

Who were you with?

Where was this video taken?

2013 ⬍   April ⬍   5 ⬍   + Add hour

⚙ Custom ▾   Done Editing   Cancel

Like · Comment · Unfollow Post · Share · Edit

Write a comment...

The Edit Video screen has several fields to fill out; most of these are optional:

- ✔ **Title:** Name your video. You can be artsy and name it something like *Boston Cream Meets a Bitter End* or something descriptive like *Pie in the Face.* If you don't choose a title, the video is automatically titled with the timestamp of when you recorded or uploaded it.

- ✔ **Description:** This field is for you to describe what's happening in your video, although frequently videos speak for themselves.

- ✔ **Tags** *(Who were you with?):* This option is similar to tagging a photo or a post. Simply start typing the names of all the friends who are in the video and then select the correct friends from the list that displays. Your friends are notified that they've been tagged in a video and can remove the tag if they decide they don't want to be forever remembered as *The one who got pied in the face.*

- ✔ **Location** *(Where was this video taken?):* You can enter a location such as a city or a place of business. Facebook attempts to autocomplete as you type.

- ✔ **Date:** As with any post, you can add a date to make sure it appears in the right place in your Timeline.

- ✔ **Privacy:** Your privacy options for videos are the same as for any post: Public, Friends Except Acquaintances, Friends, Only Me, or Custom. By default, whatever the privacy was on your last post will be the privacy for the video you added. For all-around privacy info, be sure to read Chapter 5.

Click Done Editing when you finish filling out these fields.

Discovering Privacy

While privacy is covered in detail in Chapter 5, it's worth going over a few settings again now that you really understand what it is you're choosing to show or not show to people.

Album and video privacy

Each time you create an album, post a photo, or add a video to Facebook, you can use the Privacy menu to select who can see it. These options are as follows:

✔ **Public:** This setting means that anyone can see the album. It doesn't necessarily mean that everyone *will* see the album, though. Facebook doesn't generally display your content to people who aren't your friends. But if, for example, someone you didn't know searched for you and went to your Timeline, she would be able to see that album.

✔ **Friends:** Only confirmed friends can see the photos or videos when you have this setting.

✔ **Friends Except Acquaintances:** People you've added to your Acquaintances list will not be able to see the photo or video. The rest of your friends will be able to see it.

✔ **Only Me:** Only you will be able to see that photo or video.

✔ **Custom:** Custom privacy settings can be as closed or as open as you want. You may decide that you want to share an album only with the people who were at a particular event, which you can do with a custom setting.

Another way to control who sees an album or video is to share it using Facebook Groups. So, for example, a video of your kids playing might be of interest only to people in your family. If you have a group for your family, you can share it from the Share box in the group, and then only people in the group will be able to see it.

If you're brand new to Facebook and have never changed a single privacy setting, by default, all posts you add — including photos and videos — are visible publicly. If you aren't comfortable with this, remember to adjust your Privacy settings accordingly when you add new photos and video.

Privacy settings for photos and videos of yourself

The beauty of creating albums on Facebook is that it builds a giant cross-listed spreadsheet of information about your photos — who is in which photos, where those photos were taken, and so on. You're cross-listed in photos that you own and in photos that you don't own. However, you may want more control over these tags and who can see them. To control this, go to the Privacy Settings page from the Privacy Shortcuts menu (which you access by clicking the lock icon next to your name in the left menu). From the Settings page, click the Timeline and Tagging section on the left side of the page.

The top two settings in the section labeled How Can I Manage Tags People Add and Tagging Suggestions are particularly relevant to setting privacy for photos of you:

- ✔ **Review tags people add to your own posts before the tags appear on Facebook?** Turning this option from Off to On means you get to make sure you want to be tagged in photos (and other posts) before anyone can see that you've been tagged.

  In other words, say that I tag my friend Eric in a photo.

  - If this option is *Off,* as soon as I tag him, the photo is added to his Timeline and (usually) his friends will be able to see that he's been tagged in their News Feeds.

  - If this setting is *On,* he has to approve the tag before it appears on his Timeline and in his friends' News Feeds.

- ✔ **When you're tagged in a post, who do you want to add to the audience if they aren't already in it?** Another way to limit who can see that you've been tagged in a post is to change this setting from Friends to Only Me or Custom.

  By default, if I tag Eric in a photo, his friend Dave, whom I'm not friends with, will be able to see the photo. If Eric changes this setting to Only Me, then when I tag Eric, Dave still will not be able to see that photo.

Additionally, the Who Can See Posts You've Been Tagged in On Your Timeline setting allows people to tag you in photos, but prevents certain groups of people from seeing those photos on your Timeline. So, if I tag Eric in a photo that I shared publicly, someone he isn't friends with who visits his Timeline wouldn't see that photo unless Eric allows everyone to see posts he's been tagged in.

Chapter 11

Scheduling Your Life with Events

*I*n the real world, just because all your friends are on Facebook doesn't mean that it's the only place you interact with them. In fact, the people you interact with most on Facebook may be the same ones you see at PTA meetings or at a book club or have over for barbecues. Facebook Events can help you bridge the divide between all the things that happen online and all the things you want to have happen when you're not anywhere close to your computer.

Facebook Events work really well for the same reason lots of other Facebook features work: Your friends are here. You can invite them to events, keep track of RSVPs, and use Facebook to send updates or coordinate participants in an event to help out. Facebook's Event Calendar also helps you keep track of upcoming events and your friends' birthdays.

You're Invited!

The first way you'll most likely find out about an event is through a notification. When a friend invites you to an event, a small red flag appears over the notifications icon in the big blue bar on top. Click the icon to open your notifications menu; then click the invitation to be taken to the event.

A sample event appears in Figure 11-1. The event photo appears at the top of the page, much like the cover photo does on your Timeline. Beneath the event photo is the event's name, host (which can be a person, group, or page), and privacy info.

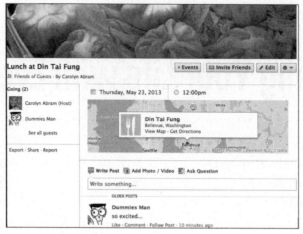

Events have three privacy settings:

- **Public:** Public events are just what they sound like: open to the public. Anyone can see the event with or without an invitation, view the guest list and posts, and join the event herself.

- **Friends of Guests:** Events with this privacy setting are slightly more private than Public events. Any friends of guests — whether or not they received an invitation — can view and join the event.

- **Invite Only:** These are the most private events. Only people who have been invited are able to see the event and join it.

The left side of the event page shows the progress of the RSVPs. Three categories are shown (although this may depend on the settings of the event, as decided by the event admin): Going, Maybe, and Invited.

The most important info about any event is in the center of the page: where, when, and what. There's a spot here for the date and time of the event, the location, and any info the event creator wants to share with guests. If the creator put in a specific address or location, a map may also appear so that you can easily get directions.

Below the event info is the Posts section of the event (see Figure 11-2). The Posts section is where people can post messages and communicate with other guests (and potential guests) of that event. Event hosts use this section to post important updates — for example, a reminder to bring a sweater in case the weather is cold, or to let people know at which section of the park they'll be meeting. Guests' RSVPs appear here as they come in, as do posts that people actively make to communicate with other guests. Depending on the event, the posts may be from people just saying how excited they are or from people coordinating rides or the food they'll bring to a potluck.

Figure 11-2:
Post here
to com-
municate
with other
guests.

To post to an event, follow these steps:

1. **Click in the Share box (where it reads Write Something).**

   This is the same way you update your status or post to group.

2. **Type your message in the Share box.**

3. **(Optional) Add tags, location information, or photos by clicking their respective icons at the bottom of the Share box.**

4. **Click Post.**

   Your message is posted to the Posts section of the event. Depending on settings, guests may be notified about it or see a News Feed story about it.

Within the Posts section, you can click the link to View Declines (not shown in Figure 11-2), which will show you all the posts people left when they said they wouldn't be able to attend an event. Seeing all the declines in the Posts section can be a bit of a bummer, which is why Facebook sequesters them away from the more inviting and excited posts.

You actually can't post to an event until you've RSVPed. So make up your mind, and then you can start talking to the other guests.

Responding to an event is easy; just click the blue Join button if you plan on attending, the Decline button if you can't make it, or the Maybe button if you aren't sure.

After you RSVP to an event, the RSVP buttons are replaced with the following new buttons:

✔ **Invite Friends:** If you want some company at an event or know of someone who would really be interested, click this button to send him an invitation. (Some Invite Only events may not allow you to invite more friends.)

✔ **RSVP status:** If, for example, you join an event by clicking the blue Join button, it will be replaced by a gray button named Going. Click this button to change your RSVP at any time.

✔ **Settings (gear icon):** Click the gear icon to turn off event notifications, to share an event on your Timeline, or to export an event to your calendar or e-mail.

Viewing Events

From your Home page, you can see reminders about upcoming events (including friends' birthdays) on the right side of the page. Clicking on an event opens a slightly larger preview that includes times and locations, as well as events that are slightly further into the future. The right-hand preview of Events is shown in Figure 11-3.

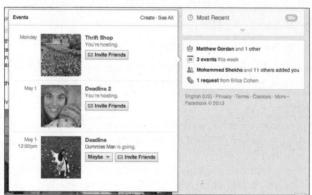

Figure 11-3:
A quick reminder of upcoming events.

You can also view a complete Event Calendar by going to the Events page. To get there, click Events in the left sidebar (you may have to expand it by hovering over the left side of the screen). The Events icon is a little calendar page. The Events page, as a calendar view, is shown in Figure 11-4. You can switch over to a list of events by clicking the List button at the top of the Events page.

At the top right of the Events page are a few more buttons to be aware of:

✔ **Invites (appears only when you have invites):** The red number in this button shows you the number of outstanding invitations you have (in other words, the number of events you've been invited to and haven't responded to). Click this button to look at event previews for these invites and respond.

✔ **Create Event:** Click this button to create a new event. I cover creating events in detail in the next section of this chapter.

✔ **Today:** Click the Today button to automatically scroll down to today's date on the calendar.

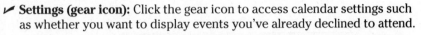

✔ **Settings (gear icon):** Click the gear icon to access calendar settings such as whether you want to display events you've already declined to attend.

You can find an option here to export your events to your computer's calendar, so all your calendars can be synced with your Facebook events.

Outstanding invitations also appear above the current month on your calendar. You can click on the event's name to be taken to the event or simply click Join, Maybe, or Decline to respond without leaving the Events page.

The calendar has events written in just as you might write in a reminder on your wall calendar at home. Click an event's name to be taken to its page. In addition to events, your friends' birthdays are marked on this calendar — look for tiny profile pictures to see whose birthday is on which day. If you forgot your reading glasses, you can always hover your mouse over the picture to see the friend's name and (if his settings allow) how old he will be.

Figure 11-4:
The Event
Calendar
helps you
keep track
of your busy
social life.

Creating Your Own Events

Eventually, the time may come when you want to organize an event. It might be a party or a barbecue or a book club or any other gathering of your friends. No matter what the context, follow these steps to create your own event:

1. **Click Events in the left sidebar of any page on Facebook.**

You may have to hover over the left sidebar to expand it. Clicking Events takes you to the Events page.

2. **Click the Create Event button in the upper-right side of the page.**

   The Create New Event window appears, as shown in Figure 11-5.

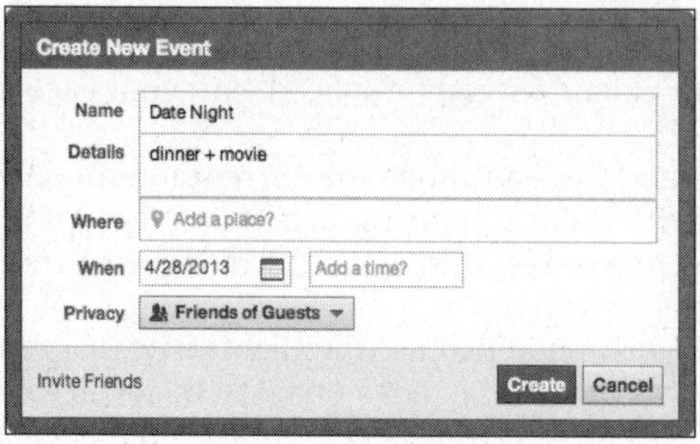

Figure 11-5:
Create your
event here.

3. **Fill out your event's info:**

   You can fill out a number of fields:

   • *Name:* Don't fill out your name here (a common mistake); this is the name of your event. Usually events get pretty descriptive names like "Carolyn's birthday party" or "Labor Day in the park."

   • *Details (optional):* This is the info guests will read about when they see the event, so provide any info that helps people understand what they're going to. For example, a bookstore event might list the readers who will be in attendance, or a party at a bar might let you know if there's going to be a cover charge to get in.

   • *Where:* Generally speaking, events are better when people know where to go. You can type an address or a location (like a restaurant or a park). Facebook attempts to autocomplete to a specific location while you type. When you see the desired location, click it or press Enter.

     When you add a location that Facebook recognizes, it will automatically include a weather forecast for that location on the date of your event. Good news for all your outdoor events.

   • *When:* By default, Facebook assumes you're an impromptu party planner, so the date in the box is today. Click the calendar icon to change the date. Next to the date box is a text field that reads Add a Time? Start typing a number to select your event's start time, down to a five-minute increment. After you add a start time, a blue link appears that reads End Time? Click that link to also add an end date and time.

4. **Select your event's privacy from the Privacy menu in the bottom of the Create New Event window.**

   The three privacy levels for events are Public, Friends of Guests, and Invite Only.

   If you choose to create an Invite Only event, you can still allow guests to invite more people by leaving the Guests Can Invite Friends check box selected. This lets you expand your guest list without drastically increasing who can see the event.

5. **Click the Invite Friends button to add guests to your event.**

   You can select friends from the interface that appears. I cover this process in the next section.

6. **Click the Create button to create your event.**

   You're taken to your event's page. Even though your event is created, you still need to make a few finishing touches, such as adding an event photo — oh, I don't know, maybe inviting some people.

Inviting guests

Trust me, your party just won't be the same unless some people show up, and the number one way to get people to show up is to invite them. Inviting people to your event isn't a one-shot deal. You can follow these steps at any time to invite people to your event:

1. **From your event's page, click the Invite Friends button in the top-right portion of the page.**

   The Invite Friends (or *friend selector*) window appears, as shown in Figure 11-6.

2. **Click a friend's name or face to select her.**

   Because you may have a lot of friends, you can use the Search box at the top to search for people by name. You can also use the drop-down menu in the top-left corner of the window (set by default to Search by Name) to zero-in on members of a particular Friend List or group you've created.

3. **Click Save after you make all your selections.**

   At this point, your guests receive the notification of a new invitation and will probably start to RSVP.

Adding an event photo

Although not required, adding an event photo to your event helps make the invitation feel a bit more official. Although it's not quite the same thing as sending out letter-pressed, hand-addressed invitations, it's the next best thing.

Figure 11-6:
The Friend
Selector
helps
you invite
guests.

To add an event photo, follow these steps.

1. **From the event's page, click the Add Event Photo button in the top-right corner.**

   A menu with two options appears: You can either select from photos you have already added to Facebook or you can choose a photo from your computer's hard drive. Either option opens an interface for browsing photos.

2. **Select a photo from your hard drive or from Facebook.**

   After selecting a photo from your hard drive, you may need to click Open. After you select your photo, it should appear at the top of the event with white text that reads Drag to Reposition Event Photo.

3. **Use your mouse to drag the photo in order to position it properly on the screen.**

4. **Click the Save Changes button.**

   After you add your event photo, the Add Event Photo button is replaced with a Change Event Photo button that appears when you hover your mouse over the photo. Click this button to choose a new photo, reposition the existing photo, or remove the existing photo entirely.

Managing Your Event

After you set up your event and people start RSVP-ing, you may need to manage some things. You might need to provide more info or change the location to accommodate more people. If it's a large public event, you may need to do some moderation of the people posting. Here are some common management issues you might face and how to deal with them.

Editing your event's info

Need to update the event time or add info about a dress code? You can do so at any time by clicking the Edit button at the top-right of the page, below the event photo. This opens the Edit Event Info box, which looks exactly like the Create New Event box. You can change the name of the event, the date and time, add more event details, change the location, and choose a new privacy setting for the event. You can also add more hosts to the event (by default, as the creator of an event, you're already its host). Hosts have the same capabilities you have in terms of editing the event.

Click Save when you're done editing.

Canceling the event

If your life has gone a bit awry and ruined your event plans, not to worry — it's easy to cancel your event:

1. **From your event's page, click the gear icon in the upper-right corner, below the event photo.**

    A menu of options related to your event appears.

2. **Select Cancel Event.**

    A window appears asking whether you're sure you want to cancel the event.

3. **Click Yes.**

    The event is immediately canceled, and notifications will be sent to guests letting them know.

Messaging your event's guests

The most common way of communicating with your guests is simply to post something to the Posts section of the event. Much like posting something to your Timeline, you can simply click in the Write Something box and start typing.

Additionally, you can start a group message thread with members of your event:

1. **Click the gear icon in the upper-right corner of your event, below the event photo.**

   A menu of options related to your event appears.

2. **Click Message Guests.**

   A Chat with *<Event Name>* window appears.

3. **Select which guests you want to receive your message by clicking their faces.**

   You can also check the Select All box in the bottom-left corner of the Chat with *<Event>* window to select all your guests.

   You can select people who have joined the event or just people who have said maybe, using the drop-down menu in the top-left corner of the Chat With window — by default, this menu says Search by Name. Click Search by Name to open the menu and choose Going or Maybe and then only message people with those RSVPs.

4. **Click the Start Chat button.**

   This opens a chat box at the bottom of your screen. Guests who aren't online will see these messages in their Inboxes the next time they log in.

Removing guests

Although removing guests isn't something that happens often, if you're hosting a large event (say, a big public fundraising effort for a charity you head), you may find that certain guests are undesirable, especially in the Posts section of the event. You can remove any posts that are inappropriate (as well as reporting spam or abuse should that happen). If there's one bad egg in particular, you can remove him from the event:

1. **On the left side of the event, click Going, which should have a number next to it representing the number of people who have RSVP-ed Yes.**

   The Guest box opens.

2. **Click the X next to the name of the person you'd like to remove from the event.**

   A confirmation box appears.

3. **Click Okay to confirm you really do want to remove this person from your event.**

   The person won't be told he was removed from the event; he'll just stop receiving notifications about the event.

Chapter 12

Facebook on the Go

Throughout this book, you discover how Facebook enriches relationships and facilitates human interaction. But what can Facebook do to enrich your relationships when you're *not* sitting in front of a computer? Life is full of beach weekends, road trips, city evenings, movie nights, dinner parties, and so on. During these times, as long as you have a mobile phone, Facebook still provides you a ton of value.

Don't take this as license to ignore a group of people you're actively spending time with to play with Facebook on your phone (unless, of course, you *want* to ignore them). Moreover, don't think you can tune out in class or in a meeting to poke your friends. But knowing the ins and outs of Facebook Mobile actually enriches each particular experience you have — while you're having it. With Facebook Mobile, you can show off your kids' new photos to your friends or broadcast where you're having drinks, in case any of your friends are in the neighborhood and want to drop by.

Facebook Mobile serves another function — making your life easier. Sometimes you need *something,* say, a phone number, an address, or the start time of an event. Maybe you're heading out to have dinner with your friend and her boyfriend whose name you can't, for the life of you, remember. Perhaps you hit it off with someone new and would like to find out whether she's romantically available before committing yourself to an awkward conversation about exchanging phone numbers. (Just a heads-up: This conversation can be awkward even *if* you find that person is single. Facebook can do a lot for you, but not everything.)

In this chapter, I make a foolish assumption: I assume that you have a mobile phone and know how to use its features. If you don't have a phone, you may consider buying one after reading this chapter; this stuff is way cool. Mobile Texts simply require that you own a phone and an accompanying plan that enables you to send text messages. Facebook Mobile requires a mobile data plan (that is, access to the Internet on your phone). Facebook Mobile applications require that you own any one of the several types of phones or devices that Facebook can currently support.

Is That Facebook Mobile in Your Pocket?

In many ways, using a mobile phone can augment your experience of using Facebook on the computer. This first section is about how you can easily add information to and get information from Facebook when you're on the go and not physically in front of the computer. These features are primarily for people who do most of their Facebooking on the computer, but sometimes interact through their phone.

Getting started

This chapter gives you almost everything you need to know about using Facebook with a mobile device. However, if you ever find yourself asking questions about it while near a computer but *not* near this book, you can go to www.facebook.com/mobile for much of the same information. To get started with Facebook Mobile, you first need to enter and confirm your phone number in the Settings page:

1. **Choose Settings from the Account menu (down arrow) in the upper-right corner of the big blue bar on top.**

2. **Click the Mobile tab on the left side of the page.**

3. **Click the green Add a Phone button.**

   You may be prompted to reenter your Facebook password. When that's all squared away, the Activate Facebook Texts dialog box appears.

4. **Choose your country and your mobile carrier.**

   If your carrier isn't listed, you may be out of luck using Facebook from your mobile phone.

5. **Click Next.**

   This brings you to Step 6, which you actually have to do from your phone.

6. **From your phone, text the letter** F **to 32665 (FBOOK).**

   FBOOK texts you back a confirmation code to enter from your computer.

   This can take a few minutes, so be patient.

7. **Enter your confirmation code into the empty text box.**

8. **Choose whether you want your phone number added to your Timeline via the Share My Phone Number with My Friends check box.**

   I find it very useful when friends share their mobile numbers on Facebook because it allows me to use Facebook as a virtual phonebook. If you're not comfortable with that, simply deselect the check box.

9. **Click Next.**

   This confirms your phone.

Mobile Texts

After your phone is confirmed, Mobile Texts are the most basic way to use Facebook on your phone. You don't need a camera on your phone or a smartphone to use Mobile Texts. Using just a simple Short Message Service (SMS) or text message, you can update your status to let people know where you are and what you're up to.

Here are the various actions you can take on Facebook via SMS:

✓ **Update your status:** Type any sort of phrase into a text message. Your status will appear on your Timeline and in your friends' News Feeds with a little mobile icon next to it so people know you're on the go.

✓ **Add a new Facebook friend.** Send the word **add** followed by the person's name or the word **add** followed by the person's phone number. Using your phone to immediately friend a person you meet is less formal than exchanging business cards, less awkward (and more reliable) than exchanging phone numbers, and gives you more flexibility later for how you want to get in touch.

   Friending someone from your phone has all the same implications as friending someone from your computer, so friend wisely.

✓ **Subscribe to a friend's status updates.** Send the word **subscribe**, followed by your friend's name. If you have a few friends whom you like to hear absolutely everything from, this is a great way to keep up on the go.

   If you subscribe to a lot of friends' statuses, make sure you have unlimited texting; otherwise, charges could pile up quickly.

TIP

✔ **Unsubscribe from a friend's updates.** Send the word **unsubscribe** followed by the friend's name.

If you realize you want fewer people's statuses sent to your phone, just unsubscribe from the ones you don't want to see regularly.

✔ **Stop getting texts.** Text the word **stop**.

✔ **Restart getting texts.** Text the word **on**.

What's all the buzz about?

An old wives' tale claims that when you feel your ears burn, someone is thinking about you. Here's a slight modification: Someone, somewhere, is thinking about you when your phone starts vibrating. Turning on Facebook Mobile Texts means that you can be notified via SMS when someone requests to be your friend, sends you a Facebook message, comments on your photos, writes on your Timeline, or pokes you.

If you haven't already, you can activate Facebook Mobile Texts from the Mobile tab of the Settings page. To start, click the green Activate Text Messaging button. The next few steps should look familiar; they're the same as the ones you took to add your phone number. Figure 12-1 shows your Mobile tab after texts are turned on. You probably notice a few new settings that weren't there before. Click the Edit link next to each setting to change it.

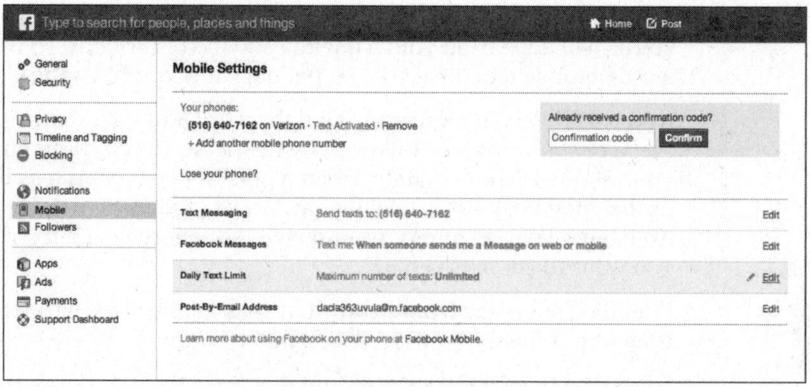

Figure 12-1: Set your preferences for receiving texts on your mobile phone.

Type to search for people, places and things	Home · Post

Mobile Settings

Your phones:
(516) 640-7162 on Verizon · Text Activated · Remove
+ Add another mobile phone number

Lose your phone?

Already received a confirmation code?
Confirmation code   Confirm

Text Messaging	Send texts to: (516) 640-7162	Edit
Facebook Messages	Text me: When someone sends me a Message on web or mobile	Edit
Daily Text Limit	Maximum number of texts: Unlimited	✏ Edit
Post-By-Email Address	dacia363uvula@m.facebook.com	Edit

Learn more about using Facebook on your phone at Facebook Mobile.

✔ **Text Messaging:** Decide which phone number you want your texts to be sent to. You need to change this setting only if you have more than one mobile phone number listed for your account.

✔ **Facebook Messages:** Click Edit to open a drop-down menu where you can specify which actions warrant a text. You can choose to receive a text whenever someone sends you a Facebook message from either his computer or his mobile phone, whenever someone sends you a Facebook message just from his mobile phone, or never.

✔ **Daily Text Limit:** The Daily Text Limit allows you to modify the number of text messages you receive per day.

If you have a mobile plan for which you're charged per text message (and you're exceedingly popular), use the settings that limit the number of messages Facebook sends you per day. Otherwise, you may have to shell out some big bucks in text message fees.

Remember to click Save Changes after updating this setting.

✔ **Post-By-Email Address:** Your Post-By-Email address enables you to upload photos and videos to Facebook from your phone. Check out the Mobile Uploads section of this chapter for more information on how to post photos and videos via e-mail.

Mobile notifications

Just when you thought you were done with Mobile Text settings, I introduce a whole 'nother bunch of settings to further fine-tune your Mobile Texts experience. To get started, head to the Notifications tab of the Settings page and click Edit next to the Text Message section. Figure 12-2 shows this expanded menu.

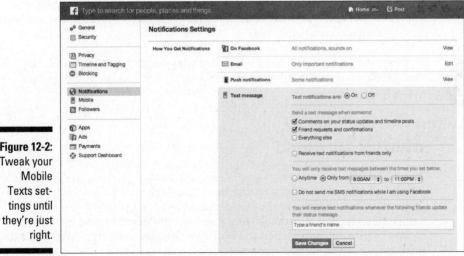

Figure 12-2: Tweak your Mobile Texts settings until they're just right.

From this section, you can change the following settings:

- ✔ **Turn text notifications on or off.** Fairly self-explanatory, although it's worth noting that even if you turn off Mobile Texts, you can continue to use the SMS commands I describe earlier in this section to update your status, add a new friend, and so on.

- ✔ **Decide which actions are text-worthy.** Choose to be notified when someone comments on your posts or status updates, when you receive a Friend Request or have a Friend Request you sent confirmed, and everything else, which encompasses actions like being tagged in a photo or receiving an Inbox message. You can select anywhere between none to all three of these options.

- ✔ **Receive text notifications from friends only.** This check box controls whether you want to receive a text only when you receive an Inbox message from a friend. This means that if, for example, a non-friend sends a message to your Inbox, you will not be notified by text.

- ✔ **Text times:** From here, you can specify a window of time when you'll gladly receive text notifications. So, for example, if someone pokes you at 2 a.m., you don't have to wake up for it. (Maybe you want to know *only* who's trying to poke you at 2 a.m. No judgment here.)

  Additionally, you can opt not to receive text notifications (via the Do Not Send SMS Notifications check box) while you're actively using Facebook because that can get a bit redundant.

- ✔ **Which friends' status updates should go to my phone?** This is another channel for specifying which of your friends' statuses you want sent to your phone. Simply type the name of the friend you want to subscribe to in this text box and choose the correct name from the autocomplete menu Facebook generates.

If you subscribe to the status of someone who doesn't spell very well but is conscientious about it, you may receive several texts as he tries to get his status just right.

Mobile uploads

Two types of people can be found at social events. There are the scrapbookers who always remember to bring their fancy-schmancy camera to every gathering. (You know who they are because they tell you to smile a lot or sometimes say "Act natural.") Then there are the people who never intend to take photos but who, when the birthday girl blows out her candles, the host spills wine on himself, or someone arrives wearing a hilarious T-shirt, is ready with his mobile phone camera. (Hey, it captures the moment, right?)

To the scrapbookers of the world: Facebook Photos was built for you, so be sure to read Chapter 10 to get the most out of Facebook Photos. However, if you're the mobile photo taker, Mobile Photos is for you. With no time for weeding, editing, or second thoughts, mobile photos allow for instantaneous documentation.

Here's how to upload a mobile photo:

1. **Make sure you have a phone with a camera and you know how to use it to take a picture and/or take a video.**

   If you're unsure, check your phone's instruction manual or ask just about any teenager.

2. **Go to the Mobile tab of the Account menu and look for your personalized Post-By-Email address toward the bottom.**

   This e-mail address — in this case, dacia363uvula@m.facebook.com — makes it possible for you to upload photos to your Timeline from your phone. Be sure to add this e-mail address to your phone's contacts so you can easily message it in the future.

3. **Wait for something hilarious or beautiful or awesome to happen and then take a picture or video of it.**

4. **Send an e-mail to your address with the picture or video attached.**

   The subject line is the caption, so choose wisely.

5. **(Optional) To make edits or changes to your mobile photos, go to your photo albums and click the Mobile Uploads album. To make changes to your video, go your photo albums and click the Video album.**

   The default visibility of your mobile uploads is Public/Everyone.

Using Facebook Mobile

Viewing a web page from your phone can be extremely difficult because the information that is normally spread across the width of a monitor must be packed into one tiny column on your phone. Facebook is no exception to this, which is why the very first tip in this section is: Never go to www.facebook.com on your mobile phone. You'll regret it.

But fear not, you still have a way to carry almost all the joys of Facebook right in your purse or pocket. On your mobile phone, open your browser application and navigate to m.facebook.com — a site Facebook designed specifically to work on a teeny-tiny screen.

The first time you arrive at m.facebook.com, you're asked to log in. After that, you never (or rarely) have to reenter your log-in info unless you explicitly log out from your session, so be sure you trust anyone to whom you lend your phone.

If you plan to use the Facebook Mobile site frequently, I recommend you have an unlimited data plan that allows you to spend as much time on the Mobile Web as you like for a fixed rate. The Facebook Mobile site is nearly as comprehensive and rich as the computer version. You can spend hours there — and if you're paying per minute, spend your life savings, too.

Mobile Home

After you log in, you see the mobile version of the Facebook Home page. The design of the mobile site closely resembles the design of the regular website, with some minor differences. Some differences exist simply because of less space; the mobile site must cut to the chase while allowing you to get more information on a particular topic.

The other differences arise because people using Facebook on a phone often have different needs than those at a computer. For example, you'll see an additional "mobile menu" in the blue bar of your friends' mobile Timelines with options to call or text them.

To follow along with this section, you can navigate to m.facebook.com on your web browser. Just imagine what you see on about one-tenth of the screen.

In this section, I detail what you see on the Mobile Home page, shown in Figure 12-3; I cover the other pages in the following sections.

From m.facebook.com, you'll see these items in your Mobile Home page:

- ✔ **Facebook menu (three horizontal lines):** Click the three horizontal lines at the top-left corner of the screen to open a drop-down menu with links to the usual Facebook suspects: News Feed, Messages, Check In, Events, Groups, Friends, Notes, Settings, and Help.

- ✔ **Friend Requests, Messages, and Notifications:** The three icons across the top of your screen are used throughout the Facebook experience: Friend Requests, Messages, and Notifications. New or unread actions are marked by a red flag in each category, just like when you log in to your Facebook account from a PC. Tap any of these icons to review that category.

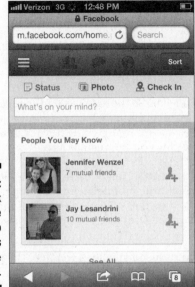

Figure 12-3:
Facebook
Mobile
Home, also
known as
`m.face`
`book.com.`

✔ **Sort:** This button, at the top-right of the screen, lets you choose how to view your News Feed. You can either display Top Stories (stories Facebook has deemed most engaging to you) or Most Recent stories (appearing chronically from newest to oldest).

✔ **Events and Birthdays:** When you reach the mobile site, you find any upcoming events right at the top of the Home page. You are also notified of any friends celebrating their birthdays today, so you can easily hop over to their Timelines and wish them a happy day.

✔ **Status:** When you use Facebook from your mobile phone, you're probably not sitting at your home office, workplace, or school. You may be trapped in jury duty, hanging with friends at a bachelorette party, or waiting in line for a roller coaster. Facebook makes it super-easy to update your status so you can spread the news the moment you're doing something you want people to know about.

✔ **Photo:** If you want to upload a photo to your Facebook account, you can tap this button and either use your built-in camera to take a photo (or video) or pick a photo from your phone's photo library to upload to your Timeline.

✔ **Check In:** If you want to let people know where you are, through Facebook, tap the Check In button to share your location on your Timeline.

✔ **Mobile News Feed:** Shows you the same stories that you would see on your computer. As you scroll down, you'll see more and more stories, so you can keep reading to your heart's content.

Mobile Timeline preview

Timelines on Facebook Mobile appear slightly different than Timelines on the regular site. The structure is ordered such that the information you're after is closest to the top.

Access to information on mobile Timelines is the same as on the regular site — when you look at your Timeline on the mobile site, you see your information, but that doesn't mean everyone has access to it. People have access only to what you specify via the privacy settings on the regular site:

- **Mobile Menu:** When viewing a friend's Timeline, three white dots in the top right of the blue bar represent the mobile menu. Clicking this menu opens a drop-down menu with shortcuts to message, call (if that person has her phone number listed on the site), text, or poke the friend whose Timeline you're viewing.

- **Profile picture and cover photo:** Just a smaller version of the profile picture and cover photo you see on the regular site.

- **Action buttons:** On the regular site, the Friends, Message, and Gift buttons appear within the cover photo, but for the mobile site they are directly below the cover photo.

- **Basic Information:** Below the action buttons is some of your friend's basic info, such as where she works and where she went to school.

- **Sections:** Below Basic Information, you see a row of boxes labeled About, Photos, Friends, Music, and so on. Tapping any of these sections takes you to their respective page. Tapping Photos allows you to see all your friend's tagged photos as well as photos she's uploaded by album.

- **Timeline and Share box:** As on the regular site, the star of the show is your friend's Timeline, where you can see her most recent posts, whether that's a status update or a photo. You can also see how many people liked or commented on her posts, and you can add to those counts yourself by doing the same. Or use the Share box to add a post on your friend's Timeline to say hello.

Mobile Inbox

The Mobile Inbox functions the same as the Inbox on the regular site, but in a more compact view. In the Mobile Inbox, your messages are sorted by the time the last message on a thread was sent. Each thread includes the sender's name, the date or how recently the message was sent, and a preview of the message.

When you open a mobile thread, similar to regular Facebook, the newest message is at the bottom with the Reply box beneath it. You can access a drop-down menu with action links from the blue bar at the top of the message (it's the white arrow in the upper-right corner). You can Mark Read/Unread, Delete, Report Spam or Abuse, Move to Other, Archive, or Forward. The Mark as Unread option is particularly handy because often you read a message on your mobile phone, but don't have time or energy to type a response right then. Marking it as Unread reminds you to respond when you return to your computer.

Mobile Apps

Mobile Web and Mobile Texts are generally pretty flexible systems. You can use them from almost any type of phone, with any sort of plan, and they generally look and work the same way. However, mobile apps are a different breed. They are tailor-made by Facebook for specific devices, and the way they work from device to device can differ greatly depending on factors like whether there's a touch screen or not. Right now, Facebook has apps available for the following phone types and devices: iPhone, Palm, Sony Ericsson, BlackBerry, Nokia, Android, Windows Phone, Sidekick, and iPad.

The mobile app for each device may look and operate differently. The following section focuses on how the Facebook for iPhone app works, which looks nearly identical to the Facebook Mobile site. If you don't use an iPhone, play around with your own phone; chances are, there are a lot of similarities.

If you find the mobile site a little slow, but don't use one of the preceding devices, you may still be in luck. Facebook for Every Phone is a downloadable app that works with Java-enabled phones (Java is a specific programming language). It's faster than the mobile site and functions similarly to the iPhone app. You can download Facebook for Every Phone at m.facebook.com.

Facebook Home

You may have read about the recent launch of a new mobile version of Facebook called Facebook Home. I won't go into too much detail because as of this writing, it's available only to Android users, but Facebook Home is essentially software built to seamlessly run on top of Android's mobile operating system.

A main benefit of this software is the capability to interact with your Facebook friends while using other parts of your phone. For example, the Chat Heads feature allows you to keep up with ongoing chats on Facebook even when you have another app open, such as a game or news reader. Facebook Home places friends at the center of your daily mobile interactions.

iPhone layout

The Facebook app for iPhone is organized much like the Mobile Home page for Facebook (refer to Figure 12-3). When you tap the top-left corner (represented by the three horizontal bars) of the screen, you see the drop-down menu to access the different parts of Facebook, as shown in Figure 12-4.

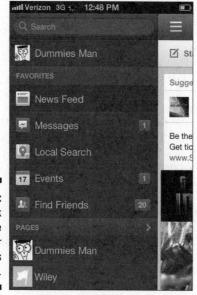

Figure 12-4: Facebook for iPhone menu for Dummies Man.

The different parts of Facebook you can access from this menu include the following:

- **Search:** At the top of the menu is a blank Search box. Type the name of any person, object, or thing you're looking for, and Facebook will attempt to autocomplete as you type. Tap the correct result when it comes up.

- **<Your Name>:** This menu option takes you to your own Timeline. In general, Timelines are organized into the same format as Timelines on the regular site, with a few stylistic changes to make sure all the information can fit on the screen. Use the Write Post or Share Photo buttons located below your profile picture to add something to your Timeline.

- **News Feed:** News Feed is the same News Feed you see on your computer screen, a constantly updating list of what your friends are up to at this moment. You can comment on and like posts from News Feed, as well as use the Status, Photo, or Check In buttons at the top of the page to add your own status update or mobile upload.

✔ **Messages:** This is where you access your Messages Inbox. From here, you can compose a new message, delete a message, or reply to one. The number of unread messages is listed to the right of this option.

✔ **Events:** This lets you view any events you've RSVPed to. This is incredibly useful when it turns out neither you nor your significant other remembers the exact street address of the dinner you're going to.

✔ **Nearby (or Local Search):** An extension of Facebook Places that lets you use your phone's GPS check-in and share where you are with your friends. It's so special that it gets its own section later in this chapter. If you see a number next to Nearby, it's the number of friends who have checked in close to you recently.

✔ **Pages:** This option takes you directly to any pages on Facebook that you admin or manage.

✔ **Groups (not shown):** This lets you interact with any groups you are a part of. This way, you don't miss out on discussions when you're out and about.

✔ **Apps (not shown):** This brings you to your own Facebook apps, like Photos, Notes, and anything you installed on your Facebook account that will work on a mobile device.

✔ **Friends (not shown):** The Friends section of the iPhone app should resemble your phone's contact list. You can scroll through your friends from A to Z or search for them from the Search box at the top of the list.

The final section of the menu contains the settings and maintenance links you've grown to love. From here, change your account or privacy settings, reach the Help Center, or log out of your account.

Posting from the iPhone

To update your status from the iPhone, follow these steps:

1. **Open the Facebook app.**

   Your News Feed appears. Three buttons are at the very top of News Feed: Status, Photo, and Check In.

2. **Tap Status.**

   This expands a large text box, as shown in Figure 12-5.

3. **Type your status.**

4. **(Optional) Tap the person icon and/or the pin icon to add tagging and location information to your status.**

5. **(Optional) Tap the Privacy menu (represented by any of the privacy icons — in Figure 12-5, the gear icon represents custom privacy) to choose who can see this status update.**

   You can choose from the usual options (Public, Friends, Friends Except Acquaintances, Only Me) as well as choose from any Friend Lists you've created.

6. **Tap Post in the upper-right corner.**

   The post is added to your Timeline and your friends' News Feeds.

Figure 12-5:
iPhone status updates start here.

Given how great an iPhone camera is, chances are you may want to add a photo to Facebook. Here's how to do that:

1. **Open the Facebook app.**

   Your News Feed appears. Three buttons are at the very top of News Feed: Status, Photo, and Check In.

2. **Tap Photo.**

   You may be prompted to grant the app permission to access your photos. After this happens, you're taken to your phone's photo library.

Choose a photo from the library or tap the camera icon at the bottom-left of the screen to take a new photo.

From your library, tap the photo or photos you want to upload. For each open photo, tap the gray check mark in a circle in the upper-right corner of the screen. The check mark turns green, and the photo is added to the Create a Post queue at the bottom-right of the screen.

3. **Tap the Create a Post button (pencil in a box) in the bottom-right corner of the screen.**

   If more than one photo is in the queue, all the photos will appear in the post.

4. **Write a caption to go along with the photo.**

   Type your caption into the Write Something text box that appears.

5. **(Optional) Tap the person icon and/or the pin icon to add tagging and location information to your photo.**

6. **(Optional) Select which photo album you'd like the photo to be added to.**

   Tap the square-within-a-square icon to the right of the camera icon to add this photo to a specific photo album. If you don't choose an album, the photo will automatically be added to your Mobile Uploads album.

7. **(Optional) Tap the Privacy menu to choose who can see this post.**

   You can choose from the usual options (Public, Friends, Friends Except Acquaintances, Only Me) as well as choose from any Friend Lists you've created.

8. **Tap Post in the upper-right corner.**

   The post is added to your Timeline and your friends' News Feeds.

Part of the greatness of Facebook on your mobile phone is that you can share the things that are happening to you as they happen. Don't be shy about documenting the funny/cool/interesting foibles of your daily life.

Checking in to Places

These days, most mobile devices have some sort of GPS functionality built in. This means you, via your phone, can easily locate yourself on a map. Facebook Places is a way for you to connect to your friends who are physically nearby.

Facebook Places works like this: When you go someplace using your Facebook app or Facebook Mobile, you choose from a list of possible locations. These might be restaurants or parks or buildings. Facebook generates this list based on the location it's getting from your phone. When you select a location, you *check in* to that location. Checking in basically means actively telling Facebook that you're there. Facebook won't share your location unless you check in.

You can tag friends in your check-ins or add photos or a few words about what's going on. After you check in, your friends can see where you are in their News Feeds. If they're out and about and also using Facebook on their phones, they can see if they are near you by tapping Nearby from the Facebook menu.

Checking in to Places leads to all sorts of nice serendipitous encounters. When I was in Boston recently, I checked in to a few different restaurants. An old friend I hadn't seen in ten years sent me a message asking how much longer I'd be in town. I didn't even know she had moved to Boston. We had brunch the next day.

To check in from your iPhone, follow these steps:

1. **Tap Check In at the top of News Feed.**

   This brings up a list of nearby places. These places may range from official businesses (Peet's Coffee) to people's homes (Carolyn and Eric's Place) to shared spaces (Dolores Park, San Francisco Airport Terminal 2).

2. **Select the name of the place you'd like to check in to.**

   If you don't find what you're looking for, type the name of the place you want to check in to in the search bar above the list of suggested locations. If it's not found, Facebook brings you to the Add a Place page, shown in Figure 12-6, and you can tap the Add button to add the place to the list.

3. **(Optional) Type a comment into the Check In box.**

   The Check In screen appears, as shown in Figure 12-7. Check-ins with comments tend to feel a lot like status updates, with a little additional information.

4. **(Optional) Tap the person icon to tag friends.**

   Your list of friends appears. Tap the ones you want to tag.

   Some people are very private about their location information, so it's considered appropriate to ask people before you tag them.

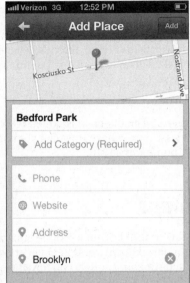

Figure 12-6:
The Add
Place page.

Figure 12-7:
Tell people
where you
are and
why.

5. **Tap Done when you're done tagging.**

6. **(Optional) Tap the Privacy menu to choose who can see this post.**

   You can choose from the usual options (Public, Friends, Friends Except Acquaintances, Only Me) as well as choose from any Friend Lists you've created.

7. **Tap Post in the upper-right corner.**

   This officially marks you as "here." The check-in is added to your Timeline and your friends' News Feeds, where they can comment or like your check-in, or maybe even pop by to say hi.

Additional Mobile apps

iPhone and Android users have a few other Facebook Mobile apps available to them. Each of these apps offers a pared down version of Facebook that focuses on one or two features or functionalities. Read on for a brief description of these apps.

Facebook Camera (iPhone only)

If you find photos to be the most engaging part of Facebook, you may want to download this application, which organizes all your friends' photo stories into a single photos feed. You can also post your own photos from the app.

Messenger (iPhone and Android only)

If you use Facebook Inbox as your personal messaging center, you may want to check out this app, which allows you to text friends using your phone's data plan as well as help you stay on top of multiple message threads via in-app notifications.

Facebook Poke (iPhone only)

With Facebook Poke, you can send pokes, messages, photos, and videos to individual friends or groups of friends. This doesn't seem too exciting until you learn that if you send a message, photo, or video, you can choose the length of time (from one to ten seconds) the content will be available for your friends to view. After the time has elapsed, the content disappears from the app.

A final word to the wise. If you use multiple versions of Facebook (computer, mobile, mobile app), you may find yourself inundated with repetitive notifications about the same action. For example, if my friend posts a photo to my Timeline, I might receive one notification in my e-mail, another through my phone's push notifications, and still another in the Facebook app. To cut down on the potential spam, go to the Notifications tab of the Account menu and adjust the settings in the How You Get Notifications section.

Chapter 13

Creating a Page for Promotion

*P*icture your town or city. Besides the occasional park or school, it's primarily made up of buildings in which people live (like houses) and buildings in which people buy things (like stores). When you drive around town, you see all sorts of activities happening — whether people are throwing a Frisbee around, arguing politics over a cup of coffee, or working out. The world we live in is composed of people, the stuff they do, and the stuff that they need or want. People have real connections to all this stuff: the shops, the brands, the bands, the stars, the activities, the passions, and the restaurants and bars — things that are important. Facebook is all about people and their real-world connections, including the connections that aren't just friends.

Facebook offers a way for these non-friend entities to be represented as part of your life — namely, *Facebook Pages.*

"Page" is a pretty common word on the Internet, so I always capitalize the *P* in Pages when talking about Facebook Pages.

There are two main types of Pages: *Community Pages,* which are collectively updated and managed by its fans, and *Official Pages,* which are updated and managed by authorized representatives of any business entity. People who manage a Page are known as administrators or *admins.*

This chapter is all about understanding the world of Facebook Pages. If you just want to know what these things are that you've been liking and that have been showing up in your News Feed, check out the next section, "Getting to Know Pages." If you're looking to represent your business, brand, band, or anything else on Facebook, start with the "Do I need a Page?" section and read on from there.

Getting to Know Pages

You can do many of the same things with Pages that you can do with friends — write on their Timelines, tag them in status updates, and so on. The main difference is that instead of friending Pages, you like them (thus, instead of becoming a friend, you become a *fan* of a Page).

When you like a Page, your information and access to your Timeline isn't shared with the Page and its admins, although any posts you make to a Page are public.

Anatomy of an Official Page

Official Pages are meant to be like Timelines, but they're intended for organizations. So if you've already read Chapter 4, most of the following will sound familiar. Figure 13-1 shows a sample Facebook Page from *The New York Times*.

Here's the anatomy of an Official Page, across the top from left to right:

✔ **Profile picture and cover photo:** Just like you and your friends, Pages use one photo to represent them across the site. Usually, it's a logo or an official press photo. Pages also have a cover photo, often an image that more broadly represents the organization's brand.

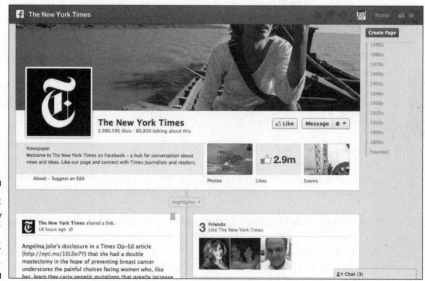

Figure 13-1: *The New York Times'* Facebook Page.

✔ **Like button:** The Like button is located at the right of the Page's name. To become a fan, click this button. (See the "Connecting and interacting with Pages" section for more on this topic).

✔ **Message button:** Click the Message button to say something directly (and more privately) to the admins of the Page you're looking at.

✔ **Options:** Clicking the gear icon opens a drop-down menu from which you can report, share, unlike, or send feedback about a Page.

✔ **About, Photos, Likes, Events:** Below the cover photo is a bit of basic information and links to see more content — photos the Page has added, other Pages it likes, and events it's promoting.

✔ **Timeline (and Share box):** The Timeline is the heart of a Page — it's where the admins post updates and where fans can leave posts and comments. Pages may or may not have a Share box here, although most choose to let their fans interact as though they were friends (although the Share box on Pages has fewer options than on your Timeline — usually just Post and Photo/Video). Scroll down to see posts the Page has added, as well as information about interactions between any of your friends and the Page. For example, Figure 13-1 contains a box with thumbnail photos of my friends who also like *The New York Times'* Page.

Community Pages

Community Pages, or Pages that don't officially represent something or some-one, tend to cover a wider range of things, from basic activities to political statements. Often, the object represented by these pages is something that simply can't be owned by a corporation or individual — things like "Cheese" or "Ultimate Frisbee" or *Pride and Prejudice* (though, interestingly, a new movie version of *Pride and Prejudice* would almost certainly have an Official Page, as opposed to a Community Page).

Community Pages can be further categorized into two distinct subsets. For clarity, I refer to these subsets as Topic Pages and Community Pages, but both fall under the Community Pages umbrella. Topic Pages differ from Official and Community Pages in key ways:

✔ **Topic Pages don't have a Timeline.** Instead, they show you a list of your friends who also like that topic and related topics as well as any relevant content about your friends and that topic.

✔ **Topic Pages pull basic info from sites like Wikipedia to explain what they represent.** Topic Pages function mostly as badges on your Timeline, appearing in your Interest boxes. A sample Topic Page is shown in Figure 13-2.

The layout of Community Pages, on the other hand, is identical to that of Official Pages. These Pages tend to be more specific than their Topic counterparts, but the admins are not official representatives. For example, a fan of the TV show *Modern Family* may admin a Page that's focused on discussing a specific season with fellow fans. You'll know you're looking at a Community Page if you see the word "Community" labeled directly below the cover photo.

Connecting and interacting with Pages

Wherever you go on Facebook, and in many places across the entire Internet, you'll see links and buttons prompting you to like something. You can like photos, statuses, comments, articles, websites, videos . . . if it's online, you can probably like it.

You can also like Pages, and doing so is the way that you become a fan; as I say earlier, a *fan* is a person who likes a particular Page. Being a fan accomplishes a few things:

✔ **Gives you a News Feed subscription.** After you like a page, you may start seeing its posts in your News Feed. If you don't like what you're seeing, you can remove that Page from your News Feed. To do so, go to the Page and hover over the Like button; from the drop-down menu, click Show in News Feed to uncheck it. Re-click to turn News Feed stories back on.

✔ **Provides access to the Timeline.** Just as when you add a friend, liking a Page lets you post on its Timeline, usually with the capability to add photos, links, and videos. Not all Pages allow fans to post on their Timeline, but many do.

✔ **Displays the Page you liked on your own Timeline.** Keep in mind that when you like a Page, it appears in the Recent Activity section of your Timeline, and by default, this section is visible to Public/Everyone.

So what does this all mean for you? Basically, when you like something, you're starting a relationship with it that can be as interactive or as hands-off as you want. Frequently, people like a lot of Pages simply as a signifier or badge on their Timelines. However, just because you like *Modern Family* doesn't mean you want to read episode recaps or watch interviews with the cast. And that's fine. On the other hand, if you like seeing those sorts of things, or interacting with other fans on the show's Page, you can do that as well. It's a pretty flexible system.

Creating a Facebook Page

A Facebook Page isn't equivalent to an account. Rather, it's an entity on Facebook that can be managed by many people with their own distinct accounts. This section takes you through all the steps of Page creation, administration, and maintenance.

Do I need a Page?

In other words, should I be creating a Facebook Page for my *<local business/band/charity/product/school>* and so on? The short answer is probably. Facebook Pages, at their most basic level, are for anything that's not an individual person and can even be useful for individuals who are celebrities or who have a public presence beyond their friends and family.

So whether you have a small consulting business, are fundraising for a local organization, or are a member of a performance troupe, creating a Facebook Page can work for you. You *do* need to be an authorized representative of any larger entity (for example, you shouldn't create a Page for a local congressperson unless you're working for her). But assuming that part is all squared away, you're ready to find out how to create and manage a Page.

Creating your Page

Before you get started, I recommend you read the Facebook Pages Terms at www.facebook.com/terms_pages.php. The terms clarify some of the expectations for owning a Page and who can create a Page for a business. There are also a few notes about who can see your content when you create a Page and age restrictions on your Page. I cover these topics throughout this chapter, but the terms provide a nice summary. If you violate these terms, your Page may be disabled, which could negatively impact your business. On the same note, if you use a personal Timeline to do the work of a Page (as I describe here), your Facebook account will almost certainly be disabled for violating the Statement of Rights and Responsibilities (which you can read at www.facebook.com/terms.php).

If you haven't already created an account on Facebook, I highly recommend you do that first before creating a Page (although you don't have to). If you don't want to, you can still create a Facebook Page at https://www.facebook.com/pages/create.php. If you go this route, you'll have an additional step of entering your e-mail address and creating a password for your Page's account.

Pages can have multiple admins. If you plan to have other people managing the Page you're creating, they can do so from their own accounts. There's no reason to share the e-mail address or password with anyone. In fact, doing so violates the Statement of Rights and Responsibilities. So use your real e-mail address and birth date; don't create a fake persona just for the Page. Your information won't be revealed to anyone else, and it makes your future interactions on Facebook much easier. To create your own Page, follow these steps:

1. **Log in to Facebook with your username and password.**

2. **Navigate to the Account menu (down arrow), located at the right corner of the blue bar, and choose Create Page from the drop-down menu.**

   The Create a Page page appears, as shown in Figure 13-3.

Figure 13-3: What kind of Page do you need?

3. **Click the category your Page falls under.**

   Figure 13-3 shows the chosen category as Artist, Band or Public Figure. You can choose from the following:

   - Local Business or Place
   - Company, Organization, or Institution
   - Brand or Product
   - Artist, Band, or Public Figure
   - Entertainment
   - Cause or Community

   When you choose your category, a registry field appears.

4. **Choose your subcategory from the Choose a category menu.**

5. **Enter the name of your Page into the Name text box.**

   Use the exact name of your business, just as you need to use your real name on your Facebook account.

   Good examples of names for hypothetical Facebook Pages are

   - Amazon
   - Anthony's Pizza
   - Stephen Colbert
   - Buffy the Vampire Slayer

   Bad examples of hypothetical Facebook Page names are

   - Amazon's Facebook Page
   - Anthony's Pizza at 553 University Ave.
   - Stephen Colbert, Politician & Comedian Extraordinaire
   - Buffy the Vampire Slayer Is Awesome

6. **Select the check box to agree to the Facebook Pages Terms.**

7. **Click Get Started.**

Getting started

In this section, I go through the steps Facebook takes you through to get your Page set up, as shown in Figure 13-4.

The first step is required to begin using your Page. You can skip the other steps and return to them at any time from your Page's Admin Panel or Edit Settings page (more on those later in the section, "Managing your Page").

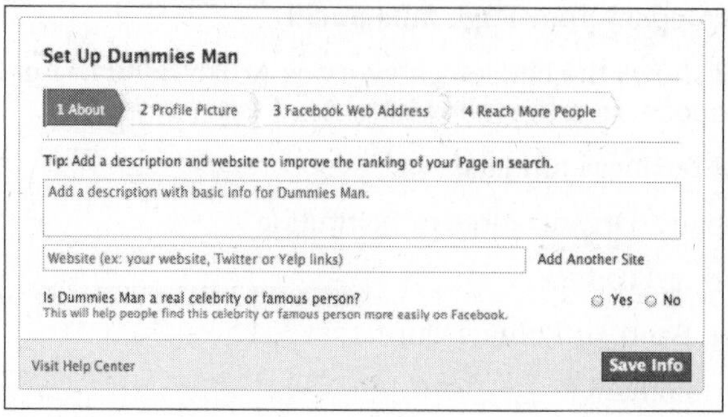

Set Up Dummies Man

| 1 About | 2 Profile Picture | 3 Facebook Web Address | 4 Reach More People |

Tip: Add a description and website to improve the ranking of your Page in search.

Add a description with basic info for Dummies Man.

Website (ex: your website, Twitter or Yelp links)   Add Another Site

Is Dummies Man a real celebrity or famous person?   ○ Yes   ○ No
This will help people find this celebrity or famous person more easily on Facebook.

Visit Help Center   **Save Info**

Figure 13-4:
Begin set-
ting up your
Page.

Step 1: Tell everyone about yourself

First, you're prompted to add a short description of yourself/business/orga-
nization/band/and so on and a link to any other websites that represent you.
This can be anything from a Twitter feed to your personal website. You also
establish whether your Page is official.

Step 2: Add an image

The second step is to get your Page's profile picture in place. You have two
options for selecting an image:

- Click Upload from Computer; then click Choose File or Browse to select
  an image from your computer's hard drive.
- Click Import from Website to choose from the images Facebook finds on
  your website.

When the photo is successfully uploaded, it replaces the default profile
picture on the left side of the Page.

Step 3: Get a Facebook web address

Facebook allows you to select a unique web address to help direct people
to your Facebook Page. It's much easier to tell people to like you at `www.`
`facebook.com/myname` than it is to tell them to go to `www.facebook.`
`com/8u53285y2lefsjlf0?fjdklfs`.

You can change this address only once after your initial pick, so take your
time thinking about it before committing.

If you have an address in mind, type it in the text box and click Set Address
to confirm.

Step 4: Reach more people

If you plan to advertise your Page on Facebook, you can add a payment
method, such as a credit card, to make the process of creating an ad easier
when you're ready. Click Skip if you'd rather add this info later.

Step 5: Like yourself

Now that your Page is live, you can be the first person to like it! Just click the Like button when prompted to become your first fan.

Step 6: Invite your friends

One of the first steps in starting your Facebook account was to get some friends. This is even more important for Pages: Without fans (the Pages equivalent of friends), your updates and information won't reach anyone. A good way to start looking for fans is to suggest your Page to your own friends. You may be prompted to suggest your Page to your e-mail contact list (similar to using the Friend Finder I discuss in Chapter 2). You can also jump to the Invite Friends section of your Admin Panel and select friends to suggest your Page to. Your friends receive a notification that you invited them to like this Page.

Step 7: Share something

Updates and posts are how your fans find out what's going on with you because these updates appear in their News Feeds. Make them interesting and engaging to get conversations started.

Congrats! You successfully created a Facebook Page.

Using your Page

After completing the previously described steps, you'll be looking at a fairly empty Page Timeline. If the idea of filling it up with posts gets your blood pumping, read on. If you need to take a break, you'll want to know how to get back to the Page.

The fastest way to get to your Page is to search for the Page name in the blue bar. Because you're the Page's admin, it should be one of your top results.

The Timeline

If you have a personal Timeline, your Page's Timeline will feel very familiar; it's the virtual scrapbook of posts you've added to Facebook. In Chapter 4, I describe the Timeline in detail as a place that tells the story of you. That story still needs to be told for you, even when you represent something other than yourself.

People are going to want to hear from you and learn about you, and the place they go to do so is your Timeline. Any content you post to your Timeline also shows up in your fans' News Feeds. In other words, it's a very important place to represent yourself honestly and engagingly through continual updates.

Check out the Timeline for George Takei of *Star Trek* fame in Figure 13-5 to get a feel for how a Page can use its Timeline to showcase what it cares about and to engage its fans.

Figure 13-5:
George
Takei on
Facebook.

As a Page admin, the most important part of the Timeline for you to understand is the *Share box.* The Share box, as shown in Figure 13-6, is where you and your fans create the posts that populate your Page.

Figure 13-6:
Use the
Share box to
send posts
out to fans.

The most basic post you can make is a *status update,* a short message letting people know what's going on, what you're up to, thinking about, and so on. To write a status update, follow these steps:

1. **Click in Share box (where it reads Write Something at the top of the Timeline).**

2. **Type your update.**

3. **(Optional) Target your update by clicking the cross-hair icon to the left of the Post button.**

   Status updates you make from your personal Timeline have privacy rules about who can and can't see them. Status updates you make as a Page have *targeting* — limitations for who can see which posts. By default, everyone can see all posts, but you can control who can see your posts in their News Feeds from the drop-down menu, as shown in Figure 13-7.

Figure 13-7:
Target your
posts to
specific
groups of
fans.

You can target posts to people by age, location, language, gender, and more. This is really useful if, for example, your band is going on tour and you want to let people in a specific city know when you're going to be there. Language targeting can also be useful if you have an international presence.

Keep your eye on the Targeted To number to the right. As you adjust targeting, this number changes to show you how many fans you'll theoretically be able to reach with those settings.

4. **Click Post.**

   The post you've created appears on the Page's Timeline and in your fans' News Feeds.

In addition to posting status updates, you can post photos, links, videos, and events to your fans.

By default, people who have liked your Page can post on your Timeline and like and comment on your posts. This is a chance to engage with your customers and fans. If someone asks a question, answer it. If they report that they had a problem with your product or experienced bad customer service, let them know that you're listening and will do your best to correct the problem.

Photos

Use the Photos application to post images and albums for your fans to enjoy:

- ✔ If you own a restaurant, you may want to take photos of your most popular dishes, creating one album for breakfast, one for lunch, and one for dinner.
- ✔ Bands might publish albums from their various concerts and events.
- ✔ Brands might use photos to show people engaging with their products.

  For example, Nike might post an album of athletes wearing its shoes, Starbucks might post a photo of a kid with whipped cream on his nose, and Netflix might post a photo of friends watching a movie.

Add photos by clicking the Photo/Video link in the Share box and selecting a photo from your computer to upload.

If you choose to, you can allow fans to add photos to your Page (you can do this from the Manage Permissions tab of the Edit Settings screen). These photos are shown in a separate section from the photos you add, which helps viewers distinguish between the content you're adding to your Page and what your fans add. Posting photos is a great way to keep your Timeline looking dynamic and to generate interesting posts for your fans' News Feeds.

Video

Just like with Photos, you can upload videos to your Page. For example, a coffee shop might show a video of a barista making latte art, a singer might show clips from a recent concert, and a movie theater might show a trailer for an upcoming film. The online retailer Zappos has an album of some pretty funny videos that include interviews and short skits done by its employees. It's a great way to put a human face on a brand. You can add videos by clicking the Photo/Video link in the Share box, and selecting a video to upload from your computer.

Event

If you ever host an event for your business, you'll get a ton of value from using Facebook Events. Stores create events for their big sales, comedians create events for their shows, and clubs create events for their special-party nights. To create an event, click Event, Milestone + or Offer, Event + in the Share box. The Create New Event window appears. Fill in the Event info and click Create. Head on over to the event's page to invite your friends and add an event photo (see Chapter 11 for more details on event creation). Events you create for your Page are Public by default, meaning anyone can see and join the event.

Other Posts: Milestone, Offer, Question

Pages can use three other types of posts. You may find yourself using these posts less often, but they can provide a lot of value and engagement when used strategically:

- ✔ **Milestones** appear larger than other posts in the Timeline and highlight a date or event that's important to your business.

  For example, a recording artist might list the date her first album went platinum.

- ✔ **Offers** let you to reward fans with in-store and online promotions.

- ✔ **Questions** are helpful for quickly gauging customer feedback by allowing you to create a poll.

  For example, an ice cream company might poll its fans to find out what the next new flavor should be.

With all your posting, you may have noticed a clock icon among the other icons in the Share box. Clicking this icon allows you to schedule a post up to six months in advance. Choose the year, day, and time you want that post to appear and click Schedule. Facebook takes care of the rest!

Applications

Photos, Events, and Notes are applications that Facebook has built to integrate with Pages and Timelines alike. But what about specific features for specific types of Pages and specific needs? What if you want people to have access to coupons at all times? Or you're a band and want information about your upcoming tour to be discoverable? Well, as they say, there's an app for that. Facebook has the capability to integrate with applications built by developers outside of Facebook.

Rather than browsing the App Center for good applications, some Page admins check out their competitors' Pages to see what kinds of applications seem to be working well for them. When you find an app you want to use on your Page, follow these steps to start using it:

1. **Search for the app's name in the blue bar and click on the correct result.**

   Select the result that reads App Page underneath the name of the app. This takes you to the App Page.

2. **From the App Page, click the gear icon and choose Add App to Page from the drop-down menu.**

   The Add Page Tab window appears.

3. **If you are the admin for more than one Page, choose which one you'd like to add the app to.**

4. **Click the Add Page Tab button.**

Not all apps work on Pages.

Using Facebook as your Page

After you get going with your Page, you may want to use Facebook as your Page. In other words, you can take actions and interact on Facebook as though your Page, not you, is the main user. Your Page has its own News Feed, where you can catch up on your Page's favorite Pages and leave comments that come from the Page (in other words, instead of a comment being next to the name and profile picture of Carolyn Abram, it is next to the name and profile picture of *Facebook For Dummies*). You will have easy access to your Page-related tools and settings on the left side of your Home page, instead of getting distracted by your friend's photos of her trip to Greece.

Switching from your personal account to your Page (you can see a sample Home page for a Page in Figure 13-8) is especially useful for big companies or brands that want a full-time presence on Facebook. This way, the notifications coming in are all about your Page, instead of mingling with the personal stuff.

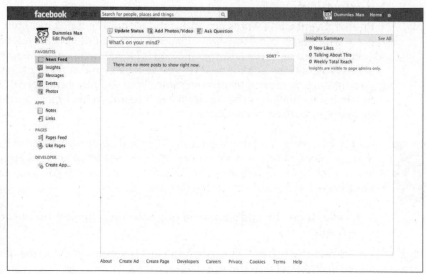

Figure 13-8:
Using
Facebook as
a Page.

To make the switch, open your Account menu (the down arrow found on the blue bar) and select your Page name from the Use Facebook As section of the drop-down menu. You're now using Facebook as your Page. Follow the same steps to switch back to your personal account.

Managing Your Page

As the creator (and therefore admin) of your Page, you have a lot of control over how people see and interact with your Page. You can manage your Page from one of two places: the Admin Panel at the top of the Page or the Edit Settings page.

Admin Panel

The Admin Panel is a box at the top of your Page. It provides a snapshot of how your Page is doing, as well as links to manage your settings, build your audience, and see all your Page Insights. Figure 13-9 shows the Admin Panel for the Dummies Man Page.

Figure 13-9:
The Admin
Panel is the
control
center of
your Page.

The top section of the Admin Panel shows you new notifications and messages from fans (if you opt to allow fans to send your Page private messages). Interacting with fans and responding to comments or messages are vital parts of keeping people engaged with your Page.

The bottom section of the Admin Panel shows New Likes and a preview of your Page's Insights — or data about how people are interacting with your Page. For more information on Insights, skip ahead to the section, "Know-It-All: Finding Out Who Is Using Your Page."

Activity Log

The Activity Log is a chronologically ordered list of every action your Page has taken (such as posting a photo) as well as every action involving your Page (such as being tagged in a status update).

Admins can access the Activity Log by clicking the Edit Page button at the top of the Admin Panel and choosing Use Activity Log from the drop-down menu. From the Activity Log, you can click the star icon next to posts to highlight them, hide posts, change the dates of posts, remove spammy posts from your Page, and so on.

Page settings

To get to your settings, click the Edit Page button at the top of the Admin Panel, and select Edit Settings from the drop-down menu. This brings you to the Manage Permissions section. Use the menu on the left to navigate to the different sections. The first section is at the very top: Your Settings.

The Your Settings section has three different controls you can turn on or off:

- ✔ **Similar Page Suggestions:** After you like a Page, you're often presented with some thumbnail photos of similar Pages you might also want to like.

  After liking the TV show *Downtown Abbey,* for example, I saw Page suggestions for the TV show *Mad Men,* the PBS series *Masterpiece Theatre,* and the film *Fried Green Tomatoes.* Keep this check box selected if you want your Page to be included in these suggestions. Deselecting keeps your Page out of suggestions on other Pages and also turns off suggestions for people who like your Page.

- ✔ **Email Notifications:** Select this check box if you want to receive e-mail notifications whenever someone posts, likes, comments on, or messages your Page.

  Depending on how busy your Page is, the amount of e-mail may become overwhelming, so remember where this setting is in case you need to turn it off.

- ✔ **Onsite Notification:** Select this check box if you want to receive Facebook notifications whenever someone posts, likes, comments on, or messages your Page.

Manage Permissions

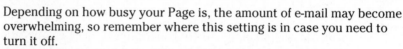

The Manage Permissions section controls who can see your Page and how they can interact with it:

- ✔ **Page Visibility:** This check box allows you to unpublish your Page, which hides it from everyone except admins. Doing so is useful if the Page is under construction because you're adding some new stuff to it.

  Don't accidentally leave it in this state when you're done making updates or your fans won't be able to find you.

- ✔ **Country Restrictions:** Leaving this box empty means everyone everywhere can see your Page. Entering specific countries lets you decide if your Page will be available or hidden for the people in those countries.

- ✔ **Age Restrictions:** By default, anyone on Facebook can see your Page. If your Page deals with adult products or themes, you may want to consider age restrictions. There's a specific Alcohol-Related option in the drop-down menu if your Page is related to alcohol products.

- ✔ **Posting Ability:** Select these two check boxes to allow fans to post to your Page as well as add photos and videos.

  Select at least the first check box because without interaction, your Page won't feel as Facebook-y. (And yes, *Facebook-y* is a word — Google it.)

✔ **Post Visibility:** Select this check box to choose whether posts from your fans appear in a special Recent Posts by Others section at the top of your Page's Timeline.

If you want these posts to appear, but prefer to first review and approve them, use the drop-down menu to change the default visibility setting to Hidden from Page. If you choose to review posts, they appear in your Admin Panel for you to approve.

✔ **Tagging Ability:** Selecting this check box allows your fans to tag themselves or others in photos that you post from your Page.

✔ **Messages:** Selecting this box adds a Message button to your Page and allows fans to send you private messages.

If you feel like you have the time to respond to these messages, it's probably a good idea to leave this check box selected because it's the sort of thing that builds rapport between you and your fans.

✔ **Moderation Blocklist:** If your Page is seeing a lot of debate, and some of it is simply offensive or not productive, you can create a moderation blocklist. If words added to the blocklist are found in a post, the post is automatically marked as spam.

✔ **Profanity Blocklist:** You shouldn't need to come up with your own blocklist for the most commonly offensive terms (none of which I can print here as an example for you). If you want at least a little sanitization of your Timeline, choose Medium from the drop-down menu. If you want it to be as PG as possible, choose Strong.

Even with your blocklists on, you should still be diligent about checking your posts, comments, and fan-uploaded photos and videos for the types of offensive language and images that can't necessarily be caught by these automated systems.

✔ **Post Privacy Gating:** Select this check box for the capability to choose your audience for each post you make.

✔ **Replies:** Selecting this check box turns on replies for future posts from your Page. Comments now display an option to Reply. Other fans click Reply to direct their responses to a specific comment or fan. Replies are displayed below comments to help clarify who is responding to what.

✔ **Delete Page:** If at some point you decide you don't want your Page anymore, you can delete it here.

Basic Information and profile picture

You can go to these sections to change these settings at any time.

Featured

Acting as your Page, you can like other Pages. Then you can feature particular Pages on your own Page by clicking Add Featured Likes and choosing the Pages you want displayed there. The Pages you feature appear in the right column of your Page.

You can also feature yourself or other Page owners (admins) by clicking Add Featured Page Owners and selecting people whose profile pictures and names you want displayed on your Page's About section.

Resources

The Resources section provides you with some helpful links to things like best practices to make your Page engaging or a link to Twitter (so when you update Twitter, you also update Facebook). If you find yourself with questions after reading this chapter, this section is a good place to look for answers.

Admin Roles

The Admin Roles section displays a list of current admins. You can remove an admin by clicking the X next to his name or add new admins by typing a name or e-mail address into the text box. You can also assign or change specific admin roles (choose from Manager, Moderator, Content Creator, Advertiser, or Insights Analyst) from the drop-down menu under an admin's name. Remember to click Save when you're done.

Apps

The Apps section shows you all the applications your Page is using. If you no longer use some of these applications, click the x to remove them. Note that Photos, Events, and Notes are considered integrated applications by Facebook, and you can remove these applications just like you remove others.

Some apps may have a little link beneath them labeled Link to This Tab. Clicking this link provides you with a URL you can share. When people click that link, they go to that specific tab on your Page, as opposed to the Timeline, which is what people see by default when they arrive at your Page.

Mobile

The Mobile section gives you information about the various ways you can use your mobile phone to control your Page. If you attach a particular mobile phone number to your Page, you can use that number to update your status and post photos.

Additionally, if you have many different admins who want to post updates on the go and who have smartphones, you can use your Page's unique Mobile Email Address (usually one that's hard to memorize, so be sure to save it to your phone's contact list) to e-mail posts to add to your Page.

Insights

The little arrow icon next to the Insights section signifies that it takes you away from the Edit Settings page to the Insights page. Insights are a way of tracking metrics about your Page and are detailed in the next section of this chapter.

Help

Clicking this section takes you to the Help Center, where you can search for any questions you couldn't get answers to here.

Know-It-All: Finding Out Who Is Using Your Page

Forty-eight hours after creating your Official Page, you start to see exactly how people are engaging with it. From the Admin Panel, look for the graph at the bottom, and next to Insights, click See All. You are brought to the Insights page, where you can see valuable metrics about how people are interacting with your Page.

Overview

When you navigate to the Insights page, by default, you land on a page showing an overview of activity on your Page. You can see an example of an Insights Overview in Figure 13-10.

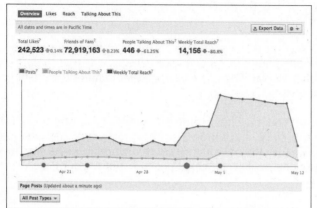

Figure 13-10:
View your
Page
Insights
here.

At the top of the Overview page are some numbers:

- ✔ **Total Likes?** This shows the number of likes your Page has — in other words, how many fans you have.

- ✔ **Friends of Fans?** This shows how many friends your fans have — in other words, the people who might like your Page simply because one of their friends recommended it.

- ✔ **People Talking About This?** Unlike the previous two numbers, this number is calculated weekly. It goes up every time someone likes your Page, tags your Page in a photo, posts on your Page's Timeline, and so on. In other words, every time a fan creates a story that goes into his or her friends' News Feeds, it counts as talking about your Page.

- ✔ **Weekly Total Reach?** This shows you the number of people who saw any content associated with your Page in the past week. That can mean a post, a photo, an ad, or any number of other things.

Next to each of these four numbers is an arrow indicating whether this number is going up or down, and by how much. In general, you want all your numbers to be going up or remaining constant.

The main graph on the Overview page, if you enjoy pretty pictures, shows three basic trends over time:

- ✔ The number of posts you made to your Page

- ✔ The people talking about your Page

- ✔ The weekly total reach

In general, posting content leads to more people talking about your Page, which leads to a greater weekly reach, which is why it can be helpful to look at these graphs as one.

If you scroll down, you can see just how each post increased your Page's traffic and reach. This can help you understand the kinds of posts people like and respond to, and which ones actually harm you. For example, if posting too many events is annoying people, chances are you're losing fans. On the other hand, if your events are legendary and never fail to get your fans talking, your reach and engaged users increase.

Likes

Find out more about your fan base by clicking Likes (to the right of Overview). This section shows you breakdowns by gender, age, nationality, city, and language of those people who like your Page. By default, it shows you data over the past month. You can adjust the timeframe from the drop-down menu at the top.

If you scroll down, you can see where your likes came from. It may be from people recommending your Page to others or from people searching for you on Facebook. Again, this can help you figure out if you need to grow your fan base and how you might reach more people.

Reach

The next section shows the demographic breakdown of your reach, meaning the number of people who saw any piece of content associated with your Page. They don't have to like your Page to see something a friend posts to your Timeline. This section offers the same breakdown as Likes, but for all the people who see your content, not just your fans.

Talking About This

Use this section to look at who is talking about you, demographically speaking.

Talking about a Page includes anything that creates a News Feed story.

Things get interesting when you look at the comparisons — are you reaching lots of men but only women are talking about your Page? Or are you doing better in certain cities than others? These types of questions can help you further build your audience or just cater better to the needs of your audience. If your Page's most vocal fans are people aged 18 to 24, make sure you post content that 18- to 24-year-olds will like and want to share. It keeps everyone wanting to see more.

Promoting your Page through advertising

Creating and maintaining a Page on Facebook is free. However, if you want to promote it more aggressively or bring attention to a specific event, you can consider running advertising on Facebook as well.

Head to the Ads Create tool at `https://www.facebook.com/ads/create` to get started.

1. **Create your ad:** Ads on Facebook have fairly standard formats. Your ad needs a title or headline, body text of fewer than 135 characters, and an image. You also need to decide where you want your ad to take people when they click it. A Page might choose to have an ad link to its Timeline.

2. **Choose your audience:** Here is where advertising on Facebook can become most efficient. You can target an ad based on location, age, and gender, as well as by specific interests. Narrowing down the people who see your ad to those people who are likely to want your product or service makes your advertising more effective.

   Say your band has a performance you'd like to promote. You could walk around town distributing flyers, but wouldn't it be better if you gave flyers only to people who like the type of music you perform? That's what Facebook ads allow you to do. You can type virtually any terms and use them to get your ads in front of the right eyes.

Depending on what you're promoting, you can also target your ads to your fans, to your non-fans, or to friends of fans.

3. **Budget and schedule your ad:** You can spend tons of money on your ads or very little. Facebook's ad system offers both cost per thousand impressions (CPM) and cost per click (CPC) models. If you choose CPM, you pay every time your ad is seen. If you go with CPC, you set a bid for how much you'll pay for a click. Your ad goes into rotation with other ads based on the targeting you choose, and you pay only for the number of times your ad is clicked (it's up to Facebook to show it enough times to get more clicks). With either choice, you can set a maximum daily or lifetime budget so you won't ever be surprised by how much you're spending. You can schedule your ad to run continuously or to stop after a certain date.

Remember that the key to effective Facebook advertising is knowing what you want to accomplish with your ads. Do you want more fans for your Page? Do you want to distribute a coupon to get more customers in the store? Do you want to bring attention or solicit donations for a cause? Knowing the answers to these questions helps you create and target the best ads.

Chapter 14

Games, Apps, and Websites on Facebook

In This Chapter

▶ Understanding what apps are and how they work on Facebook

▶ Seeing how apps can enhance your Internet experience on and off Facebook

▶ Discovering good, trustworthy apps

*I*f you're familiar with Apple's iPhone commercials, you've probably heard the phrase, "There's an app for that." In iPhone-land, an *app* is a kind of program you add to your phone that suits your particular needs. It might help you track what you eat, or it might be a game you can play alone or with friends. iPhone apps take something that is already useful (your phone) and make it even more useful and fun.

Similarly, apps on Facebook take something that is already useful (Facebook) and make it even more useful and fun. They can take advantage (with your permission) of some of the parts of Facebook that are hard to replicate elsewhere, things like your Friend List, the things you like, and News Feed.

On Facebook, apps can exist for a whole host of reasons. They may be related to sharing things like what you're reading or listening to. They can be games you can play with your friends — both on Facebook and on your mobile phone. And they are actually found on other websites, because you can use your Facebook information, like your name and profile picture, to skip over setting up multiple profiles on multiple sites.

Understanding What an App Is

For a long time, Facebook was the only company that could build apps for Facebook. And it did; it built Photos, Events, and Groups. All these are considered applications because they use the same core set of information to function: the connections between you and your friends. Building these apps on Facebook made them easier for people to use and also better. Using

Facebook Photos is great because of tagging — the connections between the people in them. Events and Groups are great because the invite lists are easy to access, and you know who everyone is. Additionally, News Feed helps spread information about photo tags and events and so on, meaning more people can find out about cool things.

The thing to remember about the apps and games I talk about in this chapter, however, is that they weren't built by Facebook. Why does this matter? It matters because sometimes some apps may behave differently than Facebook does. Things may look or function differently, and unfortunately, sometimes the apps you use may be less inclined to offer you a useful product and more inclined to spam you (and your friends) or do shady targeting with your information. That's why when you use applications, you need to authorize their use of your information and why you should know how to get rid of applications that are behaving badly (which is covered in the "Managing Your Apps" section later in this chapter).

Getting Started

Getting started using an app is often as simple as clicking a button. A lot of things happen behind the scenes when you click those buttons.

What apps need from you

Before you can start using most applications within Facebook, you need to grant the applications permission to interact with your Timeline, account, and information. When you start using a new app, you must grant it permission to access your information.

The basics

All apps need your basic information and your e-mail address if you want to use them. In other words, if you're not comfortable sharing this information with an app, you can't use it. Your *basic information* refers in this case to any information about you that is set to Public. For everyone on Facebook, this includes

- Your name
- Your profile picture
- Your gender
- Your user ID (This is the number associated with your Facebook account; everyone has a unique ID.)

✔ Your list of friends

✔ Any other information you have shared publicly

In addition to this, when you start using a game or app, most apps will request that you share your contact e-mail address with them. It will be allowed to store that e-mail address in order to contact you in the future. This allows you to establish a direct relationship with the app because the developers can always get in touch with you, without Facebook acting as an intermediary.

Giving your e-mail to an application means you can get e-mail newsletters and other updates direct from the source without logging in to Facebook. If at any time you don't want to share your e-mail address with a certain application anymore, you need to unsubscribe from its e-mail list through *the app developer* as opposed to through Facebook.

The slightly less basic

In addition to basic information, apps might require specific types of information that is not publicly available. What information this includes depends entirely on the app and what it does. Here are some examples of information an app might want to use:

✔ Things you like (books, music, movies, Pages, and so on)

✔ Things your friends like (books, music, movies, Pages, and so on)

✔ Your location

✔ Your birthday

✔ Your photos

✔ Your posts

✔ Posts that have been shared with you

✔ Other profile info, such as your education, work history, and relationship information

Permission to act

In addition to all the types of information apps need from you, apps also need permission to take certain actions, including things such as the following:

✔ Posting to your Timeline on your behalf (for example, creating a post when you win a game). You can choose who can see these posts using the regular Privacy menu, which I discuss at length in Chapter 5.

✔ Accessing your information when you're offline (for example, looking up some of the information just listed, even when you aren't using the app).

App Install Screen

The *App Install Screen* is a blanket term I use to talk about the place where you're notified that a particular action (such as clicking a button) will share your information with an app. For example, say that you click a News Feed story and an alert window pops up asking whether you want to continue playing a game or asking whether you want to start using a game on your phone and prompting you to log in to Facebook. Figure 14-1 shows one incarnation of the App Install Screen; in this case, it's on the right side of an app's page on Facebook. Notice particularly the blue buttons, which you'll see anywhere you encounter these screens.

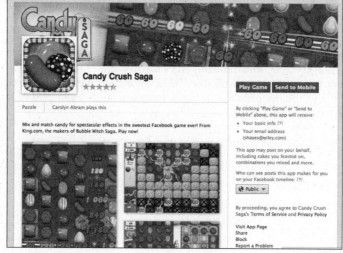

Figure 14-1:
Want to use
this app?
Make sure
you know
what it's
asking for.

Here are the most common variations of the blue buttons:

- ✔ **Play Game:** For apps that are games (for example, "Words with Friends" or *Candy Crush Saga*), you click the Play Game button to begin playing right away.

- ✔ **Visit Website:** This button appears for apps that work primarily as an outside website that sends information back to Facebook. Clicking this button takes you to the website, where you're prompted to set up an account.

- ✔ **Send to Mobile:** Many apps these days have a mobile integration as well as a Facebook integration. If you have a phone number linked to your account, you can click this button to send a link to your phone, where you can install the mobile app and link it to your Facebook account.

✔ **Go to App:** Some apps don't maintain separate websites. When you use these apps, you'll still feel like you're on Facebook; you'll still see the blue bar on top and the sidebar on the left. What you see in the center of the page, however, is dictated by the app developers, not by Facebook. Clicking this button starts your use of an app within Facebook.

✔ **Okay:** This button usually appears when you're already on another website and click to log in to Facebook. Clicking this button gets you started on that website. I talk more about this topic in the "Using Facebook Outside of Facebook" section later in this chapter.

Although these buttons vary based on the kind of app and what it does, the same thing happens when you click any one of them: You agree to share your information with that app. That's why you need to pay attention to what the app is and what it's requesting before you agree.

Clicking *any* of these buttons has the same result: Your info will be shared with the app asking for it, and you'll be able to begin using that app.

In Figure 14-1, below the buttons and the list of information the app requires is a privacy drop-down menu (set on Public in this figure). This menu is a familiar one because you use it to select your privacy setting every time you post something to your Timeline. For apps, you can actually select a blanket setting just for posts from that app. In other words, even if I share all my posts publicly, I can choose to share my *Candy Crush Saga* posts just with friends. You'll find the following privacy options: Public, Friends of Friends, Friends, Friends Except Acquaintances, Only Me, or a custom set of people.

Sometimes, when I want to use an app but I don't want it posting back to Facebook on my behalf, I set the privacy to Only Me. For example, when I started using the Hulu app (Hulu is a website that streams television shows online), I decided I didn't need my friends knowing just how much I like teen dramas. I still wanted to use the app for creating a profile on Hulu and easily posting clips to Facebook. So I set the privacy to Only Me, which means I'm the only one who can see the automatically generated posts about my *Gossip Girl* marathon.

Now What? Using Apps on Facebook

Because there are so many different apps answering so many different needs, it's difficult to tell you what to do next. However, there are some common prompts and onscreen actions. Read on to find out what form these might take.

Application Home pages on Facebook

When you click a Play Game or Go to App button, you'll likely be taken to the app's Home page. When you click a Visit Website button, you'll be taken to the app's website in a separate browser tab or window.

You can see a sample Home page (for *Candy Crush Saga*) in Figure 14-2. Its Home page basically prompts you to start playing the game. Notice that the blue bar is still at the top of the screen, which means that if you get bored playing this game, you can easily go back to your Facebook Home page or Timeline.

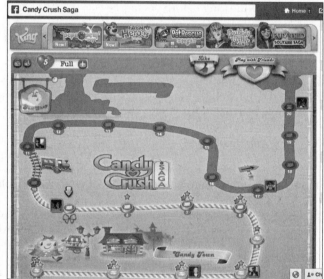

Figure 14-2:
The Home
page for
*Candy Crush
Saga.*

Sidebar links

The left sidebar on your Home page is where you go to get to different parts of Facebook: your groups, News Feed, events, and so on. Links to the apps you use most often will also appear in the sidebar, with the ones you use most often at the top. Click the See More link in the sidebar and scroll down to see all your apps and games.

If you've used lots of apps over time, you might not even see all of them when you click See More. After you expanded the sidebar, scroll down to the Apps section and click the triangle icon next to the word Apps. The triangle should be pointed down when all your apps are displayed.

Invitations and requests

Just like you can invite friends to events; you can also invite friends to play games or use apps with you. After your friends are playing the same game as you or using the same application, you can send them requests for specific actions. For example, within many games, you can send requests to people for specific items they may have accumulated through their own play.

The beauty of games on Facebook is that you can play against your friends, which means they can be opponents in word games, generals in your online armies, or tellers in your online banks. When you ask them to take part or send them something within the game, the game can send them a request on your behalf. Figure 14-3 shows the confirmation dialog box that you need to approve to send a request to a friend. That dialog box shows what the actual request will look like.

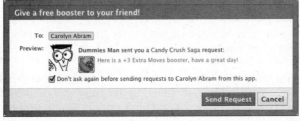

Figure 14-3: Sending requests.

In Figure 14-3, note the Don't Ask Again before Sending Requests to *<friend>* check box below the preview. If you leave this check box selected, the app will be able to send that friend requests on your behalf as often as it wants. Clear this check box so that you always know when an app is sending your friend a request.

Posts

As you play games and use apps, you may also be prompted to post things to your Timeline. Figure 14-4 shows what one such prompt might look like. In this case, it's a game prompting you to share that you completed another level. If you want to share these achievements with friends, that's great; click the Share button and feel free to add your own comments to the text field.

If you'd rather not post to your Timeline about something like this, just click Cancel and continue on with whatever it was you were doing.

Figure 14-4:
Posting
to your
Timeline
(formerly
known as
the Wall).

Extra Credit

Lots of games on Facebook allow you to purchase virtual goods within the game. For example, if you haven't yet gotten to the level needed to unlock an advantage in *Candy Crush Saga,* you could purchase that advantage (extra moves!) for a dollar or two. Some games create their own currency, which you buy, and some use Facebook Credits.

Facebook Credits is a payment system built by Facebook that other applications can incorporate into their service. Purchasing Facebook Credits is a way to purchase goods without sharing your credit card information with a million different game developers. Each credit costs ten cents, so one dollar gets you ten credits. Games may require different numbers of credits for different items.

Facebook Credits is just one of many payment systems you may come across while using apps.

Using Facebook Outside of Facebook

Imagine all the things you do on the web. Maybe you buy gifts for friends at Amazon. Or perhaps you blog or like to comment on blogs that others write. Maybe you look up movie reviews. Maybe you rent movies through Netflix. You do any number of things, all of which could be better if your friends were there.

Facebook offers websites multiple tools to make the time you spend on their sites more meaningful. There are four main ways to use Facebook on other websites, and each interacts with your account and information a little differently: logging in with Facebook, Social Plugins, sharing back to Facebook, and Instant Personalization.

Log in with Facebook

The first way to improve your web experience is to eliminate the need to create and register a brand new account for every Single. Website. Ever. The web forms that ask for your name, your e-mail, and subsequent prompts to upload a profile picture and find friends are things of the past. As an example, check out how you can create a new account on Quora, a question-and-answer site.

When you go to the Quora sign-up page at `https://www.quora.com`, you'll notice that it shows that you can register by using an existing Facebook or Twitter account. Clicking the Sign Up With Facebook button brings up an App Install Screen in a new window. This one simply asks you to click Okay on sharing your public profile, Friend List, e-mail address, and likes. Figure 14-5 shows this version of the App Install Screen.

Figure 14-5:
Connect your Facebook account with Quora.

Here are a few important things to notice about this screen:

- ✔ The Dummies Man name and profile picture are already displayed because I was logged in to Facebook when I clicked the sign-up prompt. If you aren't logged in to Facebook, you see a Facebook log-in screen in this space, where you have to enter your Facebook log-in e-mail and password. Also, if you share a computer with other Facebook users, make sure that the name displayed is, in fact, yours.

- ✔ Just like clicking any of the App Install buttons I go over earlier in this chapter, the moment you click Okay, your information will be shared with this site. Make sure you trust the site that you're using before you click Okay. `WellknownMcgoodreputation.com`? Probably okay. `SleazyMcSpamerson.com`? Maybe do a little more research first.

After clicking Okay to share my information, Quora goes on to ask permission to post to Facebook on my behalf. I can set privacy on who sees those posts or, in this case, choose not to let Quora post by clicking Skip. After I go through these install screens, I can begin using Quora, including, in this case, selecting topics I'm interested in learning about.

The sign-up process will be slightly different for each site that uses Facebook as a log-in option, so don't worry if the site you're using has a slightly different look and feel than Quora.

Each time you return to a site like Quora, you'll be able to log in by clicking the log-in button. You may also see mini thumbnail photos of friends who have previously logged in or registered through Facebook.

Often when you log in with Facebook, you will be asked to create a new password for that website. Do not use the same password you use for your Facebook account. That lowers the security of all your online accounts.

Social Plugins

Wish you had a better sense of whose Yelp reviews you could trust? Looking for a movie recommendation? Don't actually like dealing with strangers on the web? Welcome to Social Plugins.

Social Plugin refers to websites that use Facebook information within their own websites. These plug-ins may or may not be similar to the applications you use within Facebook; however, you do not need to allow access to your Facebook information in order for a Social Plugin to work (you do, however, usually need to be logged in to your Facebook account). It may be more accurate to say that these plug-ins use a Facebook link that you establish to make your experience on their sites more social. I touch upon these sorts of plug-ins in earlier chapters — liking and commenting on other websites, for example.

The following subsections briefly discuss some of the integrations for social plugins you may see as you use the Internet.

Like and Send buttons

With Social Plugins, you can like virtually anything, anywhere on the web. Facebook has made it very easy for companies to add Like buttons to their online content. Many blogs and news websites put Like buttons, along with a count of likes, alongside every single article. If any of your friends have liked something, you may see their names in addition to the number of likes.

Some sites may prompt you to share that you have liked something, as io9. com does in Figure 14-6. When you click Like, a window pops up prompting you to post the like to Facebook. When you do this, the fact that you liked it is shared on your Timeline (in the Recent Activity section) and may appear in your friends' News Feeds.

Figure 14-6:
The Like button and prompt to post on a post on io9.com.

Similar to the Like button, some websites feature Send or Share buttons. Likes are shared publicly through Timelines and News Feeds, but sending or sharing something allows you choose how you want to share it and with whom. As shown in Figure 14-7, the Share box looks pretty similar to the Share box on your Timeline. You can choose to share it on your Timeline, on a friend's Timeline, with a group, or as a message. You can also adjust the privacy using the Privacy drop-down menu next to the blue Share Link button.

Figure 14-7:
The Share box allows you to make posts from any website.

Any content you like from Facebook may be shown on your Facebook Timeline and may appear in your friends' News Feeds. If liking a controversial article might make waves with some of your friends, you can instead choose to send it as a message or share it with specific privacy as a post. In either case, you can tailor who sees that link.

Comments

Figure 14-8 shows a Comments box powered by Facebook. In theory, any blog, whether a big name or just your friend's little hobby, can add a

Comments box so people can quickly sign in and leave comments. If you're logged into Facebook in the same browser as whatever you're reading, you may not even have to log in to use the Comments box. If you leave the Post to Facebook check box selected, your comment will also be posted back to your Timeline.

Figure 14-8:
Comment on
a blog using
Facebook.

Feeds

Virtually every news site is a feed of updating posts, so it makes sense that you might want some help from your friends in understanding what to read or pay attention to. A few types of plug-ins help with this:

- **Recent Activity or Activity Feed:** Recent Activity boxes on websites display recent actions taken by your friends on the website in question.

- **Recommendations:** Recommendations shows similar information to recent activity, although instead of what's most recent, it shows what's been liked by the most people in order to show what you might like as well. A recommendation box on the *L.A. Times* website is shown in Figure 14-9.

- **Like boxes:** Like boxes can show who has liked a website's page on Facebook, as well as display a feed of recent posts from that page. A sample Like box from the PostSecret website (www.postsecret.com) appears in Figure 14-10.

Figure 14-9:
Find out
what you're
likely to
want to
read.

Figure 14-10: Shhh, it's a secret!

Sharing back to Facebook

When you link up your Facebook account with your account on another website, that site has the capability to send info back to your Timeline on Facebook. Usually it goes to the Recent Activity section of your Timeline, and it can appear in your friends' News Feeds as well. For example, if Dummies Man adds two TV shows to its favorites on the website www.hulu.com, that action appears in its Recent Activity section (not shown) and in the News Feeds of its friends (shown in Figure 14-11).

Instant Personalization

Instant Personalization is Facebook's way of connecting accounts to trusted partners on behalf of its users. There are approximately 20 partner sites at the time of this writing. They include sites such as Bing, Pandora, Yelp, TripAdvisor, Rotten Tomatoes; and several social gaming sites like Zynga, GSN, and EA.

Dummies Man favorited **2 TV shows** on Hulu.

The Mindy Project
Like · Comment

New Girl
Like · Comment

14 minutes ago · Hulu

Figure 14-11:
Just added
some favor-
ite shows.

Unlike Social Plugins, Instant Personalization requires little work on your part. When you go to a partner site for the first time, you receive a notification on the screen that Instant Personalization is at work; usually this notification is in the form of a banner across the top of the screen, saying something like, "We're using Facebook to personalize your experience." Instant Personalization automatically shares your public information (name, profile picture, gender, and other info you've shared publicly) with that site. In other words, the partner site doesn't have to wait for you to click a log-in button. As soon as you arrive, you're logged in. The idea of Instant Personalization is to make the social aspect of these websites completely seamless. As you use the Internet radio station Pandora, for example, you see which of your friends like the artists and songs that appear on your screen. You can instantly find all the people on Yelp whose reviews matter most to you: your friends.

If you don't use any of the partner sites mentioned and don't like the idea of your information being shared in this way, you can opt out of Instant Personalization. Go to the Settings page by clicking the arrow icon on the far right of the blue bar and selecting Settings. Then, click Apps on the left side to go to the Apps section. Scroll down to the Instant Personalization section of the page and click Edit. You may be prompted to watch a video explaining instant personalization; you can click the Close button on this video to view an expanded list of partner sites. Deselect the check box at the bottom of the page to opt out of Instant Personalization.

Mobile apps and Facebook

If you have an iPhone or other smartphone that uses apps, you can connect your Facebook account with mobile apps. Mobile versions of games like *Words with Friends* use Facebook information to help you find friends to play with. Photo-editing apps like Instagram use Facebook to help you share cool photos with friends. You need to approve applications on your phone the same way you do on the web. Figure 14-12 shows an App Install Screen on an iPhone. Just like on the web, it tells you what information it's asking for. When you tap OK, that information will be shared with the app.

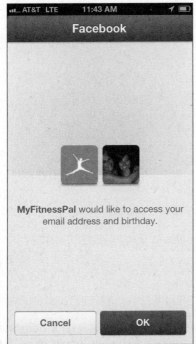

Figure 14-12:
Facebook
+ mobile =
better apps.

Managing Your Apps

Depending on how you wind up using apps and how you feel about the ones you've added, a time may come when you want to change some things. To do so, go to your App Settings page by following these steps:

1. **Click the down arrow on the right side of the blue bar on top to access the Account menu.**

2. **Select Settings.**

   The Settings page appears. The different sections of this page are shown on the left side.

3. **Click Apps on the left side of the page.**

   The Apps tab of the Settings page appears.

On the Apps tab, you can see a list of all the apps you use, in order of which you've used most recently. Click Edit, located next to these apps, to see more information about how they work with Facebook. You can see the expanded information about an app in Figure 14-13. You can adjust the settings related to each app a number of ways, which I explain next.

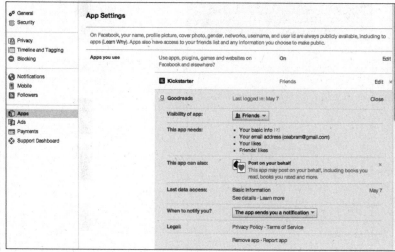

Figure 14-13: Check out the apps you use and how they use your info.

Removing apps

The simplest way to adjust how an app interacts with your information is simply to revoke its capability to interact with your information. This option makes sense only if you are 100 percent done with an app — that is, you don't plan to use it again in the future.

To remove an app, click the X next to its name in the list of your apps. A window pops up explaining that doing so removes it from your Facebook account, but that the app may still have some of the data you shared with it (it just won't get any new data going forward). You can then choose to delete all the app's activity on Facebook by selecting the Delete All Your <*app*> Activity on Facebook check box. Clicking the Remove button finishes the process.

When you remove an app, you will no longer be able to use the app, and it won't be able to send any information or posts to your Timeline or invitations to your friends. At the same time, because so many apps exist outside of Facebook, you have to keep in mind that it will still be able to contact you via your e-mail address, and it may still have an account for you created via Facebook. If you want to cut off an app completely, you may have to delete your information and close your account on another website entirely.

Changing who can see an app's posts on your Timeline

If you're concerned about who can see the content an app is posting to your Timeline, you can always change the visibility of that app (and its posts) so fewer people can see it. To do so, follow these steps:

1. **Click Edit next to the app's name in the Apps You Use section of the App Settings page.**

   This expands details about the ways this app can interact with your information and Timeline.

2. **Click the Privacy drop-down menu.**

   It's next to the section Visibility of App.

3. **Select who can see posts from this app.**

   You'll find the following privacy options: Public, Friends of Friends, Friends, Friends Except Acquaintances, Only Me, or a custom set of people. Selecting Only Me is a quick way to make sure that no one will see posts that the app creates on your behalf.

Preventing an app from posting and accessing info when you're not using it

As an alternative (or in addition) to changing who can see posts an app makes, you can revoke an app's capability to post to your Timeline altogether.

1. **Click Edit next to the app's name in the Apps You Use section of the App Settings page.**

   This expands details about the ways this app can interact with your information and Timeline.

2. **Look in the This App Needs and the This App Can Also sections to see what permissions the app has.**

   Every app will list here that it can access your basic information and send you e-mail (Instant personalization apps such as Pandora or Yelp do not list your e-mail here). Depending on the app, it will also list any other Timeline info it requires and whether it can post on your behalf or access your information when you're not using the app.

3. **Click the X next to Post on Your Behalf or Access Your Data Any Time to revoke these permissions, respectively.**

If you revoke the Post on Your Behalf setting, the app will no longer be able to make posts on your Timeline; if you revoke the Access Your Data setting, the app will no longer be able to access your data when you are not using it.

Changing notification settings

Apps may contact you via the Notifications section of your Home page. If you're being bothered by too many notifications, you can turn off this capability from the App Settings page.

1. **Click Edit next to the app's name in the Apps You Use section of the App Settings page.**

   This expands details about the ways this app can interact with your information and Timeline.

2. **Use the drop-down menu in the When to Notify You section to select Never.**

   If you previously turned off notifications and want to turn them back on, select The App Sends You a Notification.

Other app privacy settings

In addition to the Apps You Use section of the App Settings page, two other sections control how apps interact with your information.

✔ **Apps Others Use:** When your friends use other websites and apps in conjunction with Facebook, they may find it useful to see their friends' (in this case, your) information — for example, a birthday calendar application, which may alert them when a friend's birthday is on the horizon. In this section, you can determine the information about you that your friends can allow sites to access. If you want your friends to be able to use a birthday reminder website to remember your birthday, you may want to allow them to give your birthday to the sites they trust. If you want to deny an application's access to some of your information, such as your education and work history, deselect the check box next to Education and Work History. Your friends won't be able to import that information into their apps.

✔ **Instant Personalization:** Instant Personalization is a way of instantly linking your Facebook account to partner sites (I go over how this works in the earlier "Instant Personalization" section). If you don't want Facebook doing this on your behalf, you can opt out here.

Opting out

If you've been reading this chapter and you're getting more and more queasy about the idea of using games and apps, you can consider opting out of using apps entirely. This isn't a step I personally recommend because applications can be a lot of fun and very useful. But if you're very protective of your information, you can effectively turn off apps.

From the App Settings page, look at the top of the Apps You Use section. The first line item is not an app but a setting labeled Use Apps, Plugins, Games and Websites on Facebook and Elsewhere?" Next to this question is the default setting of On. Click the Edit link to the right of this item to expand more information and a Turn Off Platform button.

Clicking this button effectively removes all the apps you have used and prevents your account information from being used by any application ever again.

If, at some point in the future, you find an app you do want to use and you click any of the App Install Screen buttons, this setting will automatically turn back on.

Controlling what you see from friends

News Feed can be a great way to discover what apps your friends use, but it also can be overrun with app stories, blocking out the interesting content that's not related to those games and apps. Here are a few tips to keep your News Feed (and the rest of your Facebook) from being cluttered by apps:

✔ **Hide from News Feed.** If your News Feed is inundated with posts from apps, click the small gray arrow that appears when you hover over that post. A menu of options appears, including Hide. When you click Hide, the post disappears from News Feed and is replaced by text confirming that it has been hidden. Click the black Hide All Stories from <app> text to hide all future posts from that app.

✔ **Block an app.** If you find an app offensive or it keeps sending you invites or requests, you can block it. From the Settings page, navigate to the Blocking tab using the left menu and enter the app's name in the text field in the Block Apps section. The app will no longer be able to contact you via Facebook or see any of your info.

✔ **Block a friend's invites.** Sometimes just one person is the problem. The person may be sending you invites or requests from multiple apps, and it's driving you nuts. Navigate to the Blocking section of the Settings page, and enter your aunt's name into the text field in the Block App Invites section. Then, any invites or requests she sends you will automatically be ignored and won't generate any notifications on your Home page or in your e-mail. You'll still be friends with her, and you'll still see posts from her such as status updates and photos; you just won't get the app stuff anymore.

The App Center

Most of the time when you start using an app, it will be in this context: You'll go to sign up for a new website and realize you can log in with Facebook. Or a friend will invite you to play a game with him. But if you're in the market for new games and apps to try out and don't know where to start, check out the App Center. You can get to it by clicking the App Center link in the left sidebar on any page of Facebook. (You may have to click the See More link in the top portion of the sidebar to see the link to the App Center.) The App Center, shown in Figure 14-14, gives you the tools you need to find games and apps that are popular across Facebook and with your friends. App pages within the App Center are also how you can assess whether an app is one you want to be using.

When you land in the App Center, you may notice it has a distinct bias toward games. The navigation menu on the left side of the page lets you browse games by category, such as strategy or sports. All the rest of the apps I've been talking about — ones that work on other websites, for example, or ones that are meant to connect you to friends around things like giving to causes or creating a family tree — are under the blanket category of Apps (though when you click this category, several subcategories appear, such as Travel or Entertainment).

The App Center also displays Top Games and Friends' Games to try to expose you to the games that are most popular across Facebook and with your friends. When you click a particular category on the left, the display in the center of the page changes to show you suggested games in that category. Suggestions are created based on games and apps you've used as well as games and apps your friends have used. You can click the tabs at the top of these suggestions to view Top Rated, Trending, and Friends' Games in that category.

Figure 14-14:
The App
Center.

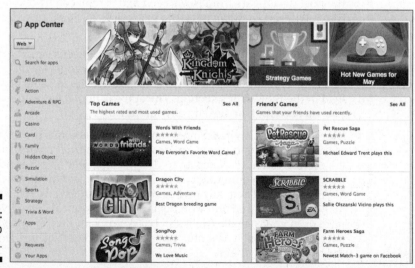

Click any app to check out its page and learn more about it before you begin using it.

App pages

A sample app page is shown in Figure 14-15; it works a bit like a Timeline for an app, complete with a cover photo, profile picture, and name. You might actually recognize this image from earlier, when I talk about App Install Screens.

Figure 14-15: A sample app page.

The app install information is on right side of the app page, but this page has a lot more information that may be relevant as you seek to learn more about an app.

- ✔ **Ratings:** As people use apps, the app may prompt them to rate it on a five-star scale. You can see the rating right under its name at the top of the page.

- ✔ **Category:** Underneath the app's profile picture is the category (or categories) that it fits into — just in case you aren't sure a game is going to have enough sports or strategy in it.

- ✔ **Who uses it:** Next to the category is a list of which of your friends (if any) use that game or app.

- ✔ **Description:** The text under the category and who uses the app explains what the app does and what people use it for.

✔ **Screenshots:** If the description doesn't quite communicate what an app or game will be like, then hopefully the screenshot(s) can help you get a sense of it.

✔ **Info:** At the bottom of an app's page in the App Center, basic info like who created the app and other platforms where the app is available (for example, if it's available as an Android or iPhone game as well as a game on Facebook) can help you find out just a little more about the app.

Assessing an app's trustworthiness

App pages are meant to be a way to learn about a game or app and assess whether you want to use it. Remember, when you use an app, it receives your information and some of your friends' info. So make sure you want this to happen! Here are some ways to assess whether an app is going to be one that will be fun, useful, and respectful of your data and how it is used:

✔ **Your friends are using it.** The first mark of a good application is that your friends are using it. This usually means it's fun, useful, and generally good. One note of clarification: When I say your friends, in this case, I mean *the friends you interact with most on Facebook*. If that guy you met that one time (TGYMTOT) sends you an invitation and you think, "Weird, I haven't spoken to TGYMTOT on Facebook in ages," there's a good chance that this is a bad application using nefarious methods to get invitations sent.

✔ **It has a good rating.** You can see an overall rating of an application right under its name. A good rating — around four stars, in my book — means the app is likely to be really fun and enjoyable to the people using it. These ratings don't always account for bad app behavior like spamming of friends, however, so it's not the *only* thing to look at.

✔ **The info it's asking for makes sense.** The App Install Screen is on the right side of an app's page. When you click any of the blue buttons here, you agree to give your info to the app, and listed below the blue buttons are the parts of your Timeline the app wants to access. If it's asking for something that seems out of place — a game asking for access to all your photos, for example — it's worth pausing before you agree to give it this info.

Many of the reasons you'd need help with an app are the same reasons you'd need help on Facebook: harassment, spam, something not working or being broken. However, because apps and games are built by outside developers, Facebook can't help you with these problems. You will need to contact the developers of whatever app or game you're using. Look around on the website or app for links that say something like Help, but if you come up empty, you can always get in touch this way:

1. **Navigate to the app's page in the App Center by searching for it in the search bar at the top of every Facebook page.**

   When you see the app appear in the menu of results, click it to go to the app's page.

2. **Click the Report a Problem link on the right side of the page.**

   This link is below the App Install section of the page. When you click this link, a window opens with a menu of options for reporting problems. The top portion, Report to Facebook, is for reporting disingenuous, spammy, or otherwise offensive apps to Facebook. The bottom part, Contact the Developer, is for getting in touch with the developers of that app.

3. **Select the appropriate category of report in the Contact the Developer section.**

4. **Click Submit.**

   Each app or game has different protocols for helping you. When you click some, they take you to an outside website or forum where you can search for answers to your questions or solutions to your problems. Others, when clicked, display a pop-up window where you can submit information about your issue.

If an app or game is doing something really bad, you can also report it to Facebook. Reasons for reporting an app include things such as pornographic content, misleading or deceptive content (promising free iPods in exchange for you taking an action, for example), or using your information without your permission in ads. Follow the preceding steps and select the reason for your report in the Report to Facebook section of the window. You'll then be asked to provide more information about why you're reporting the app and what it's done wrong. Facebook investigates these reports and removes apps that have violated its policies.

Part IV
The Part of Tens

Visit www.dummies.com for great Dummies content online.

In this part . . .

- ✔ Super uses
- ✔ Safety secrets
- ✔ Common questions
- ✔ Visit www.dummies.com for great Dummies content online.

Chapter 15

Ten Great Games, Apps, and Websites

As I discuss in Chapter 14, apps use Facebook information to provide some sort of service to you. That might be the capability to battle your friends in a game of chess or poker or it might be the capability to vote up content on another website. Here are ten apps that are popular among my friends or among Facebook users. You might want to check them out, too.

To find these apps, you can type their names into the Search box in the big blue bar on top of any Facebook page. Click the correct search result when it comes up to be taken to the app's Page in the App Center. From there, you can learn more and find instructions for beginning to use the app.

Spotify

Spotify is a music service you can actually download to use on your computer and on your mobile phone. Regardless whether you use the Spotify app on Facebook, you can use Spotify to build playlists, listen to specific songs or artists, and follow music from your favorite artists.

When you start using the Spotify app on Facebook, you can enjoy even more features of Spotify. When you listen to songs or create playlists on Spotify, this information is shown to your friends on Facebook. When your friends look at the Music view of News Feed they can see what you've been listening to, click Play, and start listening to the same song right away. It's a great way to discover new music and share the joy of music with your friends.

If you have a friend you think has particularly great taste in music, you can follow his playlists on Spotify, instead of trying to figure out for yourself what you want to listen to.

Goodreads

Goodreads is a website that enables you to list books you're reading, write book reviews for the books you've read, and share reading lists and suggestions with friends. When you sign up for Goodreads using your Facebook information, you will easily be able to share books with your Facebook friends, post your reviews to Facebook, and feature your favorite books on your Timeline — either by adding a new Goodreads section to your Timeline or by adding all your Goodreads favorites to the existing Books section of your Timeline.

Pinterest

Remember the days of tearing recipes out of a magazine to cook later? Or a cool haircut you wanted to show to your hairdresser? Pinterest is the website that allows you to do the same thing digitally. By "pinning" links and images to your various boards (think of it as the online version of tacking something to a corkboard), you can create collections of things you like, want to try, or find interesting. When you sign up with Facebook, you can automatically share your boards with your Facebook friends. If you choose, they'll also see when you pin new things to your boards in their News Feeds. From there, they can easily like your pins or comment on what you've been pinning.

Instagram

Instagram was acquired by Facebook in 2012. However, it continues to operate as an independent mobile app for taking, editing, and sharing photos. Instagram works with the camera on your mobile phone, allowing you to add filters to the images you take and then share them via the Instagram app. People can follow each other's photo streams and comment on the photos they like.

If you choose to sign up with your Faceboook information, you can post your Instagrams to Facebook, where your friends can see your photos in their News Feeds. This means you can share with followers on Instagram and with your Facebook friends without having to post the same photo twice. Instagram photos automatically are compiled in an Instagram album on your Timeline.

Someecards

Someecards is a website that creates witty, darkly funny e-cards in honor of all the typical holidays — birthdays, anniversaries, Mother's Day, Valentine's Day, and so on. You can always visit the website to send a card by e-mail, or you can use the app on Facebook to browse the cards and then post them to you or your friends' Timelines. This allows all your friends to be in on the occasion, even if it's just a "thinking of you on a random Tuesday." After e-cards are posted to a Timeline, friends can like and comment on them.

Candy Crush Saga

Candy Crush Saga is a matching game that takes place entirely in a world full of candy and candy shops. You can play it on your computer or on your mobile phone. The goal is to create clusters of certain candy types to score points. As you progress through the levels, you can see how you're stacking up against your friends. As the levels get harder and harder, you may find that you need a few extra turns, which your friends can then gift to you to help you win. You can also send each other gifts within the game to help you get higher and higher scores. So it's not just about crushing the competition, but also helping your friends. How sweet.

Scramble With Friends

Scramble With Friends is a mobile game that you can choose to join through Facebook. Once you do, you can easily challenge friends to games of Scramble (a Boggle-like word game). Much like other games on this list, you can use your Facebook information to easily find opponents and then post your victories (or losses) to your Timeline so everyone can see your prowess with letters.

Scramble With Friends and many of the other most popular Facebook games are owned by Zynga. The Zynga games are often known for their addictive nature, their entertainment, and unfortunately, sometimes spamming people's friends. As you're playing these games, make sure you pay attention to your Timeline and the number of posts the games make to it. You can remove posts you don't want or report spam by clicking the downward-pointing triangle that appears on the right corner of the post when you hover your mouse over it.

MyFitnessPal

MyFitnessPal is a diet and exercise app that helps you keep track of the food you eat and the calories you burn. When you sign up with Facebook, you can easily get support from any of your friends who are also working to lose weight or just be healthier. When you add Facebook friends as friends in MyFitnessPal, you can share your goals with them and collaborate as you all work to achieve them. You can also post fitness-related updates back to Facebook, such as a weight loss or a particular workout you just completed. As an added bonus, MyFitnessPal works on your smartphone, and can sync with activity tracking devices like the Fitbit and Jawbone UP.

Kickstarter

Kickstarter is a website that enables people to *crowdsource* funding for a project. In other words, many people can donate small amounts to a project like a film, book, product, or idea. For example, fans of the television show *Veronica Mars* recently banded together on Kickstarter to fund a follow-up film. When you sign up for Kickstarter through Facebook, there's no need to create a new account. In addition, you can easily check out what projects your friends are supporting and see if you want in on any of those. Additionally, sharing projects on Facebook is a great way to garner support for a project that is near and dear to your heart.

SongPop

SongPop is a game you can play on your phone or on your computer. It centers around identifying song titles and artists as quickly as possible based on a snippet of music. Of course, once you sign up through Facebook, you can challenge your friends to see who can identify the most songs the quickest.

I really like this game because it provides easy links to find the songs in the game in Spotify, iTunes, Amazon, and YouTube.

Chapter 16

Ten Ways Facebook Uniquely Impacts Lives

Sometimes people are dismissive of Facebook, saying, "I keep up with my friends by calling them and visiting them. I don't need a website to do that for me." And you don't *need* a website to do that for you. At the same time, though, Facebook can supplement your existing relationships in very real ways. Here are some ways that maintaining a friendship on Facebook can have big impacts in the real world.

Keeping in Touch with Summer Friends

I once spent a summer leading a troop of sixth graders into the wild. After two weeks of backpacking, kayaking, climbing, and bonding, the kids were given a big list of e-mail addresses and phone numbers, said their good-byes, and were packed off to their respective homes. I, about to head out west to work at Facebook, lamented the fact that the kids were too young to be on Facebook because they almost assuredly would lose that sheet of paper. I quickly friended my co-counselors (who were all old enough to be on Facebook) and kept up with them through photo albums, messages, and the occasional poke war. As an added bonus, years later, when one of my co-counselors needed a reference, he knew exactly where to find me.

Not just for me, but for thousands of high school students, the best-friends-for-the-summer — who had a tendency to fade away as school and life took over — are now a thing of the past. Camp friends immediately become Facebook friends, and on Facebook, no one gets lost. Plus, it's easy to share the memories of a fun summer via Facebook Photos.

Preparing to Head Off to School

Everyone has a story about leaving for college. Whether they're dropping off a child or an older sister or heading off themselves, people remember some form of anxiety, nervousness, or blinding fear of the unknown. Who were these people in the hallway or sharing the bathroom? Who was this so-called roommate?

In fact, there are special groups on Facebook for colleges and universities that only students and faculty can join. As soon as incoming freshmen receive their .edu e-mail addresses, they can join this group and start connecting with other students. As they get to know the people in the group, they may find that by the time they arrive on campus, they already know some people. Instead of wandering into the great unknown, college students go off to school having been introduced to their future roommates, classmates, and friends.

Going on Not-So-Blind Dates

Ever been a matchmaker? Ever had a particularly difficult "client" — a friend who has a million requirements for "the one"? Ever been embarrassed because you didn't realize just how picky your friend was until after the date? Enter Facebook. Now, "He's smart, funny, has a great job, lots of cool hobbies, a nice family, and nice friends" can be condensed into a Facebook message with a shared Timeline. From there, both parties can decide based on the Timelines — looks, interests, or the combination of all the information — whether they want to go on a date.

While showing a friend someone else's Timeline can be the right way to prevent a complete disaster, don't let your friend get too picky with the information there ("I could never date someone who listens to Britney Spears!"). Encourage her to take a glance at a few photos, point out some of the things the two have in common, and then point them to a coffee shop or bar where they can meet in person.

Meeting People in Your New City or Town

Heading off to college isn't the only time in people's lives that they find themselves someplace new without a lot of friends. But active Facebook users often find that there are many ways Facebook can help alleviate the confusion. I got the following message from my friend Shelby, who was living in Abuja, Nigeria, at the time:

> *So I was friends with this Marine in Liberia. We lost touch when I left Liberia. He joined Facebook two weeks ago, and requested me as a friend. We started talking again. He put me in touch with a friend who works for the U.S. Consulate in Lagos, Nigeria. I Facebooked her. She found my blog address on my Facebook profile, and forwarded it to her friend who works for the U.S. Embassy in Abuja.*
>
> *Tonight, I went out with this girl from the Embassy and a bunch of other Embassy people. And I have plans (finally!!) for a couple of days next week with these people.*
>
> *And all of this is because of Facebook.*

Shelby's story is just one example of how Facebook makes moving less of an ordeal — a neighborhood is waiting for you when you arrive. When I moved from California, I used Facebook Search to look for friends of mine who lived in Seattle. To my surprise, more than a few friends from college and people I used to work with had settled there as well. It was wonderful to feel like I wasn't surrounded by strangers, but by friends.

Reconnecting with Old Friends

Long-lost friends. The one who got away. I wonder whatever happened to her. Have you heard about him? These are just some of the ways people talk about the people they somehow lost track of along the way. Whatever the reason for the loss, this sort of regret can be undone on Facebook. Finding people is easy, and getting in touch is, too.

Many recent graduates exclaim that going to a reunion is unnecessary — you already know what everyone is doing five years later; you found out from Facebook. But even for the not-so-young alums, the Find Classmates and Find Coworkers features provide a direct line to search anyone who's on Facebook that you remember from way back (or not so way back) when.

Facebook gets e-mails every so often about people who find birth parents or biological siblings on Facebook. However, the majority of the time, people are looking for and finding their old classmates and reminiscing about the good old days. Better yet, they are re-igniting a spark in a friendship that can last far into the future.

Keeping Up with the 'rents . . . or the Kids

Face it: Keeping your parents in touch with everything that's going on is difficult. However often you speak, it sometimes feels as though you're forgetting something. And visits often feel rushed, as though you don't have enough time to truly catch up.

I've found that Facebook Photos is one of the best ways to easily and quickly share my life with my parents. Because I can upload photos so quickly — both from my mobile phone and from my computer — they can feel as though they were present at the *<insert activity here>*. Whether that's the walk I took around the lake, the concert I attended, or the really tasty pie I made, it's as though I called to tell them about it right after it happened. And of course this can happen in the other direction as well: I can see when my parents post photos of their own adventures in the world.

For new parents, Facebook is invaluable for connecting kids with their grandparents. There are few things grandparents like more than photos of their grandkids being brilliant, and you can have those in spades on Facebook. The more generations you have on Facebook, the more fun it can be for all.

Facebook Networking

If you've ever found yourself job hunting, you probably are acquainted with the real-world version of *networking*. You ask friends for their friends' numbers and job titles; you take people out to coffee; you go on interviews; you decide whether the company is right for you; you repeat the whole process.

Although finding the right job hasn't gotten any easier with Facebook, a lot of the intermediate steps have. Asking your friends for their friends' info is as easy as posting a status. You can also search for people who work at companies that interest you, and see if you have any mutual friends who can introduce you. After you receive some names, send them a Facebook message (or an e-mail, whichever is more appropriate) to set up the requisite "informational coffee date."

After interviewing, a great way to get information about a company is to talk to people who work there. Use Find Coworkers to search for people who've listed that company in their Timelines.

The only caveat to this approach is that you're now using Facebook to represent a professional portion of your life. If you contact people via Facebook and they feel a little uncomfortable with the content in your Timeline, whether that's your profile picture, a recent status that can be easily misinterpreted, or a post from a friend that reveals just a little too much information, it could make a bad first impression — just as if you'd shown up to the interview in torn jeans and the shirt you slept in. As a well-educated user of Facebook (because you *have* read all previous 15 chapters without just skipping directly to this one, right?), you're well aware of the myriad privacy settings that enable you to tailor what different parties see and don't see. However, if anything on your Timeline might be particularly misunderstood, simply hide it until you sign your offer letter.

Facebook for Freedom

If you were watching news articles about the Arab Spring sweeping through the Middle East in early 2011, you have heard frequent references to Facebook and Twitter. Young people in Egypt did a lot of their communication and coordination through Facebook. Although Facebook wasn't the source for the revolution, it was an invaluable tool in making the revolution successful (and helping people stay in touch with family across the world who might be at risk of violence).

Facebook has always been impressive at gaining support for important causes. Whether it's a monk-led protest in Myanmar, raising money to support Haiti after the devastating earthquake, creating a massive rally in Colombia denouncing a terrorist organization, or raising Autism Awareness in the United States, Facebook lets ideas spread from friend to friend to friend. Sometimes groups are the tools used, sometimes it's encouraging people to change their profile pictures to a specific image in support of their cause. There's no perfect formula for creating a Facebook revolution, but don't hesitate to share your beliefs on your Timeline or express support for causes around the world.

Goin' to the Chapel

A small bit of Facebook trivia: There has, in many circles, arisen the idea of *Facebook Official (FBO)* — the act of moving from *single* to *in a relationship* and listing the person that you're in a relationship with on your Timeline. For any fledgling couple, this is a big deal for their personal lives; however, becoming Facebook Official also serves notice to friends and anyone who happens upon one's Timeline: I'm taken.

Because of this relationship function, Facebook has become the fastest way to spread a wedding announcement to extended friend groups. Of course, people still call their parents and their closest friends, but *everyone* can find out and share in the happiness via News Feed. Congratulatory Timeline posts ensue, as do copious numbers of photos with *the ring* tagged front and center.

After the wedding has taken place, Facebook becomes a wonderland of virtual congratulations as well as photos of the big day. And in case anyone missed it, he can share in the after-party online.

Hey, Facebook Me!

Before Facebook, in both romantic and platonic contexts, it was hard to get from "Nice to meet you" to "Will you be my friend?" Now, the simple phrase, "Facebook me!" expresses this sentiment and so much more. "Facebook me!" can mean *get in touch, look me up,* or *I want you to know more about me* but in a pressure-free way. It doesn't mean *take me to dinner,* or *let's be best friends forever and ever.* It's simply a way to acknowledge a budding friendship.

"Facebook me!" can also be how good friends say, "Keep up with my life; I want you to know about it," which acknowledges that people are busy and that it's difficult to find time to see each other or talk on the phone. However, even when you're incredibly busy, a quick check on Facebook can make you feel connected again.

Chapter 17

Ten Frequently Asked Questions

Having worked for Facebook and on this book for several years, I know a lot about the specific complications, confusions, and pain-points people come across while using Facebook. At dinner parties, group functions, family events, or even walking across the street wearing a Facebook hoodie, someone always has a suggestion or a question about how to use the site. It's understandable. Facebook is a complex and powerful tool with a ton of social nuances, many of which have yet to be standardized. There are a lot of different features, and Facebook changes a lot. Each year, Facebook modifies parts of the site, redesigns how certain pages look and feel, and adds features. To keep up on what's happening with Facebook, you can like the official Facebook Page, found at `www.facebook.com/facebook`, and you'll get updates straight from the horse's mouth.

What follows are the questions I hear most often from friends and family (and the occasional message from a stranger who really needs help), often with strain in their voices or pain in their eyes. The goal of highlighting the more complicated questions is to save you the stress of encountering these issues and wondering whether you're the only one who just doesn't get it.

Do People Know When I Look at Their Timelines?

No. No. No. When people see stories about their friends pop up on their Home page, they sometimes get a little anxious that this means Facebook is tracking everything everyone does and publishing it to everyone else. That's not true. Consider two types of actions on Facebook: creating content and viewing it. Creating content means you've intentionally added something to

Facebook for others to look at or read, such as uploading a photo or a video, commenting or liking something, or posting a status. These types of actions are all publishable posts — that is, stories about them may end up on your Timeline or in your friends' News Feeds — although you have direct control over exactly who gets to see these posts.

The other type of action on Facebook is viewing content such as flipping through photos, watching a video, clicking a link your friend has liked, or viewing someone's Timeline. Unless someone is looking over your shoulder as you browse, these types of actions are strictly private. No one is ever directly notified about them, and no trace of the fact that you took that action is left on your Timeline or in your friends' News Feeds. So now you can check people out to your heart's content.

I Friended Too Many People and Now I Don't Like Sharing Stuff — What Can I Do?

The good news is, you can fix this problem by using Friend Lists. The less good news is, it's going to be a little time-consuming to set up the correct Friend Lists. Chapter 6 deals with finding friends and creating Friend Lists in great detail, but here's what you can do to deal with this exact problem:

1. **Hover your mouse over the left sidebar to expand it.**

   Depending on the width of your browser, it may already be expanded.

2. **Click the lock icon next to your name at the top of the list.**

   This opens the Privacy Shortcuts menu.

3. **Click See More Settings at the bottom of the menu.**

   This brings you to the Privacy Settings and Tools page.

4. **On the left side of the Privacy Settings and Tools page, click Blocking.**

   This brings you to all the blocklists you maintain on Facebook. The first item at the top of the page is the Restricted List. When people are on your Restricted List, they are still listed as your friends, but they see only those posts that you share publicly.

5. **Click Edit List across from the Restricted List.**

   A pop-up window displaying the people currently on the Restricted List opens.

6. **In the upper-left corner of the pop-up window, click to change the display from On This list to Friends.**

7. **Go through your friends and click the faces of people you don't want to see your posts.**

   This is the time-consuming part. If you have a lot of friends, this can take a while.

   You can always add more people to the list later if you want to stop for a break. Just click Finish to save your work so far.

8. **When you're done, click Finish.**

Alternatively, you can create a Friend List of best friends and share exclusively with them. You can also unfriend lots of people. Either way, you have to go through your long list of friends, person by person, and decide who will see your posts. I'm sorry; it's hard being popular.

What's with the New Facebook — Can I Change It Back?

Inevitably, Facebook is going to change the way it looks. You're going to log in one day, and things will look different — the things you were used to seeing on the left will now be on the right, or gone completely, or someplace hidden . . . it's confusing. Facebook changes the look and feel of either the Home page or the Timeline about once per year. And trust me when I say that when you log in and this has happened to you, you're going to hate it.

Unfortunately, no matter what you do, no matter how much you hate it, Facebook rarely goes back on a redesign like that. You won't be able to change it back, and the best thing you can do is try to figure out the new site. Check out the Help Center or Facebook's Page to read about the layout changes and how the site works. And then try to use Facebook a few minutes a day until you get used to it. Over time, it won't seem so bad any more. You'll look at a photo of the old Facebook, and you'll think how ugly it looks by comparison.

So, short answer: *No; you can't change it back.* But I have complete confidence in your ability to adapt to the new Facebook.

I Have a Problem with My Account — Can You Help Me?

I wish I could. Unfortunately, I am but a user like you, and that means although I can help diagnose the issue, I can't usually treat it. Sometimes the problems are Facebook's fault, and sometimes they are user errors, but either way, I don't really have the tools required to fix them. Most account problems can be resolved only by Facebook employees with special access to the specific tool required to fix an account. Here are a few of the account questions I've received recently, and the answers given:

- **I can't remember my password. Can you reset it for me?** *Answer:* No can do. Click the Forgot Your Password? link on the login page to start the reset process, which entails Facebook sending a reset link to your e-mail account.

- **My account was deactivated because it said I was sending too many messages. Why? Can you fix it?** *Answer:* I recently had this happen to two friends: one who was using his account to promote his music career, and one who was distributing his poetry to many, many friends through messages. This is Facebook spam detection at work. When an account starts sending a lot of messages in quick succession, especially when those messages contain links, this looks a lot like spam to the system. In most cases, the person is warned first, but if the behavior continues, his account is disabled. The only way to have this action reversed is to write in to Facebook's User Operations team and request reactivation. To write in, click Help from the Account menu — the little downward-facing arrow in the blue bar on top. Search for a FAQ entitled My Personal Facebook Account Is Disabled. Follow the instructions for contacting Facebook. The process of getting your account reactivated can sometimes take several days.

What Do I Do with Friend Requests I Don't Want to Accept?

This is a tough question. As far as I know, there isn't exactly a social convention for this yet, so the answer to this question is pretty personal. Just know that there are a number of actions you can take:

- **Many people just leave the request sitting there forever.** I don't recommend this action because it just clutters up your account — it's better to make a decision.

- **Click Not Now.** This is my favorite option. It sends the request to the hidden requests section of the Friends page, where you won't have to see it anymore. You can then go delete the request from that section of the Friends page. Although people are never directly notified that you've rejected their request, they may notice later that you're not friends and make the correct inference that you did not accept. If you do ignore a request, you also need to prepare your follow-up if she asks you why you ignored her request. Because there is no social convention for this situation just yet, most responses work well here, such as, "It's okay. I don't use Facebook often, anyway." You can try "Weird, Facebook must have messed up, I don't think I got it," but then you'll have to accept her request when she likely tries again.

✔ **If you don't want to accept because you don't want that person having access to your Timeline, you can accept the request and then add him to a special restricted Friend List (see Chapter 5).** You can go into your Privacy settings and exclude that Friend List from seeing any parts of your Timeline. Then anyone you add to that list will be restricted. In this way, you can accept the Friend Request without giving up access to your Timeline.

✔ **If you don't want to accept because you don't want to read about that person in your News Feed, no problem!** Simply click Confirm. The first time she shows up in News Feed, hover over the story and click the caron (downward-pointing triangle) at the upper-right of the story. Choose Hide from the menu that opens. The story will immediately disappear from your News Feed, replaced by this text: This Story Is Now Hidden from Your News Feed. Unhide. The line below that text reads, Hide All Stories from <*Friend's name*>. Click Hide All Stories from <*Friend's Name*> to prevent any future stories from that person from appearing in your News Feed.

Why Can't I Find My Friend?

I'm assuming you're asking this question after exhausting every possibility for finding friends, as described in Chapter 6. And I'm also assuming you're looking for a specific person, not friends in general.

You won't be able to find a friend for the following few reasons:

✔ **She hasn't joined Facebook.** Shocking, I know. If you think she'd enjoy it, you can always invite her to join and be your friend as long as you have her e-mail address.

✔ **She goes by a different name on Facebook to protect her privacy.** For example, if her name is Jane Smith, she may list her name as Janie S. Try searching for her by her e-mail address or phone number.

✔ **She has a common name.** Facebook Search tries to get you to the right Jane Smith by looking at things like friends in common and shared hometowns, but sometimes it comes up empty.

✔ **She doesn't have much information filled out on her Timeline.** If you're looking for someone you went to high school with but she never entered her high school information, you're going to have a hard time finding her.

✔ **She blocked you.** Yes, this one is harsh. I put it on the list only because I've seen it happen before. Someone says to me, "I *know* she's on Facebook. And I *know* she's friends with my friend. But when I go to find her she's not there."

While it hurts to be blocked by someone, don't drive yourself crazy looking for reasons why it happened. If she doesn't want to connect with you on Facebook, that's her loss; move on to your other friends and all the things you can share with them.

Will Facebook Start Charging Me to Use the Site?

Another simple answer: *No.*

This rumor is a particularly nasty one that makes the rounds every now and again via people's statuses. There are several variations, but they always seem to involve asking you to repost the status that Facebook is shutting down/going to start charging/running out of names. Don't fall victim to this ruse. Facebook has long maintained that it will always be free to users. Unless you're advertising something, Facebook will always have space for you for free.

How Do I Convince My Friends to Join Facebook?

Most methods for persuasion involve showing (rather than telling) your friend the value by sending him links to the photos you post on Facebook, putting his e-mail address on the invite of event and group invitations, or even sending him links and messages (again, by putting his e-mail address on the To line) from the Facebook Inbox.

You can tell her anecdotally the ways in which Facebook has enriched your life. Maybe you're interacting with your kids more, you're keeping in touch with friends you thought were lost, or you have a place to put your thoughts and photos where your friends might actually see them. You can let her look over your shoulder as you use the site so that she can see the experience herself — ask her questions about whether there's anyone in particular she'd like to look up. The more information she sees about the people she cares about, the more likely she is to take the next step.

One common complaint from people who haven't joined the site is that they "don't have time for yet another computer thing." To this concern, one common response is that Facebook is an efficiency tool that often saves a person time compared to using old-school methods. Messaging can often replace e-mail, and events are easier to coordinate over Facebook. Sharing phone numbers is easier. Sending and receiving links is easier. Finding rides to the airport, restaurant recommendations, and who is heading to the park on Saturday are all faster and easier than trying to use e-mail, phone, or other methods of communication.

Finally, for some people, it's just not their time. No matter what you say, they'll stick their fingers in their ears and sing *la-la-la* until you start talking about sports or the weather or the circus coming to town next week. You can't force them to Facebook; you have to let Facebook come to them. Over the years, I've watched many a nonbeliever eventually cross over and discover the value. Patience may be your only weapon for these diehards.

What If I Don't Want Everyone Knowing My Business?

To those who ask that question and don't have time to read Chapter 5 of this book, which goes into great detail about how to be a private person on Facebook, I simply try to impart the following message: You can be an extremely private person and still derive nearly all the same value out of Facebook as anyone else. All you have to do is learn how to use the Privacy controls and lock down all your information and access to your Timeline, ensuring that only those you trust can see your info. From there, you can interact in all the same ways as anyone else without feeling like your privacy is being compromised.

Note: Besides understanding the Privacy settings and taking the initial time to adjust yours until they feel just right, you will have to do a little extra work to be private on Facebook and still derive comparable value. You'll likely have to put in extra effort connecting with friends, because the more locked-down your information is, the harder you make it for not-yet-Facebook-friends to find your Timeline, and the harder it is for your friends to find you, identify you, and connect with you. As long as you're willing to do the work of seeking out your friends and connecting with them, however, your experience should be nearly identical with everyone else's.

Does Facebook Have a Feature That Lets Me Lock Myself Out for a Few Hours?

Short answer: *Not really.*

Long answer: Many people do *deactivate* their accounts. Deactivation is a way of shutting down your account temporarily. It means that no one will see your Timeline or be able to interact with you on Facebook. Some people will deactivate their accounts, their reason being "I spend too much time using Facebook." The benefit of such an action is that you're guaranteed not to get notifications about messages, picture tags, Timeline posts, or anything else. The downside is that it will cause a lot of confusion among your friends who suddenly can't message you, tag you, or write on your Timeline. If they have your e-mail address, they're likely to bug you anyway to ask why you disappeared from Facebook.

The reason it's not a real solution is because all you have to do to reactivate at any time is to enter your password (just like signing in), and you're completely back to normal. So if you're remotely curious how your social group has evolved without you, you may have trouble truly staying away.

Which brings me to the next suggestion: Have some self-control. Just like many good things in life, the key to keeping them good is moderation. French fries are delicious, but too many give you a tummy ache. Dancing is a blast 'til your feet are covered with blisters. Television is educational and entertaining until it's 3 a.m., you're watching your fifth infomercial, you forgot to feed the cat and put out the trash, and you find yourself wondering what life is all about. Facebook is no different. It's a brilliant utility when used to make your life easier and your social interactions richer. When you find yourself flipping through two-year-old vacation photos of a friend of a friend of a friend of a friend, it's time to blink a few times, step away from the mouse, and go out for ice cream, or dancing, or whatever else it is that gives you joy.

Index

• **E** •

● *Q* ●

About the Author

Carolyn Abram is a writer. She was the first user of Facebook at Stanford in 2004 and worked for Facebook from 2006-2009. She has used Facebook every day for most of her adult life, acquiring 767 Facebook friends and 971 tagged photos. Despite that, she managed to receive a BA from Stanford ('06) and an MFA from California College of the Arts ('12). Her short fiction has appeared in *New California Writing 2013* and *Switchback.* She currently lives in Seattle with her husband, dog, and baby.

Author's Acknowledgments

A huge thank you to a very flexible and supportive editorial staff, including Steve Hayes and Pat O'Brien. This book also would not have been possible without the herculean efforts of Amy Karasavas in both editing my work and writing two chapters when I needed help. The rest of the Wiley crew also has my gratitude.

On the home front, I have to thank Eric, who did everything possible to get me time to write while we were juggling a new baby and his own workplace stresses. Also, I should probably thank Connor for being such a good subject for Facebook posts, and for occasionally sleeping and letting my brain recover enough to write.

In closing, I'd like to thank the millions of Facebook users around the world who are busy connecting, sharing, and generally having fun on Facebook. Keep on signin' on.

Publisher's Acknowledgments

Project Editor: Pat O'Brien

Executive Editor: Steve Hayes

Copy Editor: Melba Hopper

Technical Editor: Amy Karasavas

Editorial Manager: Kevin Kirschner

Editorial Assistant: Annie Sullivan

Sr. Editorial Assistant: Cherie Case

Cover Photo: © YinYang / iStockphoto

Project Coordinator: Sheree Montgomery

Layout and Graphics: Jennifer Creasey, Jennifer Goldsmith, Joyce Haughey

Proofreader: Debbye Butler

Indexer: Potomac Indexing, LLC

Apple & Mac

iPad For Dummies,
5th Edition
978-1-118-49823-1

iPhone 5 For Dummies,
6th Edition
978-1-118-35201-4

MacBook For Dummies,
4th Edition
978-1-118-20920-2

OS X Mountain Lion
For Dummies
978-1-118-39418-2

Blogging & Social Media

Facebook For Dummies,
4th Edition
978-1-118-09562-1

Mom Blogging
For Dummies
978-1-118-03843-7

Pinterest For Dummies
978-1-118-32800-2

WordPress For Dummies,
5th Edition
978-1-118-38318-6

Business

Commodities For Dummies,
2nd Edition
978-1-118-01687-9

Investing For Dummies,
6th Edition
978-0-470-90545-6

Personal Finance
For Dummies,
7th Edition
978-1-118-11785-9

QuickBooks 2013
For Dummies
978-1-118-35641-8

Small Business Marketing Kit
For Dummies,
3rd Edition
978-1-118-31183-7

Careers

Job Interviews
For Dummies,
4th Edition
978-1-118-11290-8

Job Searching with
Social Media
For Dummies
978-0-470-93072-4

Personal Branding
For Dummies
978-1-118-11792-7

Resumes For Dummies,
6th Edition
978-0-470-87361-8

Success as a Mediator
For Dummies
978-1-118-07862-4

Diet & Nutrition

Belly Fat Diet For Dummies
978-1-118-34585-6

Eating Clean For Dummies
978-1-118-00013-7

Nutrition For Dummies,
5th Edition
978-0-470-93231-5

Digital Photography

Digital Photography
For Dummies,
7th Edition
978-1-118-09203-3

Digital SLR Cameras &
Photography For Dummies,
4th Edition
978-1-118-14489-3

Photoshop Elements 11
For Dummies
978-1-118-40821-6

Gardening

Herb Gardening
For Dummies,
2nd Edition
978-0-470-61778-6

Vegetable Gardening
For Dummies,
2nd Edition
978-0-470-49870-5

Health

Anti-Inflammation Diet
For Dummies
978-1-118-02381-5

Diabetes For Dummies,
3rd Edition
978-0-470-27086-8

Living Paleo For Dummies
978-1-118-29405-5

Hobbies

Beekeeping
For Dummies
978-0-470-43065-1

eBay For Dummies,
7th Edition
978-1-118-09806-6

Raising Chickens
For Dummies
978-0-470-46544-8

Wine For Dummies,
5th Edition
978-1-118-28872-6

Writing Young Adult Fiction
For Dummies
978-0-470-94954-2

Language &
Foreign Language

500 Spanish Verbs
For Dummies
978-1-118-02382-2

English Grammar
For Dummies,
2nd Edition
978-0-470-54664-2

French All-in One
For Dummies
978-1-118-22815-9

German Essentials
For Dummies
978-1-118-18422-6

Italian For Dummies
2nd Edition
978-1-118-00465-4

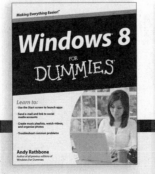 **Available in print and e-book formats.**

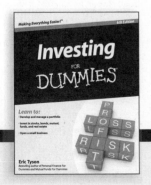

Math & Science

Algebra I For Dummies,
2nd Edition
978-0-470-55964-2

Anatomy and Physiology
For Dummies,
2nd Edition
978-0-470-92326-9

Astronomy For Dummies,
3rd Edition
978-1-118-37697-3

Biology For Dummies,
2nd Edition
978-0-470-59875-7

Chemistry For Dummies,
2nd Edition
978-1-1180-0730-3

Pre-Algebra Essentials
For Dummies
978-0-470-61838-7

Microsoft Office

Excel 2013 For Dummies
978-1-118-51012-4

Office 2013 All-in-One
For Dummies
978-1-118-51636-2

PowerPoint 2013
For Dummies
978-1-118-50253-2

Word 2013 For Dummies
978-1-118-49123-2

Music

Blues Harmonica
For Dummies
978-1-118-25269-7

Guitar For Dummies,
3rd Edition
978-1-118-11554-1

iPod & iTunes
For Dummies,
10th Edition
978-1-118-50864-0

Programming

Android Application
Development For
Dummies, 2nd Edition
978-1-118-38710-8

iOS 6 Application
Development For Dummies
978-1-118-50880-0

Java For Dummies,
5th Edition
978-0-470-37173-2

Religion & Inspiration

The Bible For Dummies
978-0-7645-5296-0

Buddhism For Dummies,
2nd Edition
978-1-118-02379-2

Catholicism For Dummies,
2nd Edition
978-1-118-07778-8

Self-Help & Relationships

Bipolar Disorder
For Dummies,
2nd Edition
978-1-118-33882-7

Meditation For Dummies,
3rd Edition
978-1-118-29144-3

Seniors

Computers For Seniors
For Dummies,
3rd Edition
978-1-118-11553-4

iPad For Seniors
For Dummies,
5th Edition
978-1-118-49708-1

Social Security
For Dummies
978-1-118-20573-0

Smartphones & Tablets

Android Phones
For Dummies
978-1-118-16952-0

Kindle Fire HD
For Dummies
978-1-118-42223-6

NOOK HD For Dummies,
Portable Edition
978-1-118-39498-4

Surface For Dummies
978-1-118-49634-3

Test Prep

ACT For Dummies,
5th Edition
978-1-118-01259-8

ASVAB For Dummies,
3rd Edition
978-0-470-63760-9

GRE For Dummies,
7th Edition
978-0-470-88921-3

Officer Candidate Tests,
For Dummies
978-0-470-59876-4

Physician's Assistant Exam
For Dummies
978-1-118-11556-5

Series 7 Exam
For Dummies
978-0-470-09932-2

Windows 8

Windows 8 For Dummies
978-1-118-13461-0

Windows 8 For Dummies,
Book + DVD Bundle
978-1-118-27167-4

Windows 8 All-in-One
For Dummies
978-1-118-11920-4

𝑒 Available in print and e-book formats.

Available wherever books are sold. For more information or to order direct: U.S. customers visit www.Dummies.com or call 1-877-762-2974.
U.K. customers visit www.Wileyeurope.com or call (0) 1243 843291. Canadian customers visit www.Wiley.ca or call 1-800-567-4797.

Connect with us online at www.facebook.com/fordummies or @fordummies